PROBLEMS IN MODERN GEOGRAPHY

Urban
Geography

PROBLEMS IN MODERN GEOGRAPHY

SERIES EDITOR: *Richard Lawton*
Professor of Geography
University of Liverpool

published

LAND AND LEISURE
J. *Allan Patmore*
Senior Lecturer in Geography
University of Liverpool

URBAN GEOGRAPHY: A SOCIAL PERSPECTIVE
David Herbert
Lecturer in Geography
University College of Swansea

in preparation

AGRICULTURAL GEOGRAPHY
J. R. *Tarrant*
Lecturer in Environmental Sciences
University of East Anglia

DERELICT LAND: ORIGINS AND PROSPECTS OF A LAND-USE PROBLEM
Kenneth L. Wallwork
Senior Lecturer in Geography
New University of Ulster

NEW COMMUNITIES
H. *Brian Rodgers*
Professor of Geography
University of Manchester

THE REBUILDING OF EUROPE: A GEOGRAPHICAL ANALYSIS
Mark Blacksell
Lecturer in Geography
University of Exeter

WATER SUPPLY
Judith Rees
Lecturer in Geography
London School of Economics and Political Science

PROBLEMS IN MODERN GEOGRAPHY

DAVID HERBERT

Urban Geography

A SOCIAL PERSPECTIVE

David & Charles : Newton Abbot

0 7153 5771 9

Set in 10/11 pt Janson
and printed in Great Britain
by Clarke Doble & Brendon Limited Plymouth
for David & Charles (Publishers) Limited
South Devon House Newton Abbot Devon

For TONWEN

Contents

Illustrations

TEXT ILLUSTRATIONS AND MAPS

Page

List of Tables

Preface

As any study of the city must be incomplete, it is perhaps wise to state one's terms of reference and to acknowledge some of the omissions which have to be made. The book is concerned with the internal structure of the city and follows a social geographical approach to its analysis. A necessary pre-occupation with the socio-spatial context allows only a limited treatment of the more economic qualities of city structure. Some aspects of land use within the city, particularly manufacturing and some business activities, are not discussed fully and much economic-based location theory is given implicit rather than explicit acknowledgement. Such selectivity has guided the text into particular approaches, literature and concepts, but it is believed that the right priorities for understanding city structure have been maintained: for the city can best be seen as a social environment which society has produced and within which it interacts.

Geographical research on the city is not inconsiderable in itself, but it has contributed only one part of a large body of literature. In attempting to trace the contribution of a geographical perspective to the study of the many aspects of urban structure, an attempt is made to tie in as many threads as possible. In consequence, there is some indication of the dimensions of an urban bibliography. Within this literature theories and even more detailed empirical studies can become unintelligible to all but the specialist. A conscious attempt has consistently been made to report research findings and to summarise main themes in a language which makes them meaningful to non-specialists. The problems of cities are amongst the most pressing which face mankind. If academic research is to make any kind of contribution towards the solution of those problems, it must report its findings in a comprehensible way.

Although an aim has been to treat the city as a global phenomenon, with as wide a range of examples as possible, inevitably the Western city receives the greatest amount of attention for the literature is dominated by case studies in advanced countries, with research in America dwarfing that of any other nation. For non-Western countries the need for more detailed studies of the city is obvious and urgent but there are many basic problems to be overcome, especially the availability of adequate data, before substantial progress can be made. Similarly, our knowledge of cities in socialist countries is severely limited. With these limitations on knowledge, an overview of the city from any point of view is largely impossible and generalisations can only be tentative.

CHAPTER ONE

Introduction

THE CITY AS A TOPIC

A RESEARCHER with the time and enterprise to count the number of words which literature affords various topics, would surely find that the city ranked high in his findings. The city has a fascination which has attracted writers from a variety of disciplines and a great diversity of points of view. By some, it has been personalised as a mammoth anti-societal force through which established orders and values will be destroyed; others identify different qualities, perhaps those of a most advanced civilisation. Which view of the city one adopts is in large part conditioned by the particular facet of urban growth with which one is concerned: a writer who extols the virtues of the cities of ancient Greece or Rome would find less to praise among the urban products of industrial England in the nineteenth century. Although interpretations of the city may vary, it is clear that urbanisation and the growth of cities have become one of the major characteristics of the present century. Societies all over the world are moving, many much later than others, along the road to urbanisation. The city demands attention as an expression of human society and settlement which cannot be ignored.

The city in its totality is incomprehensible to single disciplines, let alone to individuals: academics, planners, administrators and others stand a long way from comprehending its multi-variate complexity. No one discipline or single academic approach holds any dominant advantage in the task of studying the city; the

B

emphases in one approach are the deficiencies in another. Ideally, the contributions of different disciplines should be seen as aggregative with common frameworks of research leading towards common overall goals. There are strong and clear signs that this kind of inter-disciplinary approach is being developed; examples range from the coordinating efforts of global organisations like the United Nations[1] to those of individual companies in the planning of new cities.[2] Unfortunately the summation of all the individual parts does not necessarily constitute the whole and separate approaches must not only pool their findings but also design ways in which to integrate them and comprehend the inter-relationships which exist. These attempts have possibly been most successful in the context of smaller-scale, manageable projects which start from scratch, such as new towns, but are less successful in the large-scale, rapidly expanding metropolises which are increasingly dominant in the twentieth century. Again, although there is some evidence of multi-disciplinary and integrated studies, most academics continue to study the city—as they do other phenomena—within their own conceptual confines and with limited awareness of the ideas of others.

SOCIAL GEOGRAPHY AND THE CITY

A social geography of the city cannot claim to present a comprehensive overview, but the perspective which it offers is broader-based than most: it studies patterns of social activities in a spatial context. The patterns formed by the distribution of people and social institutions are characterised by flows or movement over space and by processes of interaction.[3] The geographer can identify spatial patterns, the structure of areas or distribution of points and their linkages, with comparative ease; greater difficulties are posed by their explanation, particularly when the necessary dimension of time is taken into consideration. An emphasis upon social activities at once places a limit upon the material and content to be discussed and also presages a treatment in depth of an increasingly focal field in urban geography. There are rich returns for the geographer interested in socio-spatial patterns and yet aware of the ideas and concepts of other disciplines, particularly sociology and urban ecology. A geographer develops his own perspective, but the problems and their context are shared.

A basic assumption in a geographical perspective is that spatial location is in itself of some significance in understanding patterns of human activity. This assumption is far removed from the cruder attempts to identify a deterministic relationship between man and environment, but has several qualities which will be developed during the course of this book. In some contexts, for example, a relationship has been hypothesised between urban environments and the society which inhabits them; in others, physical contiguity is seen as a referent of importance and the neighbourhood as a socio-spatial milieu is seen as a basic source of explanation. Although these perspectives will be demonstrated and argued, it is recognised that spatial location cannot always be propounded as the major source of explanation. It has a contribution to make, often an important contribution, but there are contexts in which it is only of minor significance, and in all cases it is never a sole factor but one which is inter-related with others.

Even within a geographical context, the recognition of a range of phenomena requires some unifying framework within which the various elements and their relationships can be correctly seen. For science as a whole, systems analysis has been proposed as the general framework which might enable different problems to be seen in a similar light through the use of a common holistic structure and a common language. Some geographers have suggested that systems analysis could form a valuable basis from which to approach geographical studies: [4] the conceptual framework allows problems to be seen as a whole and the relevant variables, including spatial qualities, are elements which must be identified and their relationships understood. Clearly the city forms a topic which lends itself to this kind of approach and the type of conceptual framework suggested by systems analysis could be a valuable aid. Also potentially valuable in this context is the proposal of a general field theory approach within geography,[5] whereby a framework is established within which the integration of formal and functional characteristics of the city may be understood.

SCALE OF ANALYSIS

The scale at which a geographical approach operates is general rather than individual, and is sometimes described as a meso-scale.

In the context of the city, it is the group rather than the individual—the neighbourhood rather than the single dwelling unit—
which forms the unit of analysis. This level of generalisation has
its caveats. Patterns of variation may be hidden within the unit
of analysis; individual qualities which might prove definitive at
a micro-scale are blurred within the general characteristics of the
group; the aggregate or ecological statistic may in fact be a crude
average summarising an internal heterogeneity. It will be argued
that these problems are exaggerated and that the real value of
this scale of analysis can be confirmed by innumerable empirical
studies. H. M. Blalock, for example, has suggested that the
ecological unit submerges the eccentricities of individuals and
offers the best measurement of a general trend:[6] it is, of course,
also the unit of analysis at which urban planners must of necessity
make their decisions, with their priorities calculated in terms of
the needs of society rather than of individuals. Although social
geography is still biased towards this scale of analysis, it should
also be stated that in recent years a trend towards study of
individual perception has developed. These behavioural studies
are highly relevant to a geography of the city and promise to
enrich the existing body of knowledge. In particular, residential
mobility has proved especially susceptible to behavioural
approaches and it is in such contexts that some general principles
can be discussed. A major quality of behavioural approaches in
geography, however, serves to maintain their alignment with the
normal scale of analysis. This is the necessity of seeking to identify
aggregate characteristics, even though the individual is the initial
unit of analysis; meaningful generalisations in a spatial context
remain the geographical perspective.

DEFINING THE CITY

A social geography concerned with the city inevitably faces
the problem of a real definition which has generated a substantial
amount of literature. A clear difference exists between the formal
city, defined in terms of 'bricks and mortar'—the physical
expression of urban growth—and the functional city, which is
defined in terms of the linkages between city and hinterland. With
both these approaches there are fringe areas of transitional
characteristics and any eventual boundary must be an approximation. In a formal definition of the city, this fringe area will have

'rural-urban' qualities in which the patterns of land use and the densities of population and settlement gradually change from being characteristically urban to rural. The fringes of the functional city cannot be measured by its visual impact upon landscape but must be identified by data on flows and movements—for example journeys to work or business—derived from field surveys. The transitional elements of this fringe are evident where movements are split between alternative centres and the functional city is normally defined in probabilistic terms to include those areas from which a specified majority of movements are city-ward. In more recent attempts at definition, the terms metropolis and city-region have been used to describe areas which are effectively functional cities.[7] The third kind of city which exists in terms of definition is the legal city, the unit of local government and administration: one of the fallibilities of the legal definition is that it has most in common with the formal city whereas it should more properly be designed in accord with the functional city.

Geographers have not been entirely consistent in defining their unit of analysis, tending to take an area which is formal rather than functional. There are, of course, variations in this depending upon the particular topic with which any individual study is concerned; whereas a study of journey to work, for example, would involve the functional city, an analysis of residential patterns might deal with the formal city. The legal city has frequently been used as the unit of analysis in the past because it has been the area for which statistical data was available. More recently, however, the availability of data by small territorial units which can be used as 'building blocks' has removed this constraint and researchers have been able to define an area more appropriate to their needs. This research trend has been matched in countries such as Britain by attempts to re-form the pattern of local government boundaries so that the legal city bears a closer resemblance to modern urban realities.[8]

The question of defining the city has further implications in conceptual terms, namely the validity of an approach which isolates the city as a discrete element from its societal context. Cities are not independent entities but are products of the particular type of society in which they are placed; a study concerned with *the* city adopts a unit of convenience within which the complexities of structure may be analysed. Geographers, perhaps more than others, have studied the relationships among cities and between cities and other areas, and well understand the necessity of seeing the city as part of an overall system. The patterns and processes which can be discerned and analysed within the city are neither unique nor particular and can best be viewed as reflections of wider societal forces with their counterparts elsewhere. Geographical studies have moved decisively from an emphasis upon the unique or the exceptional to a preoccupation with more general principles, a move sometimes described as being from an ideographic to a nomothetic point of view.

OBJECTIVES IN A SOCIAL GEOGRAPHY OF THE CITY

The study of the city as an area accepts that however it is defined the city possesses a high measure of internal variation: its anatomy is characterised by a complex and dynamic structure. In looking at the anatomy of the city, the problem arises of format and organisation of material. Geographers concerned with the city have followed both systematic and regional paths, mirroring procedures in the subject as a whole. A systematic approach might deal only with a specific element such as morphology or physical form and the way in which this has evolved over time: a regional approach would take one distinctive area within the city, such as the central business district, and study it as a functional whole. Both these types of approach have been aware of the dynamic nature of the city and have incorporated a temporal dimension. The format adopted in this book is mainly guided by regional divisions within the city, but within each of these separate approaches have to be documented and seen in relationship one to the other. In this way it is hoped to present a convenient and clear framework for studying the anatomy of the city without losing a perspective of the complexly unified structure which it represents. Some of the well-known generalised models of spatial structure are useful introductions to the city and its parts; individual areas, such as the central business district and residential districts, may subsequently be studied in more detail. Most of the text, because of the stated emphasis on social activities, is concerned with residential areas and with patterns of urban population; other aspects which are variously present, particularly manufacturing areas within the city, are not dealt with at all. It is within the context of residential districts and the particular topic of residential mobility, that behavioural approaches, dealing initially with the individual household, will be discussed. The aim is the ambitious one of representing the contribution of the social geographer at several scales, from the overall spatial model of the city to the characteristics of individual households.

Two final comments in this introduction can be briefly made. First, social geography—along with most other branches of the social sciences—has been affected by a trend towards increasing quantification in its techniques and procedures. This has been particularly relevant in the context of cities where the complexity of the topic has prompted the use of multi-variate statistical techniques. Some of the terminology is technical and an appendix outlines briefly the more important techniques used in the text and the terms which they employ. Secondly, geographers, along with other academics, can be criticised on the grounds that their studies often seem to bear little relevance to the real problems facing an urban world. It has often been observed that Chicago is the most studied city in the world and yet retains some of the greatest urban dilemmas. No attempt is made to argue the case that most of geography can be applied, nor to relate specific studies to real problems in the city. Whilst not directly forming links between research and problems, however, it is maintained that an awareness of problems must impinge upon all those concerned with the city. The chapter which follows is a brief statement of urban problems and it is hoped it will be self-evident in the subsequent text that there are significant communalities between academic studies and the practical problems of the city.

CHAPTER TWO

Urban Problems

THE development of cities has always proved a mixed blessing. Although cities are mostly acknowledged as basic to an advanced society and civilisation, they have problems, many of which have seemed to increase rather than diminish over time. Such problems inevitably affect research concerned with the city, attracting attention because of their intrinsic interest, demanding attention because of the need for practical solutions and receiving attention because of the priority afforded them. This is not to suggest, of course, that all urban research is problem orientated, but most workers concerned with the city must almost inevitably touch upon, and are often drawn more squarely into, applied rather than abstract studies. Many urban problems have not been solved and they will indeed worsen considerably before any turning point is reached, but the intense activity of the last decade has at least achieved a sound appreciation of their nature and dimensions.

Social geographers concerned with the city have for some time been more directly involved with problem-orientated research than have most other members of their discipline. Their concern with social structures and social processes and with people rather than with resources or enterprises has drawn them towards social problem areas. Even so, much of the emphasis has remained academic rather than pragmatic. Studies of residential patterns, for example, have identified socially-deprived areas, and analyses of residential change have revealed the enormous constraints upon the movement of underprivileged minority groups, but social geographers have rarely proceeded further and sought *solutions* to these problems or become involved in constructive decision-making. Recent trends suggest that awareness of these limitations as a deficiency in social geography is growing and that socially constructive research may become a priority. The theme of 'relevance' is becoming explicit in geographical research to a far greater extent. It is hoped to demonstrate in this text that for the social geographer the step from implicit to explicit and creative relevance may often be very short and that there are already topical fields in which the value of a geographer's perspective is clear.

THE PROCESS OF URBANISATION

The most basic problems of cities are those posed by the process of urbanisation itself, a process by which the world is progressively becoming a more urban society with the shift from more rural and agricultural forms of living. Estimates of the extent to which the world is now urban vary because of problems of definition, but a United Nations survey has suggested that in 1960 one-quarter of the world's population lived in cities of 20,000 or more in size,[1] a figure which had increased from 14 per cent in 1920 to 19 per cent in 1940 and was projected as 32 per cent in 1980. A shift towards really big cities was equally pronounced with the proportion of the world's population living in cities of over 500,000 changing from 5 per cent in 1920 to 12 per cent in 1960 and a projected 17 per cent for 1980. Although trends towards a completely urbanised world are present, proportionately urbanisation has not changed greatly in the twentieth century because it is relative to a world population which is experiencing rapid overall growth. Recent growth of world population from just under two million in 1920 to three million in 1960 and over six million estimated for the year 2000, is the outcome of a 'demographic revolution' as death rates, affected by improved medical science and better living conditions, fall rapidly and birth rates remain high or decline only slowly. The first occurrence of the demographic revolution coincided with the emergence of the industrial city in Western Europe and the beginnings of modern urbanisation. This urbanisation which began in north-west Europe in the early-nineteenth century has only subsequently, in recent decades of the twentieth century, begun to affect the developing countries of the world. Whilst the pattern of western urbanisation is now reasonably well under-

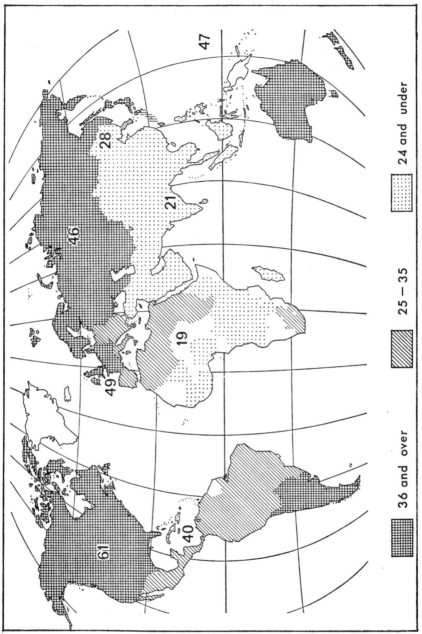

Fig 1. *World urbanisation:* Shaded categories show proportions of total population living in towns over 20,000 in 1960: figures are estimated levels in 1980. (Based on data in Breese, G. (ed) *Readings on Urbanism and Urbanisation,* 1969.)

36 and over

25 — 35

24 and under

stood, contemporary trends in non-western countries are far less clear and seem certain to diverge from western experience.[2] During western urbanisation, there was large-scale migration from rural areas, accompanied by an increase in population growth, and the proportion of population which could be classed as urban rose sharply. The later urbanisation began, the more rapidly did it take place. Using as an index the time taken for a country to change from a situation in which 10 per cent of its population lived in cities of 100,000 or over in size, to one in which 30 per cent could be so classed, this change took seventy-nine years in Britain, where it occurred first, sixty-nine years in the United States, forty-eight years in Germany, thirty-six years in Japan and twenty-six years in Australia. Comparable rates of change in the degree of urbanisation have not, however, been experienced in non-western countries. Whereas in Europe and North America the growth of the urban population was paralleled by the decline through migration of rural population, in non-western countries the rises of city populations are often matched by comparable increases in the rural areas. Migration is important in non-western countries but much of the explanation for urban population growth lies in natural increase; the experience of western cities, which periodically in modern times were not self-propagating but were dependent on migration, has not been precisely repeated as medical science has lowered the death rate and allowed a population boom in urban and rural areas alike. This contrast, added to the time lag in the onset of modern urbanisation, has produced marked differences between developed and developing countries. The advanced countries have become urbanised, but non-western countries remain predominantly rural. Since 1920, however, rates of increase in the proportion of urbanisation in the developing world have been universally faster than in developed countries outside Eastern Europe. Table 1 demonstrates these broad contrasts, though the definition of urban (proportion living in cities of over 20,000) tends to understate the process of change.[3]

These broad regional figures cloak considerable heterogeneity, particularly in Latin America where some countries are highly urbanised, and in Europe where contrasts also occur. Whilst individual European countries, such as England and Wales, are nearly 80 per cent urban, other countries in eastern Europe, such as Bulgaria or Rumania, have only one-third of their populations

Table 1   Urban Population (in cities of 20,000 or more) as a Proportion of Total Population in Major Regions

	1920	1940	1960	1980(e)
Europe	32	37	41	50
N. America	38	45	57	61
Oceania	34	38	50	50
USSR	10	24	36	46
East Asia	7	13	20	28
South Asia	6	8	14	21
Latin America	14	19	32	41
Africa	5	7	13	18
World	14	19	25	32

See also Figure 1.   *e* = estimated.

classed as urban. However, the broad contrast is between Europe and North America which are highly urbanised and Africa and Asia which are not. The figures can, of course, be misleading, particularly in relation to the varying urban definitions upon which they are based. In Britain and the United States, it could be argued that there is little rural population; there are city-dwellers together with that part of the urban population which lives in rural areas, either as commuters or as farming population with urban life-styles. The reality of urban-rural contrasts has thus become tenuous in advanced countries: even in non-western countries an analogous, though inverted, situation occurs where a large part of the city population is in fact rural in life styles. Thus the differences in degree of urbanisation between western and non-western countries are likely to be greater than the statistics suggest.

If the proportional shift towards cities in the twentieth century is undramatic, the growth of cities in absolute terms cannot be similarly described. From many parts of the world, available statistics show the rapid growth of cities. (See Table 2 on page 30.)

Further evidence on this dramatic growth of cities is provided by the emergence of cities of over one million population: in 1800, Tokyo was probably the only such city; London followed early in the 19th century but there were thirteen 'million cities' by 1900 and 133 by 1962. Moreover, there were in the mid 1960s an estimated seven megalopolises, each with at least ten million population and in aggregate around 130 million. In terms of absolute numbers, therefore, the cities of the world are moving

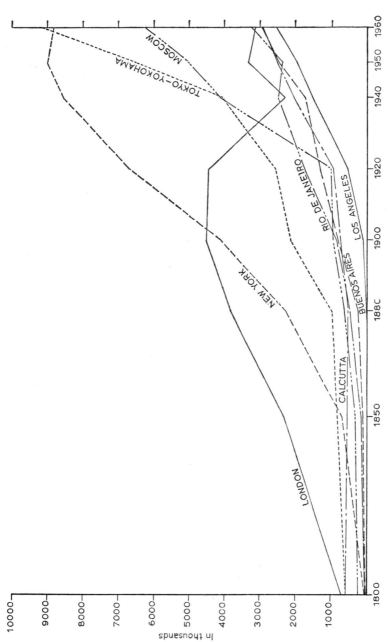

Fig 2. *Growth of selected cities:* Graph based on data in Breese. **G.** (ed) *Readings on Urbanism and Urbanisation.* 1969. The figures are for cities and not for metropolitan areas; this produces apparent declines in London and New York and understates more spread metropolises. such as Los Angeles. but patterns of absolute growth and west/non-west contrasts in timing are still evident.

Table 2   City Growth in the Twentieth Century[4]

	1900	1920	1940	1960	Metropolitan Area (1960)
Bombay	776,000	1,176,000	1,490,000	4,152,000	5,741,000
Buenos Aires	821,000	1,320,000	1,720,000	2,927,000	7,000,000
Rio de Janeiro	821,000	1,720,000	2,457,000	3,223,000	3,974,000
Johannesburg	100,000	300,000	500,000	594,000	2,000,000
Tokyo-Yokohama	2,145,000	2,596,000	4,076,000	9,118,000	11,374,000
London	4,537,000	4,485,000	2,320,000	3,195,000	8,172,000
New York	4,130,000	6,710,000	8,567,000	8,836,000	14,759,000
Moscow	989,000	1,028,000	4,137,000	6,262,000	6,824,000
Miami	2,000	N.A.	N.A.	N.A.	1,397,000
Mexico City	345,000	N.A.	N.A.	N.A.	5,150,000

See also Figure 2.   N.A. = Not available.

towards new and unprecedented size-dimensions and non-western countries may yet produce the most dramatic urban agglomerations. Projections towards the end of the twentieth century suggest that between 1960 and 2000 the world's urban population will increase from 1,000 million to nearly 3,500 million, with a continuing emphasis on really large cities. An attempt to describe these new scales of urban growth is evident in descriptions of metropolis as the product of the mid-twentieth century,[5] of megalopolis, first identified in the north-eastern United States as formerly separate cities became functionally interdependent,[6] and in C. A. Doxiadis's use of the term ecumenopolis to describe a completely urbanised world with interconnected city complexes which might emerge by the late twenty-first century.[7] (Figure 3.)

A further contrast between modern urbanisation in western and non-western countries lies in the stimuli from which they have proceeded. In western Europe and North America, the rapid growth of cities coincided closely in time with the 'take-off' phase of economic development as industrialisation gathered force: the cities emerged in response to a quickening economy and the need for a centralised labour force. Non-western countries, however, have witnessed the growth of major cities without this accompanying economic development and this has led to the assessment by most observers of a state of over-urbanisation or pseudo-urbanisation.

This diagnosis is not universally accepted and N. V. Sovani in particular has attempted to show that present-day non-western countries are comparable to European countries at a similar stage of development.[8] His arguments, however, are not convincing and the evidence of over-urbanisation appears throughout the Third World as urban populations agglomerate but expected concomitants of employment, shelter and services are deficient.

The broad pattern of world urbanisation has attracted a number of academic interpretations, some concerned with the statistical evidence, others with the impacts of this process of change upon society and economy. One largely unresolved problem which has attracted geographers concerns the ordering of cities by popula-

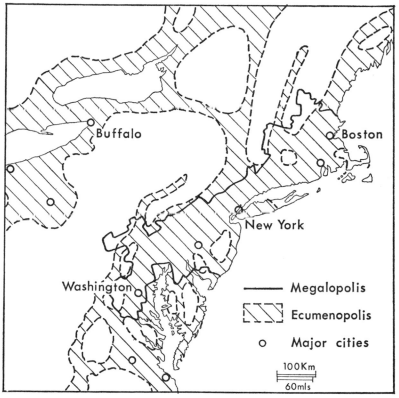

Fig 3. *Megalopolis and beyond in eastern United States:* Intensive urbanisation has begun to form one inter-connected urban system. Megalopolis is mostly associated with the work of J. Gottman; ecumenopolis is a futuristic form of the late twenty-first century. (Adapted from a map in Doxiadis, C. A., *Ekistics*, 1968, by permission of the author and of the Hutchinson Publishing Group Ltd.)

tion-size within a country. It has been observed, for example, that in any one country there will tend to be a few large cities, a greater number of medium-sized cities and a very large number of small cities. The order is thus apparent and the question is whether it can be detailed and explained. A further more tentative observation was that in many countries the largest city was disproportionately bigger than any other: in Latin America, for example, the largest city, usually the capital, contained 33 per cent of the total population in Uruguay, 29 per cent in the Argentine, 23 per cent in Chile and Panama and 21 per cent in Cuba and Costa Rica. Mark Jefferson described these as primate cities and suggested that they were a recurrent feature of urbanising countries.[9] A different pattern, called the rank-size rule, required that the population-size of any one city would bear a regular relationship to its rank relevant to the largest city.[10] Both these models of population-size distributions have some empirical credence but a succession of studies have failed to establish either their universality or their theoretical validity.[11] B. J. L. Berry and W. L. Garrison were led to the conclusion that whilst in many cases they could identify associations, such as primacy in newly urbanising 'homogeneous' countries, the patterns were not consistent and a stochastic explanation, related to the influence of a myriad of minor chance forces rather than one definitive force, was as credible as any other.[12]

Another feature of urbanisation which has attracted the attention of geographers and others, concerns the implications for societal change which the growth of cities involved. In past western urbanisation, the idea of a contrast between rural and urban life-styles was universally assumed. Louis Wirth's thesis on urbanism as a way of life was a seminal paper in which population size, density, and heterogeneity were taken as features of urbanism and an absence of face-to-face relationships was a key social effect.[13] Rural/urban differences were also proposed in the so called theories of contrast, by Tönnies, Weber, Redfield and others, but the concept has been increasingly questioned.[14] Oscar Lewis has made a detailed re-examination of Redfield's work in Tepoztlan and has also identified a more general culture of poverty, which unites poor urbanites and rural peasants throughout the non-western world.[15] Studies by Janet Abu Lughod in Cairo[16] and B. Hoselitz in Bombay[17] confirmed Lewis's analysis based on Mexico City. Janet Abu Lughod was able to show that

OPPOSITE: Pressures on space in the western city: *(above)* Manhattan, Central Park and Harlem from Empire State Building; *(below)* urban freeways and car-parking space in Los Angeles.

particular districts of Cairo drew population from particular rural areas and that traditional rural values, life-styles and forms were perpetuated in an urban setting. Differences were less between urban and rural than between rich and poor. Western countries have similarly provided evidence that urban/rural contrasts are no longer meaningful. Numerous studies have demonstrated that social cohesiveness and face-to-face relationships can exist within localised parts of the city, whilst more recently R. E. Pahl in a study of London's metropolitan fringe suggested that class, occupation and interest were much more relevant divisors of population.[18]

Urban/rural conflict, an academic problem in terms of social definition, is also a problem of a more practical kind. The growth of cities has inevitably meant a physical encroachment upon other uses of land, particularly agricultural, and European countries have proved a major arena for this conflict. Peter Hall estimated that between 1937 and 1955 the area used for building in the Ruhr increased from 24·8 per cent to 34·8 per cent, mainly at the expense of agricultural land.[19] In Britain, a strong conservation movement has existed to protect rural land in the face of urban sprawl, and R. H. Best has produced statistical evidence which suggests that the problem in Britain has been exaggerated.[20] Urban uses in 1960 only accounted for 10 per cent of the total land area of England and Wales, increasing from 5 per cent in 1900. The rate of loss of land to urban uses had decreased since the 1920s and by the year 2000 only 15 to 16 per cent of land would be urban in the United Kingdom as a whole. This fairly slow rate of growth has been more critical, however, because expanding cities have tended to be located in prime agricultural areas, and in the south-east region of England, for example, 36 per cent of the land is likely to be under urban uses by 2000.

SUBSTANDARD HOUSING IN THE INDUSTRIAL CITY

The problems discussed so far arise from urbanisation as a global and regional process. Another set of problems are generated within individual cities. The European industrial city grew in the nineteenth century as a response to the needs of an expanding and changing economy. Cities grew rapidly, with few other purposes than to house workers close to their place of employment; living standards were minimal and there was an almost

OPPOSITE: Form of the non-western city: (above) Kano, West Africa; (below) walled city: Lahore, West Pakistan.

complete absence of planning. These industrial cities became what Lewis Mumford has variously described as 'coketowns', 'man-heaps' and 'mechanicsvilles',[21] with a mounting problem of sub-standardness and a range of social dilemmas. The form of this industrial city attained universality in the western world, with some variations instilled by the historic cores of European cities. The excesses of urban growth prompted response: 'Perhaps the greatest contribution made by the industrial town was the reaction it produced against its own greatest misdemeanours.'[22] In Britain, a series of reform movements and legislative measures evolved new minimum standards for features such as street widths, sanitation, and housing, but planning in the nineteenth century was limited to the individual activities of particular industrialists with their schemes for garden villages.

Substandard housing is one of the major relics of nineteenth-century urban growth which persists in the western city, although many of the worst slums had disappeared from British cities by the 1930s and war damage in European countries effectively removed obsolescent housing. In Poland, for example, 75 per cent of the buildings in Warsaw, 65 per cent of those in Wraclaw and 55 per cent of those in Gdānsk were destroyed in the war.[23] Yet substandardness remains; it is always difficult to assess because of varying definitions, but in a British survey of 1955, Liverpool described 43 per cent of its housing as statutory slum. More recently, J. B. Cullingworth has estimated that 4 out of 18 million houses in Britain were substandard.[24] Peter Hall described a 1961 survey of the region of Paris which recorded that one-half of the dwellings had only one or two rooms, whilst 90 per cent of the city's dwellings had been built before 1914.[25] It is in the older central areas of the western city that substandardness is normally greatest and here change is most evident. Declining population densities in the inner city result from the process of dispersal: the city spreads and the urban fabric, affected by innumerable redevelopment and renewal schemes, undergoes substantial change. In many European cities, the historic nature of the inner city resists change (Figure 4); the zone of preservation in Paris, for example, includes that part in which it is intended to keep and restore buildings which constitute a city's heritage; many individual buildings, often scattered over a wide area, pose a problem of conservation. Apart from its historic elements, how-ever, most of the inner city is scheduled for replacement and

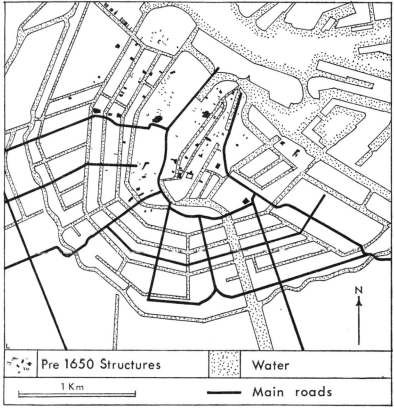

Fig 4. *Historic Fabrics in Amsterdam:* Amsterdam is a particularly good example of a European city in which historic elements remain within the city and pose problems for modern planners. Many buildings and the canal system have historic and social values and must be retained at economic cost.

innovation and the population which remains in substandard housing is that which has least choice.

TWENTIETH CENTURY HOUSING PATTERNS

Suburban growth has been a dominant feature of the western city in the twentieth century. The movement to suburbs began with the wealthy and has gradually spread down through all classes in society as improvements in transport have allowed the divorce of residence and work-place. Suburban growth has been epitomised in North America, where available land and efficient transport systems have combined with an almost universal preference for low-density living. The American city has become the spread city as the compact form of the nineteenth and early-twentieth century has dispersed. In Britain, a similar process, though at less generous densities, has occurred, added to by peripheral public housing schemes, particularly since the Addison Act of 1919.[26] Such legislation reflects the basic problem for most European countries of providing low-cost, often subsidised, housing for large sections of their populations. For reasons of economy and land shortage, many have opted for higher-density suburban expansion. The south-east extension of Amsterdam, for example, will be predominantly tall blocks of flats with not more than 10 per cent of the population in single-family homes: [27] in Poland between 1950 and 1960, over one million flats were built with nearly three million rooms (Figure 5);[28] and in Moscow by 1965, 70 per cent of housing was being constructed as four- or five-storey flats in an attempt to conserve space.[29] Tokyo, where over half the dwellings were destroyed in the 1939–45 war, probably has the severest housing problems in the western world. Good housing is astronomically expensive, living space is characteristically small, and regular lotteries are held for the right to rent single-roomed flats. Even in North America, the past decade has witnessed a boom in high-rise apartments, not merely in the central city, where they have some traditional place, but also in suburban locations and aligned along arterial highways. The explanation for this trend in Canadian cities like Toronto (Figure 6), often lies in escalating land prices and financial problems which place home-buying beyond many households. Although its form varies, suburbanisation has been the universal twentieth-century reaction of the western city to the substandardness and overcrowding bequeathed from the past. Compared to suburban growth, all other solutions to the housing problems, caused by the need to rehouse slum populations, cater for population growth and to reduce sharing of dwellings, are less significant.

In some western countries, however, particularly in Britain, new towns have provided an alternative. Ebenezer Howard provided prototypes with his garden cities at Letchworth and Welwyn Garden City and the New Towns Act of 1946 has been the legislation under which twenty-seven British New Towns have subsequently been built. Despite early setbacks and a modification of initial objectives, the British new towns have been considerable achievements in recent planning. By December 1970 the new towns had housed an extra 700,000 people[30] and many were still at a comparatively early stage of their development; most had achieved economic and social viability. In terms of design, the new towns have tended to mirror changing theories of urban planning. The first phase carried forward a garden city mode of design, with low population densities, well-defined functional

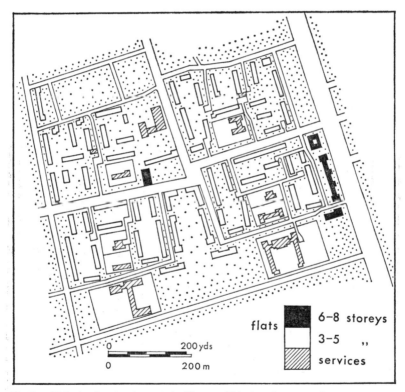

Fig 5. *High density development in Warsaw:* This housing estate for 9,000 people completed in 1956 typifies the emphasis on high-rise dwellings in Eastern Europe. Service buildings include nursery and primary schools. (Reprinted from *City and Regional Planning in Poland,* edited by Jack C. Fisher. Copyright 1966 by Cornell University and by permission of Cornell University Press.)

areas which lacked flexibility, small overall size and limited provision for cars. Cumbernauld was judged a major advance in 1957, being a distinct break from the garden city concept and a design in the urban rather than the rural tradition. (Figure 7.) Cumbernauld had relatively high densities, around thirty dwellings per acre, ample provision for car-ownership, a linear city centre within walking distance for 50,000 of its 70,000 population and an overall form strongly affected by the Scottish urban tradition. The latest wave of British new towns have shown further departures in their move towards a grid form of road system which allows for more general accessibility and easier growth than the centralised radial plan. New towns have already been adopted in other European countries such as Sweden and Holland, the latter country now using reclaimed polders for urban development including new towns, of which Lelystad is an example. Various past plans for Paris have rejected new towns but there are now nine new towns scheduled in France, five of which will be in the Paris region. The satellite towns around Moscow, planned as self-contained communities, are clearly in the mode of new town development. The first modern American new town

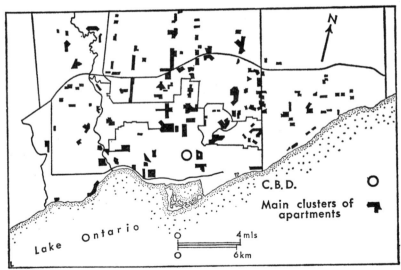

Fig. 6. *Apartments in Toronto* (1970): High-rise development is found in all parts of the metropolitan area and is often aligned along arterial roads. Most apartment blocks are of recent construction. (Based on information supplied by Metropolitan Toronto Planning Board.)

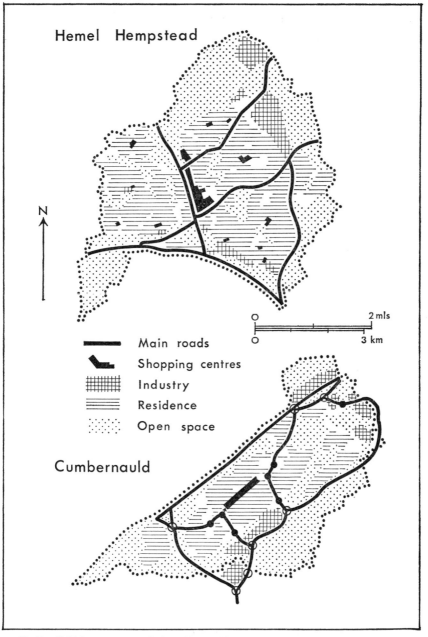

Fig 7. *British new town design:* Hemel Hempstead and Cumbernauld represent different design principles. Whereas the former typifies earlier British new towns with segmented neighbourhoods at low density, Cumbernauld, with its high density residences closely placed around a linear centre and its acceptance of high car ownership rates, is regarded as a major departure in planning. (Adapted from diagrams in Davies, L., 'British New Town Design', *Town Planning Review,* 37, 1966, 157-72, by permission of the author and the *Town Planning Review).*

was in 1958 at El Dorado Hills in California, followed by Reston, Virginia, and Columbia, Maryland. American new towns, unlike their major European counterparts, are private and not government-sponsored enterprises, typically located at the metropolitan fringe and not beyond, and forced to attract their own employment or commuter transport facilities in the absence of government direction or subsidies. Whereas in Europe new towns may have been seen as alternative strategies to suburban growth, this is less so in America: 'American new towns are a different way of developing the metropolitan fringe, not an attempt to change the megalopolitan character of the nation's urban growth'.[31]

TRANSPORT AND THE WESTERN CITY

The pressures exerted upon cities by the needs of movement seem at times to dominate policies for form and growth. Traffic congestion in western cities has become acute and the advent of motor cars has proved the major single factor. Between 1945 and 1970, the number of passenger cars registered in the United States rose from just under 26 to well over 70 million; in the latter year the total of vehicles was 105 million, expected to rise to 146 million by 1985. Although one-quarter of American households do not own cars, the number of cars per 1,000 population is 410 compared with 193 in Britain.[32] Forward plans for all major western cities include large-scale freeway systems, the cost of which becomes astronomical. The rise of the private motor car has been matched by a declining usage of mass transit systems; United States mass transit catered for 192,000 million fare-paying passengers in 1946, but this figure had fallen to 6,700 million by 1966.[33] Mass transit systems, usually subsidised, remain most important in older American cities such as Boston and New York. These two cities carry between 70 and 90 per cent of all commuters on mass transit at peak hours, compared with less than 10 per cent in Los Angeles and under one-third in Detroit and St Louis. Mass transit is still important in European cities, accounting for 90 per cent of London's peak movement. In Amsterdam, 60 per cent of present work trips are by bicycle and only 10 per cent by car but the eventual aim is 60 per cent by mass transit.[34] Most major European cities have elaborate metro and subway systems, Moscow's often being judged to be the best in the world. Many American cities, prompted by

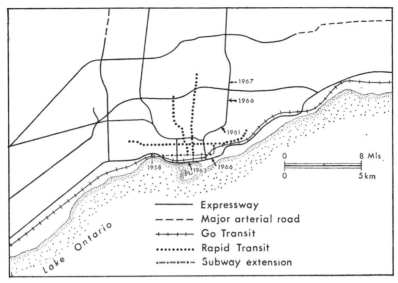

Fig 8. *Transport in Toronto:* Metropolitan Toronto has balanced massive freeway development with innovations in public transport, particularly an underground
transit system. One major road scheme, the Spadina Expressway into the central
city, has been abandoned (1971) and this is seen as a reaction against the space
demands of the automobile. (Map based on information supplied by the Metropolitan
Toronto Planning Board.)

pressures on space and the social costs of the automobile, have
ambitious mass transit plans which are, however, also usually
matched by road-building schemes. Toronto, often quoted as a
model in recent years, has since 1955 developed a subway, a
Go-train commuter rail service and a massive programme of
freeway development extending into the central city (Figure 8).
Control of private cars in cities is frequently and forcefully
advocated: 'The day cannot be far off at which every section
of the World City will have to adopt Venice's practice of making
it compulsory for mechanised road vehicles arriving at the city's
outer edge to halt and garage there'.[35]

ADMINISTERING METROPOLIS

Government poses further problems for the western city
because of an inherited mosaic of local administrative areas which
has become increasingly out of phase with an emerging metro-

polis. In Britain a long and tortuous process of boundary reform will be finalised in the 1970s. The extent of fragmentation of decision-making is exemplified by the conurbations; in Manchester, for example, until recently over 50 local authorities could be counted within a six-mile radius of the city's centre. London has already achieved a rationalisation from over 80 boroughs to 32, with one Greater London Council (Figure 9). These British examples are matched by most European countries, excepting those in the centrally controlled Communist bloc, but difficulties are probably most acute in some American cities. John Lindsay has described the relationship between municipality and state as the fundamental cause of municipal financial poverty and inefficient government.[36] A further problem is the widening gap between the central city, with its concentration of poor and the coloured population, and the suburban municipalities. The middle-class suburbs, fearful of being encroached upon by slums, have tended to isolate themselves administratively and fiscally; the result has been further fragmentation of the overall city.

URBAN POLLUTION

Although western cities have long ago overcome basic problems of sanitation and hygiene, modern life styles and economic development have brought new sources of pollution and health hazard. Waste disposal from cities is a mounting problem: the estimate for American cities by the year 2000 is 37,000 million gallons of municipal sewage per day or 132 gallons per head of population; this compares with a current British figure of thirty gallons.[37] Each American citizen produces three-quarters of a ton of solid refuse per year (growing at a rate of 4 per cent per year) and Los Angeles alone dumps 12,000 million cubic feet of waste into tips and land fills. In America, 48,000 million aluminium cans are dumped annually, along with over 6 million vehicles; besides the economic costs of dumping, there are also social costs in terms of health hazard and landscape dereliction. Water pollution is endemic both from sewage and industrial waste; in Britain some 5,000 miles of river are reckoned to suffer from pollution of some kind. Air pollution is a major result of road transport and each year in America with an estimated 200 million tons of fuel consumed on the roads, 100 millions tons are residuals in the form of carbon monoxide and another 20 million tons in unburned

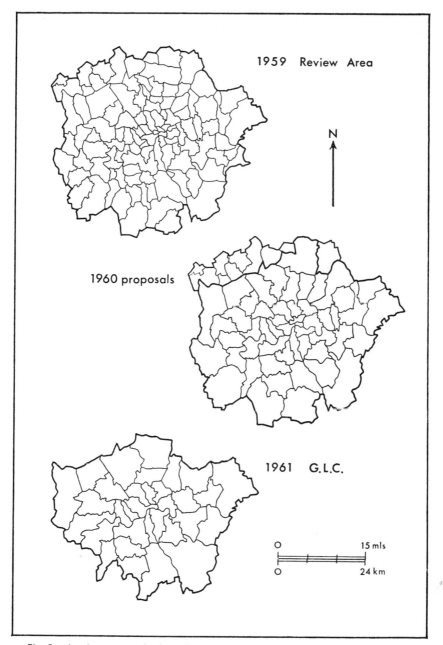

1959   Review   Area

N

1960 proposals

1961   G.L.C.

0   15 mls
0   24 km

Fig 9.   *London: reorganisation of local government:* The first major attempt in Britain to reduce the number of municipalities and allow better government in a metropolis. From an initial number of nearly 100, the independent authorities were reduced to 52 by the initial commission and to 32 in the final legislation.

hydro-carbons.[38] Ameliorative measures are possible and tests of the infamous Los Angeles atmosphere have shown that devices such as afterburners or re-cycling can eliminate 90 per cent of emission at an acceptable cost. An awareness of urban pollution, waste and congestion has focused more attention upon the quality of the urban environment and the need to plan open spaces. Space to stop urban growth has been preserved for some time: British green belts are much-used planning devices whilst the 'green-heart metropolis' of Randstad, Holland, has attracted acclaim. Urban parks also, of course, have a long tradition and Marion Clawson has described the functions of open space within the city as to provide light and air, to improve perspectives and vistas, to allow recreation in the broadest sense, for ecological purposes such as flood control, to break up the urban pattern and to reserve space for future use.[39] As western cities increase in size, so the proper management of intra-urban space becomes more critical whilst outside the limits of the physical city recreation space must be planned as a complete escape from the intensity of urban living. Recent research has shown that the concept of wilderness varies considerably among individuals and whereas many countries will be increasingly unable to cater for individuals like Daniel Boone, who felt crowded if he could see smoke from another cabin, a diversity of recreation space can be planned for cities. Dutch activities in this field are particularly far-sighted; a large proportion of new land reclaimed in the polders is being designated as recreation space for the populations of the growing cities.

PROBLEMS OF THE NON-WESTERN CITY

The problems of non-western cities are of a much more basic kind. Their concern is with the provision of an urban fabric and an infrastructure of any kind rather than with improvement or replacement. In some ways the present problems of non-western cities are reminiscent of those in European cities in the first half of the nineteenth century, but they are occurring on a scale which has no real precedent and without the wealth and expanding economy which accompanied western urbanisation. Although reliable figures are virtually absent*, unemployment is extremely

*An Oxfam statement (1971) suggested that overall male unemployment in developing countries stood at 33 per cent (near 50 per cent in the 14 to 25 age-group) and that wasted labour was near 75 per cent.

high throughout the Third World and underemployment, evidenced by the countless millions employed in useless tertiary occupations such as selling trinkets or repairing bicycles, is endemic. Overurbanisation is a fact in many non-western countries and A. L. Mabogunje has testified that there is no doubt that Nigeria's level of urbanisation is inconsistent with its level of technological development.[40] G. Breese talks of subsistence urbanisation in which the average citizen has only the bare necessities, sometimes not even those, for survival in an urban environment.[41] Lack of jobs does not deter new migrants from rural areas, much though cities would like to stop the flow: in Djakarta, for example, vagrants are regularly rounded up and sent to rehabilitation camps on the edge of the city.

Employment is a basic problem but housing is perhaps the more obvious. Charles Abrams talked about three categories of street sleepers, slum dwellers and squatters;[42] the former are exemplified in Calcutta where an estimated 600,000 are homeless. The slum dwellers occupy tenements at incredible rates of over-crowding and population densities in the central city are extremely high, running between 100,000 and 200,000 people per square mile. In south-east Asia, the Chinese quarters are often the most over-crowded with dozens of families occupying individual buildings which are divided into cubicles, many of which have no natural light. Lighting, sanitation and cooking facilities are minimal and rooms are used on a rota system: five or six people in 40 square foot cubicles in Hong Kong; an average seven persons per room in the slums of Bombay; 700 people sharing one tap in the worst part of Kingston, Jamaica; these are all not untypical features of non-western cities.

SQUATTERS AND THE SHANTY-TOWNS

Given these extreme conditions of overcrowding, it is little wonder that shanty-towns have proliferated in non-western cities, occupying any available space. These are squatter settlements, illegally occupying land, and J. F. C. Turner has distinguished between the incipient squatters of recent origin; the semi-legal squatters, where local custom enabled their initial establishment and plots are subsequently bought and sold as real estate; and *de facto* settlements, which have acquired some permanence over time.[43] Shanty-towns are endemic throughout the Third

World, housing between 25 and 30 per cent of the populations of the capital cities of south-east Asia. Hong Kong's shanty town population grew from 30,000 to 300,000 between 1947 and 1949. One-third of the population of Mexico City live in shanties, as do over two million people in metropolitan Calcutta (Figure 10). Materials from which shanties are built vary according to local circumstances; tin cans in Algeria, reed in Baghdad, and mud and straw in India. The shanties lack basic services and pose enormous risks of disease, fire and a range of social problems. In Latin America, space around any new housing project is rapidly covered with shanties which seek to share the services which must be provided: the contrasts between rich and poor become stark and immediate.

Governments have tended to oppose squatter settlements. Priorities in India, for example, have been to preserve the standards of building and thus shanties are inevitably condemned. Kuala Lumpur has squatter clearance schemes, Manila has a relocation policy, and in some Latin American countries there have been eruptions of violence between police and intending squatters. More recently, however, the argument has been advanced that this attitude towards squatters should be changed: such settlements, it is argued, are the only real form of urban growth in the non-western world. In Latin America especially, shanty towns result from a frustrated demand for housing rather than from poverty. Their occupants include professional people and the emergent middle-class and many shanties are improving *in situ* as material possessions increase and better building materials become available. The physical form of the shanty and the character of its population vary from one country to another, but Turner would argue that shanties are essential where governments cannot supply the housing need. Again in Latin American cities, a distinction could be drawn between the poor central shanties, occupied by recent migrants who needed to be close to possible sources of work, and the peripheral shanties with their more stabilised and improving population. Whereas the former might resemble the western slum, the latter had features of suburbia. Colin Rosser, from his close involvement in the planning of Calcutta, supported Turner's case.[44] Calcutta's *bustees* existed because the need for low-cost housing could not be met elsewhere and housing programmes with idealistic objectives were futile. Besides providing cheap housing, *bustees* served as reception areas

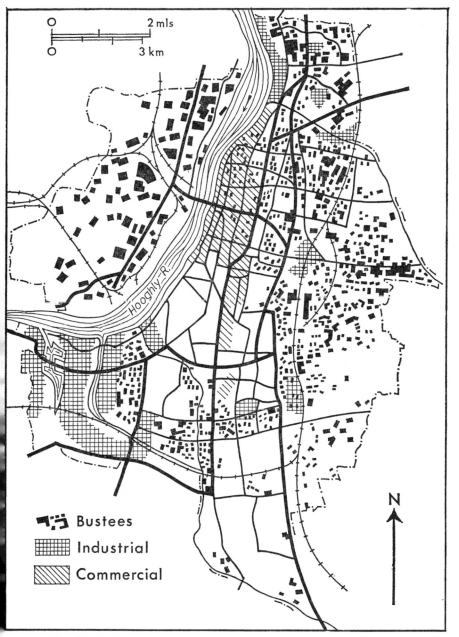

Bustees

Industrial

Commercial

N

Fig 10. *Distribution of bustees in Calcutta:* The bustees or squatter settlements of Calcutta house an estimated two million people in makeshift buildings of mud and straw which have minimal services. They are scattered throughout the city area where space is available. (Based on a map in Berry, B. J. L. and Rees, P. H., 'Factorial Ecology of Calcutta . *American Journal of Sociology* 74, 1968–69, 445–91, with permission; copyright 1969 by University of Chicago).

for new migrants, provided 'cottage industries' and catered for mobility. The planned programme for Calcutta is a massive *bustee* improvement scheme, new experimental building techniques, and the construction of model *bustees* to house one million people in ten years. Turner would advocate this role of government aimed at control and improvement, rather than prevention of shanties. There are other examples of the acceptance of those principles, such as the self-help housing of Bogota's Ciudad Kennedy, Peru's housing associations and the Chilean government's attempts to provide sites and services whilst people build their own houses. In these ways the advantage of shanties can be maintained, whilst their worst expressions can be avoided.

Some non-western countries, with advantages of organisation and investment capital, have attempted more ambitious solutions to their urban problems. Hong Kong's new town of Tsuen Wan had reached a population size of 223,000 in 1968; Singapore built 700,000 units of public housing in the 1960s in resettlement schemes, though forced to accept high density of occupance; Venezuela has a programme to build three new towns at Ciudad Guyana, Tuy Medio and El Talbazo. Western prototypes are not directly transferable and for developing countries the main objectives of new towns are often to exploit natural resources and to infuse national spirit. To date Brasilia has been a failure as a national capital but in the long run its objectives of opening up the interior may be realised.

TRANSPORT

Transport problems in non-western cities are of a different kind to those of the west: the congestion is of pedestrians, bicycles and bullock carts rather than cars. T. McGee wrote of southeast Asia: 'The breakdown of public transportation is evidenced by the frustrating lack of any timetable. The overcrowded buses pick their way through streets cluttered with pedestrians, bicycles, motor scooters and motor cars'.[45] In some cities modern transport systems are emerging, as in Lagos where a bus service moves 100,000 daily and railways increasingly transport commuters.[46] An underground mass transit system planned for Caracas by 1974 could carry 15·4 million passengers annually compared with the 5·8 million on New York's metro and the 2·8 million on the London underground.[47]

OPPOSITE: *(above)* Form of the non-western city: Local market in Nigeria. *(below)* House types and morphology in Britain: Norman castle and modern villas, Swansea.

THE URBAN PROSPECT

Urban problems in all parts of the world are still far from solution; the larger the city the more accentuated the problems become. One universal necessity must be control and organisation from which a cohesive policy can emerge and be implemented. The expressions of disorganisation, congestion and social disorder are too obvious to be ignored. Non-western cities carry the additional burdens of poverty and a lack of resources, and the fears of revolutionary outlets to urban problems are real and persistent. McGee suggests that in south-east Asia attempts to build up community and civic pride have broken down, under the impact of population growth and shared poverty, into urban anarchy.[48] L. W. Pye states that authorities in non-western countries have so far failed to demonstrate an understanding of the needs of the urban poor and the gap between the élite and the masses has widened.[49] Whatever the social implications of world urbanisation, new physical dimensions are assured. Megalopolis will characterise western countries, on a scale foreseen by Doxiadis[50] in America's Great Lakes region stretching from Milwaukee to Toronto (Figure 3); city forms are hard to imagine in non-western contexts as continuing population explosions and accelerating in-migration aggravate existing situations. Arnold Toynbee[51] accepts Doxiadis's ecumenopolis in his vision of World City and his plea is that it should be humanised by skilful administration which would create constituent parts on the scale of the contemporary local city.

OPPOSITE: House types and morphology in Britain: *(above)* Terraced rows and interwar villas, Swansea; *(below)* municipal housing, Swansea.

D

CHAPTER THREE

Some Aspects of
Urban Theory

REFERENCE will frequently be made to theories and concepts many of which are derived from other disciplines and need integrating into a geographical perspective.[1] The objective in this chapter is to provide some more general comment on theories which have broad application to the study of the city. Most of the theories described are derived from urban sociology, although economic theories of urban location are pertinent to intra-urban structure, even though geographers have relied most heavily upon location theory in studies of relationships between cities. It is argued in this text that a geography emphasising social patterns and processes offers greatest potential for understanding the anatomy of the city, as David Harvey has argued in his plea for an awareness of the sociological imagination.[2]

The difficulties involved in assessing general urban theories are considerable. All such theories have major deficiencies which arise from the attempt to generalise upon variable and complex phenomena. L. Reissman, in his lucid review of such attempts within urban sociology,[3] suggested that a systematic general theory of the city is still lacking and may now be unattainable, though there have been a number of attempts at general urban theories from sociologists. All these possess deficiencies but still serve as useful general frameworks within which to view the city. Discussion of these theories will be selective: amongst those not (fully) discussed are Reissman's own attempt at an urban theory[4]—based on the four components of urban growth, industrialisation, the emergence of the middle-class and nationalism—and the well-known theory of Louis Wirth which distinguished urbanism as a way of life.[5] Wirth's theory constructed around the qualities of population size, density and heterogeneity, has been recently closely reviewed[6] and has few claims to be regarded as a general theory because of its particularism to the western industrial city.[7]

PRE-INDUSTRIAL CITIES AND THE IDEA OF A CONTINUUM

One general theory which provides a particularly useful background for the social geographer is that based around Gideon Sjoberg's thesis of the pre-industrial city. Sjoberg saw cities as products of their societies, which he categorised as folk pre-literate, feudal, pre-industrial and literate, and urban industrial. Although too broad and oversimplified to be regarded as a successful general urban theory, and breaking down in particular empirical circumstances, Sjoberg's theory provides a most useful overall framework with a good level of application. Cities at different points in time and in different parts of the world can be seen in a general relationship to each other related to the stages of development which they have reached. There is, therefore, a global typology of societies and their urban expressions of a kind similar to that formed by Reissman. Both typologies possess a temporal dimension which can, in the case of Sjoberg's theory, be characterised as a continuum of urban development along which the pre-industrial and industrial city types are convenient main categories. The continuum can thus be used to distinguish changes in the city through time, viewed as an evolutionary process, and also to identify contemporary contrasts over space. Differences between non-western and western cities at the present time, for example, are in many ways analogous to those between pre-industrial and industrial cities. It must be emphasised that these terms are merely broad categories of convenience which contain diversities within themselves, as the concept of a continuum implies. The industrial city of America has different characteristics from those of some European countries and the non-western city of Asia is not identical to that of Latin America. Diversities may even occur within countries and whilst the major cities of Asia show evidence of change, smaller cities retain their traditional features. Sjoberg relied heavily upon technology, particularly transport and communications, as a force for differentiation and change, and possibly understated the significance of other, especially cultural, factors. Cultural factors, such as race, ethnicity and religion, were important in pre-industrial cities as Sjoberg suggested, and remain vital factors in explaining differences between modern non-western cities, even when they are at comparable stages of technological development. The analogy between pre-industrial and non-western city is a useful guideline rather than a definitive statement; the crushing problems created by urban population growth in non-western cities defy simple analogues.

Leo F. Schnore has used Sjoberg's concept of a pre-industrial city[8] but attempted to redress the balance in terms of dimensions of structure and change by proposing an ecological complex possessing four main components of environment, technology, population and organisation. Environment included those influences arising from the physical setting of the city; technology acknowledged the role of transport and communication facilities; population elements included size, rate of growth, ethnic and racial composition; organisation comprised the economic base of the city and its social structure and from its characteristics under these four headings a city could be placed in the continuum. The concept of a continuum implies open-endedness and for some time urban theorists have recognised the emergence of new urban forms beyond the industrial city. As early as 1933, R. D. McKenzie described 'metropolis' in the United States as the child of modern facilities for transport and communication;[9] many subsequent writers have attempted to define the new features which metropolis contains, its dispersed form, its regional scale and its higher tempo of mobility.[10] Metropolis is seen as a development from the industrial city in western countries and the term 'metropole' has been coined from those Asian cities which occasionally have the dimensions but not the essential functional qualities of metropolis.[11] Even beyond metropolis, megalopolis has a potential place in the continuum though its characteristics have barely been investigated let alone understood.[12]

URBAN ECOLOGY

L. F. Schnore could be described as an urban ecologist, but the field of study which is termed urban ecology considerably pre-dates his work on the internal structure of the city. Urban ecology is a part of urban sociology which R. N. Morris has suggested falls into two major approaches defined as ecological and organisational. Morris said of the ecological approach that it 'assumes that the essence of the city lies in the concentration of a very large number of persons in a relatively small space'; and of the organisational approach that it 'begins with patterns of social behaviour rather than with the size of population units'.[18] The former is closely aligned with a geographical approach in that it identifies a territory and then seeks to analyse its character-istics; the latter is more purely sociological with its initial emphasis upon societal structure. Urban ecology also possesses a stronger bias toward economic theory than other branches of sociology. Principles from land economists, dating from Richard Hurd's work on city land values in 1903,[14] have been used as an essential part of the ecological explanation of land use and social patterns within the city. Notions such as the costs of occupying a unit of space and the significance of transport costs, rents, accessibility and economic competition are implicit in the body of concepts developed by ecologists since the 1920s. There are now several authoritative statements on the development of urban ecology but some space is devoted here to an academic approach which has had a considerable impact upon geographers concerned with the city.

Urban ecology studies the total environment of the city, in which it seeks to identify the elements of its structure, recognise the patterns which they formed and understand the inter-relationships which existed. Despite these apparently laudable objectives and the general framework which it provides, urban ecology has a chequered history. Its pattern of development could be summarised into a number of phases: an early period covering the 1920s and part of the 1930s which was dominated by the so-called Chicago school; a phase of quiescence up to the 1950s when substantial criticisms of the field were not authoritatively answered; and a contemporary period of re-formulation. The main criticisms of urban ecology were aimed at its assumptive base and at its failure to develop cohesive and rigorous theory.

Although the pioneer urban ecologists did not counter these criticisms and Robert Park himself in fact denied that he had ever attempted to construct a theory, a reviewer such as L. Reissman —by no means an advocate of the ecological approach—was prepared to state that 'in spite of its errors, ecology still is the closest we have come to a systematic theory of the city'.[15] To warrant this description, urban ecology clearly achieved something in theoretical terms and beyond this few would deny the seminal quality of the empirical analyses which the Chicago school produced in relation to their parent city.

Robert Park's paper on 'The City'[16] was an early stimulus to urban ecology and included a statement on his conception of the city as a kind of social organism. A great quality of Park and his contemporary ecologists was their incredible amount of first-hand knowledge about the city of Chicago. This intimate knowledge of the city and its people, based upon intensive field-work and involvement, was reflected in their many papers on the subject. Park has been described as an undisciplined empiricist, excited by the patterns and apparent explanations which he saw in city life, but his adoption of a general framework within which to study his patterns led him into a methodology which was committed to theory-building. This framework Park derived from an analogy with the biological world and the belief that the patterns and relationships evident there could be paralleled by land use and people within cities. This enthusiasm for a biological analogy can only really be understood in the context of the early part of this century when the appeal of Social Darwinism in particular, and the guidelines of classical economics, prompted lines of thought which found expression in many disciplines. A major attraction of the biological analogy was its totality: if offered a *gestalt* model which was simple and logical, the similarities to the biological world could everywhere be observed, measured and recorded, and each segment could be seen in its relevant place within the overall broad framework and explained by the same guiding principles. The basic qualities of such a systems analysis approach (see appendix) are evident in the attractions which the biological analogy offered.

Beyond the framework, biology also provided a source of other concepts and a terminology for the urban ecologists. Symbiosis described the most basic set of relationships and the mutual interdependence of the elements of the city. Park showed how symbiosis operated in the biological world, his best known example being that of the humble bee and its place in the 'web of life'.[17] McKenzie sought direct analogies within the city: 'In the struggle for existence in human groups, social organisation accommodates itself to the spatial and sustenance relationships existing among the occupants of any geographical area'.[18] Closely allied to symbiosis was the concept of competition, translated into economic terms, whereby space would be allocated among alternative uses on a competitive basis. The essence of this kind of competition was that it operated at an impersonal level in a way reminiscent of the biological world. The concept of community, borrowed directly from biology, was applied to the city as a population group inhabiting a distinguishable geographical space and co-existing through a set of symbiotic relationships. Such a population group within the city was territorially organised and interdependent in the 'natural order' of the community. Within such a community, further symbiotic relationships and ecological processes could be identified. The 'dominance' of one particular group within a community could be ascribed to its superior competitive power. 'Segregation' of distinctive groups would occur within communities: 'Every area of segregation is the result of the operation of a combination of the forces of selection.'[19] Other crucial ecological processes were those of 'invasion' and 'succession' which described the gradual incursion of one group into the territory of another and the eventual displacement as succession took place. Invasion and succession could be viewed as a cycle which proceeded through a number of stages with, ideally, a complete change in land use or in population type between first and last stages. A clear example of the process could be seen in the territorial expansion of the commercial activities in the central city, which through their superior purchasing power were able to displace adjacent land uses. These ecological processes were most clearly derived from biology. Other more regional forces identified by E. W. Burgess and R. D. McKenzie, such as concentration and centralisation, were more related to economic factors.

The analogy provided the framework and most of its conceptual ingredients but there is ample evidence in the literature of urban ecology that differences between biological and human society were appreciated. It was never denied that human society had an extra dimension of cultural and traditional values which were not apparent in the biological world. Robert Park suggested that social organisation could be studied at two levels, the biotic in which competition was the guiding process and the cultural in which consensus and communication among members of society were the main factor.[20] Park's notion here was that the biotic level could be studied separately as an analysis of aggregate behaviour and structure, ignoring the myriad of cultural or non-rational values which might be measurable on an individual basis. Despite this acknowledgment of non-biotic factors, however, the paucity of their treatment was to prove one of the major points of criticism of urban ecology. It is clear that Park, Burgess and the others consistently understated and often omitted to include the distinctively human qualities of the city in their conceptual framework which was essentially mechanistic and generalized.

The critics of urban ecology seized on this neglect of human and cultural factors as a basic deficiency and questioned the validity of using analogues. Perhaps the best-known example of this line of criticism is the work of Walter Firey in his study of *Land Use in Central Boston*.[21] Firey found ecological laws were not satisfactory explanations of the patterns which he observed. Cultural factors, which he described variously as non-rational values, sentiment and symbolism, were the dominant influences in some parts of the city: thus the motivations of the families who acted to preserve Beacon Hill, an old and prestigious residential district, against the encroachment of commercial functions and lower-status groups, were not economic. Others have found similar evidence, for example, Emrys Jones's study of the social geography of Belfast.[22] Milla Alihan rejected the biological analogy on the same grounds but had wider-ranging criticisms of the urban ecologists.[23] She suggested that the Chicago monographs, although of lasting value as studies of urban-social structure, had not followed ecological rules, and used terminology inconsistently thus affecting the interpretation of key concepts such as community and society. This obsession with words was later to evoke cynical rejoinders: 'Human ecology has already inspired a generation of critics too easily irritated by figures of speech';[24] but contemporaneously the defences were few. McKenzie died in 1940 and Park acquired a reputation as an undisciplined empiricist. Louis Wirth, always a less committed ecologist, attempted to re-define a position for urban ecology as a perspective which focused attention upon localised or territorially-defined social structures and phenomena.[25] With this focus, he suggested, community has a central position in the conceptual framework but the term is inevitably ambiguous because all communities are also societies and all societies bear some characteristics of communities. Ecology provides a perspective but behaviour in the human world can only be understood in the light of habit, custom, institutions, morals, ethics and laws. Wirth's statement was a careful re-appraisal of ecology in which the biological analogy had no necessary part. J. A. Quinn[26] and A. H. Hawley[27] provided later restatements of ecology and the latter stressed the field as a theory of community structure. Whilst Hawley was seen by most critics as a defender of the traditional tenets of urban ecology rather than an innovator, he was impatient of suggestions that social values had not been considered and reiterated the holistic view. Indeed Hawley and others such as O. D. Duncan and L. F. Schnore were classed by G. A. Theodorson as neo-orthodox ecologists who have maintained some basic elements but have sufficiently modified their concepts to accommodate expressed criticism.[28]

A modern perspective is exemplified by L. F. Schnore's ecological complex concept as a framework within which to analyse the internal structure of the city.[29] The scale of ecology has clear attractions to urban geographers as the level of generalisation at which many of their investigations take place. In a more general geographical context Harvey talks similarly about the resolution level which falls between macro and micro, though he described this as a regional scale.[30] Concepts such as the ecological complex closely resemble geographers' attempts to study 'eco-systems' within which they can identify variables and their inter-relationships. The ecological complex approach has been criticised on a number of grounds, such as failure to explain the assumptive bases to theory and an adequate definition of its components. Although it could be argued that 'social' values are not excluded, they are not clearly specified and N. P. Gist and S. F. Fava suggested that a fifth component, namely a social-psychological component which incorporated sentiment, preferences, values, attitudes and beliefs, could be added to meet this deficiency.[31] The mixing of such dissimilar measures poses difficulties: 'Do not add cabbages to electrons and expect to get a total which means anything'.[32] It has also been argued that ecology adopts a 'normative' approach which cannot account for choice among alternatives or conformity/non-conformity.[33] How then, in the light of this debate, can the value of urban ecology be assessed?

Its value is as a perspective—not sufficient in itself—which provides valuable insights into city structure and geographical patterns of society. The scale or level of generalisation at which it operates is in itself a limitation but one in which aggregated data can be usefully analysed and valid hypotheses formed. The scale delegates analysis of individual behaviour patterns to other perspectives but is 'normative' in the sense of probability and what has been called the law of empirical regularities. For social geography the qualities of urban ecology are both familiar and attractive. The level of generalisation is compatible with geographical units of analysis; the interest in spatial patterns and the tendency to proceed from the characteristics of an *area* are common themes. However, as emphasised already, this kind of approach is not sufficient to understand the complexities of the city, and later in the book topics will be discussed in which more detailed scales of analysis are essential.

TOWARDS A GEOGRAPHICAL PERSPECTIVE

Geographical approaches to urban theory have in the past been best developed in the context of systems of cities. Walter Christaller's central place studies stood out as one of the few deductive theories in urban geography[34] and it is only recently that these have been applied to internal urban structure. Ian Burton's statement on geography as a whole in 1963: 'There is not a very large literature in theoretical geography. Our discipline has remained predominantly ideographic',[35] had general significance. Early geographical studies of cities were empirical rather than theoretical; the pre-occupation was with the historical, environmental and economic influences upon points or locations at which cities emerged and grew. As B. J. L. Berry and F. E. Horton have suggested: 'When the problem of the internal structure of the city was approached, the question of actual site became important . . . the smaller topographical details affecting utilisation, land values, and city growth and expansion became important considerations along with the grosser features which initially determined the suitability of sites and eventually affected city success or failure'.[36] Earlier urban geographies tended to

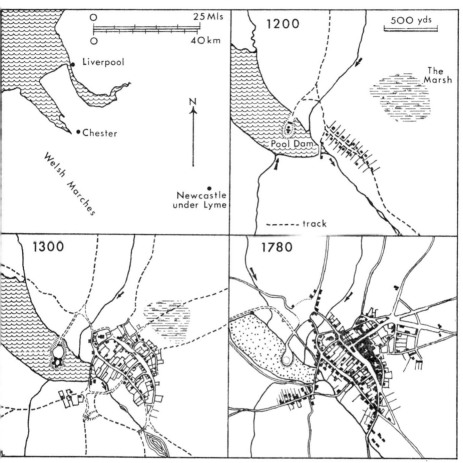

Fig 11. *Urban site and situation: Newcastle-under-Lyme:* Urban growth can often be related in a general way to the regional setting and the physical site. Newcastle's setting had effect initially through its strategic position in a zone of conflict and eventually through its convenience for routeways. Initial settlement was around a castle nucleus but urban functions emerged with market and borough status, independent of the initial defensive purpose.

concentrate upon qualities of site and setting and examples occur
in the work of European geographers such as J. M. Houston[87]
and R. E. Dickinson.[88] Typical formats in analyses of internal
structure included a detailed examination of situation and site and
their relationships to stages of urban growth and characteristics of
urban form (Figure 11). A distinctive set of academic approaches
was provided by urban morphology which although never perhaps amounting to a theory, made distinctive contributions and
was specifically concerned with internal structure.

URBAN MORPHOLOGY

Urban morphology is concerned with the physical qualities of
the urban environment identifiable in the plan or layout of a city,
composed of streets or channels of movement, plots or blocks of
space or structures, and individual buildings. It is the variation in
the characteristics of these elements and their spatial con-
figurations which form the context of urban morphology. A. E.
Smailes has provided a useful review of the development of ideas
in urban morphology.[39] Smailes considered existing deficiencies
in approaches to urban morphology and outlined some general
principles from which the field of study could develop. The
deficiencies included too great a reliance upon the techniques of
other disciplines, notably economic history, and an over-emphasis
upon the historic core of the city as an area of study. The new
principles suggested by Smailes emphasised a geographical
technique based upon field survey and the search for generalised
rather than detailed patterns of variation. The 'townscape'
analysis proposed by Smailes involved land use, street patterns
and building types and allowed the identification of sub-regions
within the city. A particular typology described by Smailes
included the kernel or historic core, together with sub-regions
composed of 'terrace-ribbing', 'villa-studding' and 'block-
clumping' (Figure 12). The aim was a generalised description of
the urban morphology of individual cities and a series of studies
followed the outlines suggested by Smailes.[40] The use of precise
techniques of measurement was limited, however, and too often
studies led to conclusions couched in terms of uniqueness. Such
characteristics led to criticisms of urban morphology at the
Lund Symposium on Urban Geography in 1960, on the grounds
that the studies remained descriptive and lacking in generality

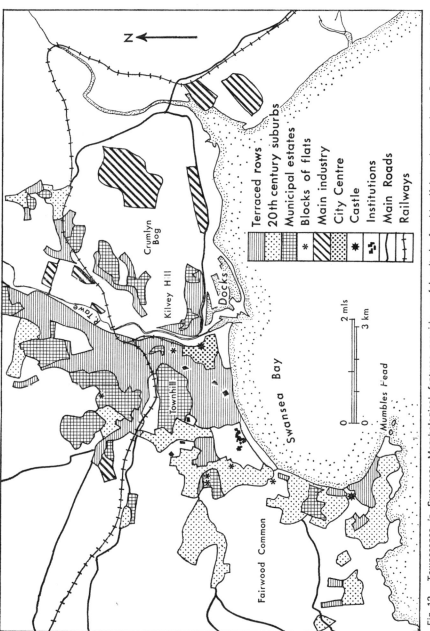

Fig 12. *Townscapes in Swansea*: Morphological features provide useful criteria for identifying urban regions. Swansea can be divided into broad categories similar to those suggested by A. E. Smailes, although its constricted coastal site and its industrial history have produced an irregular form.

Terraced rows
20th century suburbs
Municipal estates
Blocks of flats
Main industry
City Centre
Castle
Institutions
Main Roads
Railways

N

Crumlyn Bog
Kilvey Hill
Docks
R. Tawe
Townhill
Swansea Bay
Fairwood Common
Mumbles Head

2 mls
3 km

and that they had failed to develop either good measurement techniques or a substantive theory.[41] The criticisms had more than a ring of truth about them and more recent studies in urban morphology, although still largely lacking theoretical basis, have shown greater willingness to use measurement and to seek explanations which lend themselves to generality. J. Wreford Watson's study of relict morphology in Halifax, Nova Scotia, contained some extremely useful suggestions of ways in which morphological elements might be incorporated into an analysis of urban growth.[42] There were clear examples of elements in the morphology which had directed any growth or change from particular parts of the city, such as the zone of ossification (Figure 13). Similarly, the studies of urban fringe-belts have demonstrated the effects of past land-use patterns on modern urban structure,[43] whilst other studies have concentrated upon the relationship between form and function.[44] This latter type of study has several points of emphasis, exemplified by the findings of E. M. Horwood and R. R. Boyce[45] that the shape of the central shopping district had relevance to its efficiency and performance and by studies which relate traffic flow efficiency to the form of the channels of movement.[46] The relationship between form and function for individual structures is closest when the original activity occupies the original building but becomes more tenuous away from that situation. A clear indication of past functional patterns can often be obtained from the morphological evidence which is left in the urban landscape.

Urban morphology as an academic approach within urban geography has proved responsive to criticisms in the past decade and now provides an important perspective to study of the city. The necessity to incorporate the physical fabric of towns into more general theories of urban growth has long been advocated by urban morphologists in Britain and there are now clear signs that they are being heeded. An emphasis in L. S. Bourne's recent analysis of central city change in Toronto was the need to account for the effect of physical structures and real estate, the inherited urban fabric, upon modern trends for change.[47] S. T. Openshaw has shown how statistical approaches may be used to relate the urban morphology of a city to its socio-economic structure,[48] and in doing so has tested a tacit assumption in studies of socio-spatial structure, namely the link between morphological and social patterns: others—including historians—have been

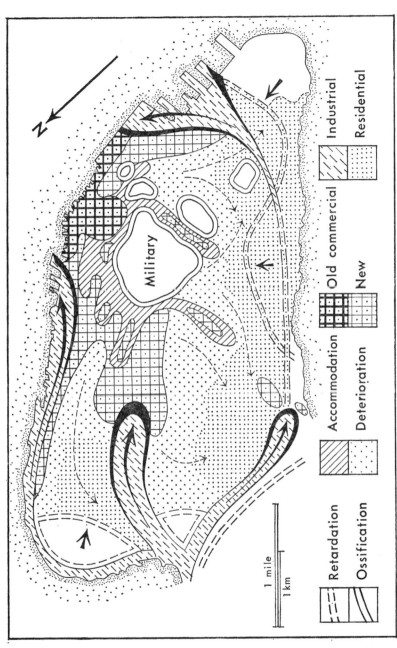

Fig 13. *Relict morphology and urban growth: Halifax, Nova Scotia:* J. Wieford Watson demonstrated that relict features could influence growth patterns with this Canadian example. Various stages of adaptation are evident with ossification or firm resistance to change, exemplified by military land-use in the city. (After Miller, R. and Watson, J. W. (eds), *Geographical Essays in Memory of Alan G. Ogilvie*, 1959, by permission of the author and Thomas Nelson and Son Ltd.)

Military

Industrial
Residential
Old commercial
New
Accommodation
Deterioration
Retardation
Ossification

N

1 mile
1 km

concerned with the processes of decision-making which underlie patterns of urban growth and have thus begun the examination of behavioural influences.[49] These more recent, innovative approaches hold promise of more significant studies for urban morphology, although its importance is likely to be as an integral part of a wider geographical perspective rather than as a systematic field in its own right. The shifts in emphasis during the 1960s, mainly evidenced in American literature on urban geography, have been towards functional analyses more closely related to concepts in land economics on the one hand and the geometries of space on the other. Process rather than static structure has offered another analytical emphasis on flows and linkages rather than on points in a distribution. Besides underlying economic postulates, it is the social dimensions of city structure which are receiving increasing attention. The qualities of these and other new emphases in urban geography can best be developed in the context of individual topics; it remains here only to identify the ways in which an overall geographical perspective of the city may be characterised.

STATEMENTS ON GENERAL THEORY

Such a perspective cannot of course be distinctively urban: it must derive its qualities and characteristics from a more general geographical theory of which it is part. Despite Burton's assessment of a deficiency of theory in geography, there are long-established approaches and concepts which Peter Haggett has categorised as areal differentiation, landscape, man/environment relationships, spatial distribution and geometry:[50] crudely stated, three are more traditional, whilst the latter two have developed more recently. Evidence of progress has been abundant in the last decade. W. Bunge's book on theoretical geography provided new insights and B. J. L. Berry and F. E. Horton were able to suggest in 1970 that: 'Not only have there been major syntheses of existing concepts, but bold new theoretical departures have been made'.[51] Progress, however, does not mean success and David Harvey[52] concluded that for the 1970s theory construction on a broad and imaginative scale should be a first priority. Harvey suggested that concepts in geography were either derivative, that is obtained from other disciplines, or indigenous, developed from within geography. Not all indigenous concepts could be justified as such because they were either simply procedural devices or were concerned with the temporal dimension and were not, therefore, geographical. The most acceptable indigenous concepts were those concerned with sets of spatial relationships; qualities such as location, distance and pattern which bore strong ties with geometry. The interaction between process and form, exemplified by T. Hagerstrand's work on diffusion,[53] W. Bunge's drawing together of flows, movements and spatial patterns,[54] and B. J. L. Berry's use of general field theory,[55] could, Harvey argued, provide a new kind of synthesis in geography, replacing the more intuitive synthesis of regionalism. Harvey believes that a general theory could emerge from an exploration of the links between indigenous theories of spatial form and derivative theories of temporal process.

Against this a perspective for studying social geography in the city can be constructed. The set of spatial elements within the city can be summarised as points, individual locations or foci; areas, such as neighbourhoods and sub-regions within the city; and flows or spatial interactions. The elements within this set provide a focus for geographical perspective which may be concerned with the patterns themselves, with their inter-relationships, and with the behaviour and activity which occur within their context. Separate topics in this text will demonstrate the various emphases and ways in which they integrate into an overall geographical perspective. Derivative concepts of importance have already been stated: principles of economic location will be implicit in many themes, particularly those concerned with the functional organisation of the central city; urban sociology, however, provides the main derivative theories. The plea is similar to that of B. T. Robson, that urban geographers should be more interested in social structure and the postulates of allied disciplines;[56] while Harvey's suggestion that any general theory of the city must relate social processes to spatial form and combine elements of the 'sociological imagination' with the 'geographical imagination' is closely aligned to the present approach.[57] In the analysis of a complex phenomenon, which increasingly demands inter-disciplinary perspectives, derivations are essential and the spirit of Sir Kenneth Clark's justification for the borrowings of Raphael, 'The great artist takes what he needs' has some relevance for the social geographer.[58] The need is for progress away from the situation which Harvey described as one of individual

E

disciplines 'ploughing lonely furrows' to one of integrated research at the inter-faces. From this a more satisfactory conceptual framework may emerge, not least for a geography of the city.

SPATIAL MODELS OF THE CITY

Generalised spatial models of the city have also been derived from other disciplines. Those which exist are only valid as very general statements of the structure and growth of cities but have proved remarkably persistent as concepts, largely because of their generality. Most of the spatial models were formed with reference to the internal structure of the American city at a particular point in time; they have become more obviously inadequate as urban systems have become more complex and as contrasts between cities in different parts of the world are more clearly identified.

The so-called 'classic' models of urban land use have had a considerable and continuing impact upon the literature of urban studies and deserve a place in any review of the field (Figure 14).[59] The best-known is undoubtedly the concentric zonal model, which, although usually associated with E. W. Burgess, had in fact several previous formulations. The concentric-zonal model, in common with the others, attempts to provide a descriptive framework for the spatial organisation of urban land use. Its solution is that, given model conditions of a uniform land surface, universal accessibility and free competition for space, land use will arrange itself in a series of concentric zones around a central point. The sequence of land uses from centre to periphery suggested by Burgess was: 1. the central business district; 2. the transition zone; 3. the zone of workingmen's homes; 4. the zone of better residences and 5. the commuters' zone. Whilst clearly acknowledging that this model would not hold for each and every city, Burgess nevertheless thought that it might have some generality within North America, and its outlines could be recognised in Chicago and some other cities in the United States. The Burgess model was a description of urban structure but was also intended to serve as a mechanistic framework for urban growth and change. The main ecological processes involved in the dynamic aspects of the model were those of invasion and succession by which population groups gradually filtered outwards from the centre as their status and level of assimilation improved.

Although many of the assumptions made by E. W. Burgess and his use of ecological processes are questionable, his simple spatial model has persuasive qualities for persistence. As R. A. Murdie has pointed out, the concentric zonal model parallels at least three other models of urban growth, which from different angles might arrive at the same basic form.[60] These are Colby's notions of centrifugal and centripetal forces; generalisations concerning urban population densities and their progressive decline away from the central city; and the more recent bid-rent models developed by urban land economists. The latter type of model attempts to measure the equation of land costs and transport costs by individuals and institutions in their location decision.

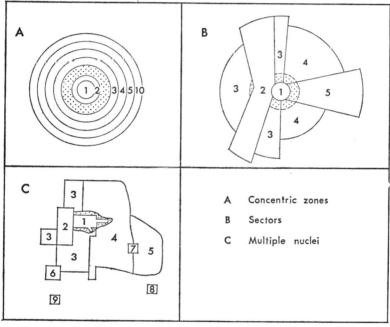

Fig 14. *'Classical' models of the city:* These models, largely intended to provide descriptive generalisations of residential structure, are often described as the classical models. 1. CBD; 2. wholesale, light industry; 3. low-status residential; 4. medium-status residential; 5. high-status residential; 6. heavy industry; 7. outlying business; 8. residential suburb; 9. industrial suburb; 10. commuters' zone (Adapted from: *(a)* E. W. Burgess; *(b)* H. Hoyt; *(c)* C. D. Harris and E. L. Ullman) Dot-shading marks the zone-in-transition.

The sector model of urban land use formulated by H. Hoyt is normally regarded as the second of the classic models of urban spatial form. The Hoyt formulation was constrained by its narrow focus on housing and rent. He obtained rental and other data which he mapped by blocks for 142 American cities and from this empirical research suggested his sector model. The model took the form of a central business district with a series of sectors emanating from it. The high-grade residential areas pre-empted the most desirable space and were powerful forces in the pattern of urban growth. Other grades of residential area were aligned around the high-grade areas, with the lowest-grade areas occupying the least desirable land, often adjacent to manufacturing districts. The various residential areas took the spatial form of sectors, extending from the central city towards the periphery, and were thus in apparent contrast with the concentric zones suggested by Burgess. The common elements were the focal nature of the central business district and the presence of a transition-zone which was clearly identifiable in American cities. The sector model was also a growth framework and Hoyt's formulations on neighbourhood change were mainly aimed at describing the dynamic characteristics of the high-grade residential areas which he regarded as key elements. The high-grade areas would move, he suggested, towards amenity land, along transport routes, and towards the homes of leaders of the community.

The third classic model was that by C. D. Harris and E. L. Ullman which they termed the multiple nuclei model. Its main distinctive quality was its abandonment of the central business district as a sole focal point, replacing it by a number of discrete nuclei around which individual land uses were geared. As the conditions for the location of these nuclei may vary, there was no one generalised spatial form which could be suggested.

The merits of these three spatial models have been extensively discussed and although further general assessment is not necessary, a number of more specific points may be made. First, although the models appear to take different spatial forms, they are not necessarily contradictory. One useful, though rather crude analogy may be formed with the J. Von Thünen model of agricultural land use (Figure 15).[61] The original formulation by Von Thünen was one of concentric zones of land use and this represented the 'purest' model of uniform land surface, single

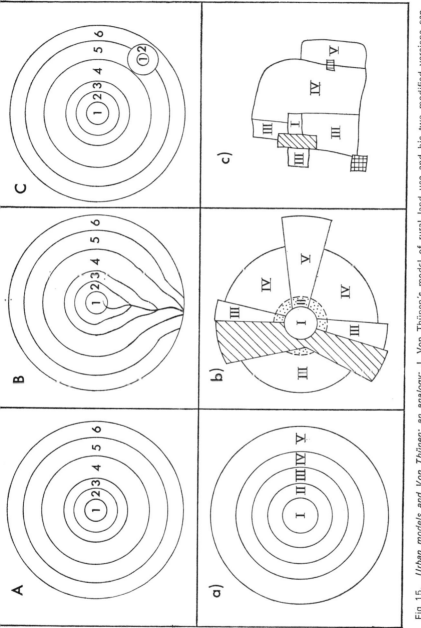

Fig 15. *Urban models and Von Thünen: an analogy:* J. Von Thünen's model of rural land use and his two modified versions can be seen as analogous to the three urban models. Aa represent the ideal models; Bb the modification imposed by specialised route-ways; Cc the effects of alternative centres. 1. horticulture/dairying; 2. silviculture; 3. intensive arable; 4. arable with long ley; 5. 3-field arable; 6. ranching. I CBD; II zone in transition; III low status; IV middle status; V high-status.

centre and universal accessibility. His introduction of a line of movement, a river in this case, distorted the zones into a form which was distorted along that line. The introduction of a second centre, a minor farm, produced a new pattern of land use. In some ways the classic models of the city conform to this succession —Burgess' being the simplest model, with sectors produced by lines of movement, and separate clusters by the distinct nuclei. The models are thus successive adaptations away from the simple state. This analogy cannot be taken too far but others have argued that the classic models are not contradictory but represent different facets of the city's spatial structure. 'The models are independent, additive contributors to the total socio-economic structuring of city neighbourhoods.'[62] This point will be elaborated in chapter 6 but for the moment it is sufficient to suggest in general terms that the two main models—concentric zonal and sector—essentially measure different aspects of the city. The concentric zonal model emphasises the urban growth pattern and was reflective in America both of population groups at various stages of assimilation and of ageing of the urban fabric; the sector model measured prestige or status ratings of residential districts.

A second specific point can be made with reference mainly to the concentric zonal model which is taken as the most comprehensive of the three. This point concerns the amount of universality which the model possesses both in terms of time and of regional variation. Reference has already been made to the work of G. Sjoberg and L. F. Schnore; their findings on the spatial structure of cities have relevance to the Burgess model.[63] Sjoberg found that the pre-industrial cities which he identified had a spatial structure which resembled a concentric form. His evidence was obtained from historical records and contemporary descriptions of pre-industrial cities in Europe and other parts of the world. The zonal pattern of land use was in many ways, however, the inverse of that identified by Burgess in North America in the 1920s and 1930s. The central city was weakly developed in commercial terms and was a place of prestige, occupied by government buildings, market place and status functions. The zones around the centre declined in terms of residential prestige from the centre towards the periphery until the poorest sections of the population were found outside the city walls. L. F. Schnore in his analysis of cities in Latin America found that the zones of land use could be crudely described as taking the form of concentric circles, but that the sequence was that of the pre-industrial city (Figure 16). The observations of Sjoberg and Schnore lead to the proposition that the concentric zonal model of Burgess was pertinent to a time-technological stage represented by American cities in the 1920s and 1930s. The assumptions which Burgess made of a mixed industrial/commercial base, free land market and heterogeneous population are those typical of the industrial city. In other parts of the world where these conditions were satisfied, perhaps Britain in the late-nineteenth century, the concentric zonal model might be applicable; elsewhere there are deviations. The differences evident in the spatial structure of pre-industrial cities in the historic sense and as they appear contemporarily in developing countries are a result of different technologies and organisations, analogous to Schnore's idea of a continuum differentiated in terms of his ecological complex.

Accepting the fact of temporal change, it is clear that the concentric zonal model may become less applicable over time as urban systems grow and as the assumptive base becomes less valid. Many American cities show increasing divergence from the land-use patterns of the 1920s as major changes in their structure occur.[64] The relative decline of the central business district and the emergence of suburban business centres create separate nuclei for development. Changes in housing styles, including the move towards apartment dwelling, redistribute status groups. Processes of assimilation become less evident as the inflow of different culture groups to American cities ceases and a contemporarily non-assimilable minority remains. As the American metropolis founded upon the new transport and communications technology becomes more clearly articulated, then the models based upon the industrial city become less relevant. A major trend to distort the classical models in many parts of the world has been the increasing level of public intervention in the forming of urban structure. Zoning laws in North America, public sector housing and development control in Britain, state control in Communist communities, are steps towards destroying the validity of a basic assumption in the classical models, that of a free market for land.

The classical models, as their description implies, were formulated some time ago and there have been very few attempts to provide alternatives in more recent years. W. Alonso provided a new interpretation rather than a new model with his structural

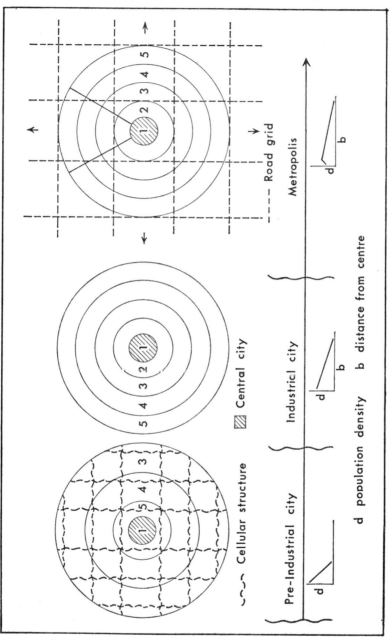

Fig 16. *Generalised spatial models and the idea of a continuum:* The three broad stages on a continuum can be given spatial descriptions. The pre-industrial city has a weakly-developed commercial centre but many local nuclei: there is functional mixture and vertical zoning. In the *industrial city*, the single centre is highly developed commercially and in the city area, economic factors assume greater importance: accessibility to the centre is crucial and functional separation occurs. *Metropolis* has a weaker centre in a more dispersed city area, with more separate nuclei; accessibility is more universal. 1. central city; 2. zone-in-transition; 3. low

theory (Figure 17). Alonso described the classic models as historic theories, committed to a pattern of peripheral expansion through the invasion-succession process, which had matched the pattern of growth in American cities up to recent decades.[65] His structural theory, however, relied not upon the mechanistic growth processes but upon the tastes, preferences and life styles of individuals choosing a place to live. Because of its flexibility, the structural theory was more able to accommodate contemporary trends such as the move back towards the central city of a limited section of the higher income groups. More obviously new models, but of a much more quantitative kind usually dependent upon high-speed computers for their construction and operation, are the wide range of experimental models developed within the context of urban planning.[66] Characteristic of these models has been their increasing complexity, as new variables measuring different aspects of reality are built in, and their

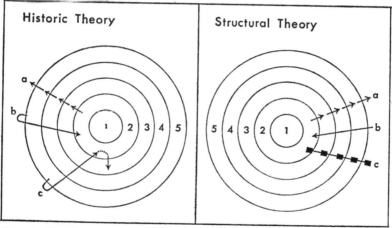

Fig 17. *Historic and structural theories of growth in the American city* (after W. Alonso). *Historic theory* is based on ageing structures, sequent occupance, population growth, available land. (*a*) Consistent outflow until 1950s. (*b*) Commitment to return flow as renewal provides space. *(c)* Continuing return flow but new shift out as renewal clears next zone. Structural theory involves same factors but is effective through taste and preference. (*a*) Consistent outflow likely to continue for most people; (*b*) Return flow will be selective (single, no family, mobile transients); (*c*) High-rise apartments may occur in any zone. In both theories an immobile group is constrained to particular central areas and there is territorial expansion with population growth. 1. CBD; 2. zone-in-transition; 3. low status; 4. middle status; 5. high status.

tendency to become specialised sub-models of the city rather than overall models of urban structure. Much progress has been made in terms of gravity models, measuring movement such as journey to work and journey to shop within the city; simulation models of urban growth have been successfully used in measuring future residential development in American cities; traffic problems have proved particularly amenable to model building and forecasting. This kind of model-building has recently been defined as a priority area for research in human geography and is already in fact a rapidly developing field.[67] As the models become more sophisticated and complex, however, they become further removed from the form and perhaps the spirit of the classical models of urban structure. A great quality of the concentric zonal model is its simplicity; it really is a model in the pure form, an abstraction from reality and it endures because at this simple level patterns can be recognised. But the simplicity is in turn a form of weakness; the concentric zonal model is a very generalised descriptive model linked to a mechanistic theory of urban structure and growth. It is useful in those terms as a way of representing land-use patterns within the city and identifying broad sections or zones. It is useless, however, to the urban planner concerned with more detailed structure and process and indeed, as indicated above, increasingly less useful even as a generalised descriptive statement of the modern city. There are of course many different kinds of models which may be formulated at various levels of generalisation and for a diversity of purposes.[68] The classical models of city structure, particularly the concentric zonal and sector models, have continuing value as points of reference, for organisation of study and for theory-testing, in the modern city as will be seen when many of the points touched upon in this discussion are elaborated in subsequent chapters.

CHAPTER FOUR

The Central City

THE central city has always been a spatial location of significance
although its characteristic qualities have varied considerably over
time and space. A most obvious broad contrast is that between
the central areas of pre-industrial cities, characterised by Gideon
Sjoberg[1] and those of the modern industrial city of North
America. Pre-industrial cities were dominated by symbolic and
social rather than by economic values; centrally-placed palaces
and temples in Oriental cities, cathedrals and public institutions
in medieval Europe, displayed priorities such as prestige, power
and defence rather than economic gain in the use of central land.
Market places and points of exchange existed within the city but
they tended to be dispersed in localised nuclei rather than concentrated at the centre. Guilds were similar multiple nuclei and a
general spirit in which competition was institutionally rejected
re-inforced the many-centred framework of the city.[2] In contrast
to this pattern, the evolution of the American central business
district epitomised the replacement of social by economic forces
in the determination of central land use. Space in the centres of
growing cities was used with increasing intensity and functional
concentration; ability to occupy a given site was determined by
purchasing power. The urban skyline of downtown Manhattan,
with its multi-storey blocks of business functions, symbolises this
pressure on central space. Elsewhere in American industrial cities,
the central districts took on a similar form as the temples of
Mammon dominated land use.

Although the comparative recency of American cities and the particularly advanced nature of the American economic organisation have tended to make them a special case, evidence from most other parts of the world suggests that as processes of economic development and modernisation have quickened, so traditional forms of the central city have been infiltrated by economic forces. European central cities, although still a paler version of the American downtown, have largely become commercialised areas and similar trends are evidenced in some of the larger non-western cities. Because of their age, European central cities still partly appear in more traditional forms: urban fabrics inherited from the past and often retaining some symbolic value are juxtaposed with modern structures which are the products of economic forces for change. Similar amalgams of the old and the new will doubtless characterise the non-western central cities as they adapt themselves to modern forms of spatial organisation. In Europe, it is the existence of these historic cores which still poses some of the greatest problems in adapting the central cities to fit new functional roles.

Change and dynamism are very clear qualities of the central city. From the descriptive statements already made, a broad trend of change is hypothesised whereby economic centrality dominates the centre and more traditional cities move towards a form resembling the American model. This statement is of course far too simple: there are fundamental differences even within one country between larger and smaller cities: older traditional cities, such as Amsterdam, can never be completely dominated by the forces of economic competition; historical urban fabrics will persist because of the non-economic values which society places upon them. Differences between large and small cities are probably going to be especially significant in non-western countries, whilst marked contrasts between different parts of the non-western world are already apparent. Change does not stop with the attainment of the American model and a major feature of American cities over the past decade has been change within the central business district. This change has meant a lessening role for the central city as its monopoly on accessibility has been broken and groups of functions have tended to migrate to the suburbs. The break-up of this single-centred dominance almost implies a return to the multi-centred form which Sjoberg identified in pre-industrial cities. J. E. Vance has summarised this process of change in the American city: 'That area of urban synthesis is the downtown. In the past we have called it the central business district but that term is hardly adequate today. There is "central business" all over the city at the same time that there is only one "downtown" '.[3]

Geographical studies of the central city have recognised, at least for the American city, two constituent areas termed the central business district and the zone-in-transition. Emphases in geographical studies have been upon characteristics of these two areas in terms of land use and activities, upon the problems of boundaries and definition, and more latterly upon linkages, interrelationships and temporal change. These emphases have been primarily academic but have in many cases lent themselves naturally to applied problems.

THE CENTRAL BUSINESS DISTRICT (CBD)

The CBD is perhaps the most obvious functional zone within the western city and is occupied by those activities which need a central and accessible urban location. Geographers have long recognised the existence of the CBD as an urban zone but detailed analyses of its structure and its dynamism have been of comparatively recent origin. M. J. Proudfoot, who analysed Philadelphia in 1937,[4] is usually afforded the status of a pioneer in more recent techniques and his emphasis was upon the differentiation of types of retail centres within the city. A more detailed CBD study was that of W. W. Olsson in Stockholm[5] in which he incorporated many techniques which have since become standard procedures. CBD expansion was an observable fact of Stockholm's urban growth and business activity had spread from the medieval town on the isthmus to the mainland. Within the CBD had developed a number of distinctive districts of specialisation, such as retail trade, wholesaling, government offices and professional offices. In a more detailed analysis of retail trade, Olsson devised a 'shop-rent index' (total shop rents in a building divided by the length of its frontage) which could serve as a measure of the varying levels of land-use intensity. This study of Stockholm, more than any other earlier analysis, indicated some of the potentialities for detailed geographical investigation of the CBD.

DELIMITING THE CBD

R. E. Murphy and J. E. Vance focused attention upon the functional structure of the CBD, its delimitation and its temporal change.[6] The problem of accurate delimitation was faced first by Murphy and Vance for a number of sound reasons which included the fact that it was a geographical problem of regionalisation and was an essential preliminary step for comparative studies. Their approach to the problem of delimitation included the development of techniques which proved suitable for other aspects of CBD analysis. A major difficulty of delimitation was that of attempting to identify a precise boundary which did not really exist: the difference between the CBD and other parts of the city is one of degree rather than of kind. High intensity of land use and high land values, for example, are both typical of CBD space but there is often a gradual transition to lower levels of intensity and value rather than a well-defined break. Occasionally, there are sharp boundaries to a CBD, provided by natural barriers such as a river or lake-shore; or man-made barriers such as parks and transport lines, but these tend to be exceptional. The difficulties of delimitation are reflected by the variety of criteria which have been adopted and the surfeit rather than deficiency of potential measures. D. H. Davies in his study of Cape Town listed sixteen delimiting criteria with which he had experimented, none of which however achieved any clear advantages over the others.[7]

Population measures offer one example in which some experimentation has been made. The crudest such measure is that based upon the assumption that the CBD is a non-residential district and that an approximation of its boundary could be obtained by plotting permanent residences. The resultant map should possess a central blank space corresponding to the CBD, though allowance would have to be made for other non-residential use such as industrial areas, parks and routeways. Associated with this particular approach, though not specifically with the identification of boundaries, have been a series of studies contrasting daytime and nighttime populations in a number of cities.[8] A more realistic technique adopting population criteria involves the measurement of pedestrian flow. The underlying principle to this technique, typical of a wide range of criteria, is that space within the CBD is more intensively used than that of any other part of the city,

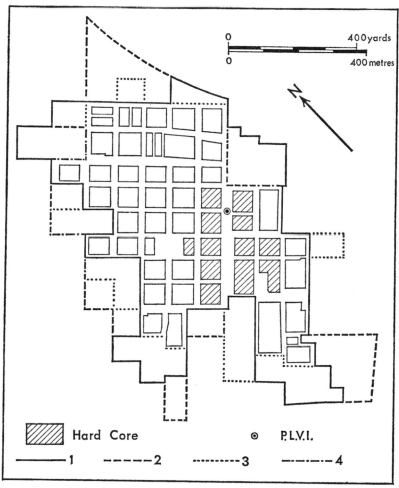

0   400 yards

0   400 metres

Hard Core   ◉   P.L.V.I.

———1   - - - - -2   ··········3   —·—·—4

Fig 18. *Delimiting the CBD: Cape Town:* 1. central business index; 2. 5 per cent land values; 3. traffic count; 4. composite index from 2 and 3. (Adapted from Davies, D. H., *Land-use in central Cape Town*, 1965, reprinted by the permission of the author and *Economic Geography*.)

a necessity arising from its high centrality and accessibility. Qualities of centrality which belong to a limited part of the central city diminish rapidly with distance from it. Pedestrian flow is one such measure of this diminution and can be expected to be extremely high at the most central parts of the CBD and to decrease rapidly towards its edges. Simultaneous counts at a large number of points throughout the CBD can be used to identify these various levels of pedestrian flow and to identify a boundary. The data are usually difficult to handle in that local factors such as transport termini or stopping points and walkways which are used in transit by non-CBD users can distort levels. In terms of finding a boundary, there is the recurrent difficulty of identifying natural breaks, as pedestrian flow is not exclusively a feature of the CBD. A similar population measure used by D. H. Davies was based on the numbers of visitors to individual stores at various points within the CBD.[9] (Figure 20.)

Measures based upon the monetary value attached to sites within the CBD have proved a useful source of experimentation both in the analysis of boundaries and of internal organisation. The basic logic is the same as that underlying pedestrian flows, that the value attached to a site will reflect its accessibility and will decline with distance from a key central point. There are numerous empirical studies to show that in terms of the general urban area, land values will be high at the centre and will decline rapidly towards the peripheries. Murphy and Vance suggested that there was within the CBD a peak land value intersection (PLVI), typically at a major road junction, around which land values were disposed (Figure 18). A number of studies have used this criterion of monetary value, such as W. W. Olsson's Shop Rent Index which has already been described. Murphy and Vance experimented with land values whilst D. T. Herbert developed a Rate Index applicable to British cities and based upon rates or local taxes (Figure 19).[10] Monetary measures, although conditioned by the availability and reliability of data, have worked reasonably well, but the familiar problem with the CBD boundary is deciding the point at which land values cease to be typical of the CBD. Murphy and Vance formulated one definition from land values, assessed on front footage, which they called a 5 per cent line. They suggested that by placing the highest valued lot within the city at 100 per cent, a line could be drawn enclosing the lots with valuations which formed 5 per cent or more of that peak

OPPOSITE: *(above)* House types and morphology in Britain: Modern private housing, Swansea; *(Below)* The Central City: Central Manhattan.

lot to give a good approximation of the CBD boundary. Applications of this particular technique showed that it did indeed provide such an approximation, though Murphy and Vance did not pursue it, mainly because it failed to distinguish between the different forms of land use.

Land use itself did in fact form the basis for the Murphy and Vance central business index (CBI) which is the best-known of the delimitation techniques. Their basic hypothesis was that the CBD was characterised by a particular set of functions which, though not exclusive to it, formed their highest expression within the CBD. The procedure began with a definition of a CBD function, 'The retailing of goods and services for a profit and the performing of various financial and office functions',[11] and the formulation of a check list which in fact pre-determined the result, in that the CBD was to be defined as the locale of those functions which were initially classed as CBD in character. Wholesaling, governmental and public institutions were excluded from the list, despite the fact that they are normally found in the CBD and are dependent upon centrality and accessibility. The CBI was composed of two other measures of land use, the central business height index and the central business intensity index with the boundary identified where blocks scored less than 1·0 on the former and less than 50 per cent on the latter. Other rules covered the contiguity of blocks with other parts of the CBD. A comparative study of nine American cities by Murphy and Vance demonstrated the viability of their procedure, whilst D. H. Davies identified a 'hard core' of the CBD in Cape Town by adopting threshold scores of 4·0 and 80 per cent[12] (Figure 20). Although the original list of functions may be questioned, the CBI provides a reasonably accurate way of eliminating the CBD. The remaining question is whether the effort is justified. Academically the justification exists both as an exercise in regionalisation, which could be developed further, and as a necessary basis for comparative studies. The academic qualifications include the accusation that delimitation imposes an artificial compartmentalisation and diverts attention from other priorities of study such as processes, linkages and interrelationships. Practically, the CBI procedure is less tenable because it requires a great deal of data and measurement to define a boundary which can never be more than an approximation. For the urban planner and administrator, a much quicker rule of thumb technique would be adequate, and both

OPPOSITE: The central city: *(above)* Central Lahore, West Pakistan; *(below)* a traditional central square with governor's palace and archbishop's palace: Quito, Ecuador.

F

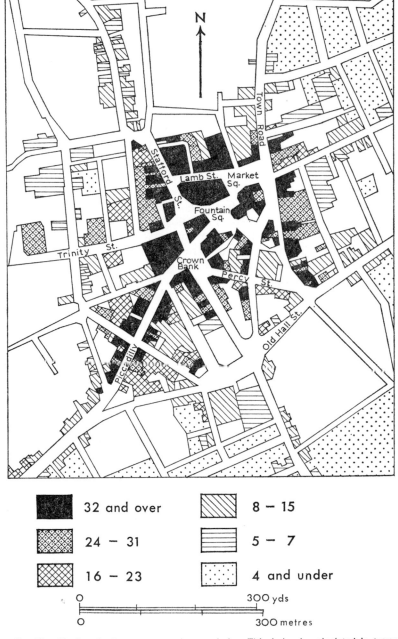

N

Stafford St.
Lamb St.
Market Sq.
Town Road
Fountain Sq.
Trinity St.
Crown Bank
Percy St.
Old Hall St.
Piccadilly

32 and over

24 – 31

16 – 23

8 – 15

5 – 7

4 and under

0   300 yds
0   300 metres

Fig 19. *Hanley, Staffs: scores on the rate index:* This index is calculated in terms of gross rateable value per unit area.

the American Bureau of Census and the British Census of Distribution offer much simpler definitional procedures for the return of statistics. These short-cut procedures lack detail but they have the merit of setting out to achieve an approximation where only an approximation is possible. The value of a simple procedure, even in the case of academic study, was recently

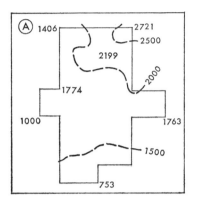

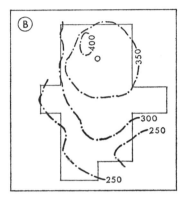

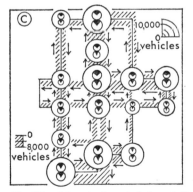

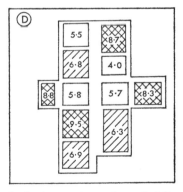

Fig 20. *Internal characteristics of Cape Town's hard core:* A. numbers of daily visits; B. land values in shillings per square foot; C. traffic flows (large circle shows 12 hours total; smaller shows a.m. (upper) p.m. (lower). Black = % commercial vehicles. Width of shaded section = % flow of vehicles. D. total height indices; shading under 6; 6–8; over 8. (After Davies, D. H., 'The hard core of Cape Town's CBD', *Economic Geography,* 36 1960, 53–69, by permission of the author and *Economic Geography.*)

suggested by A. R. Pred who emphasised that the core was not a discrete phenomenon but a 'union of sets'* for which a conventional, arbitrary, working definition would be sufficient.[13]

INTERNAL STRUCTURE OF THE CBD

Techniques developed to delimit the CBD have proved applicable to analyses of internal structure. Emphasis in past studies has been upon land use patterns, though current trends show an increasing interest in processes and functional linkages. All functions occupying space within the CBD have in common the need for centrality and their ability to purchase accessible locations. Within the CBD there are diversities which are revealed by the distinctive functional districts and by the individual locational qualities of specific functions. The functional districts or quarters are produced by what J. E. Vance has termed the segregation process,[14] and these become better defined with increasing size of the CBD. The retail trade quarter is often referred to as the node and is usually on the most central space: the office quarter is well-marked and may have sub-sections such as financial or legal districts. Besides these horizontal divisions, there are distinctive vertical variations in the distributions of functions; the ground-floors of multi-storey buildings are occupied by activities with the greatest centrality needs. With these qualities in mind, many geographical studies of CBD structure have attempted to identify and explain patterns of variation. Patterns of land use have provided the basic structure and explanation is often attempted using measures of centrality. These measures are closely similar to those used in delimitation and can provide a second dimension to the spatial distribution of activities.

Some past studies concerned with the analysis of internal variations have been content to identify broad divisions; E. M. Horwood and R. R. Boyce, for example, developed the core-frame concept in which the core was described as the central and the frame as the more peripheral parts of the CBD.[15] R. E. Murphy and J. E. Vance formulated much more detailed studies, using the Peak Land Value Intersection as a focal point around which zones placed at 100-yard intervals could be identified.

*A term employed in the mathematical theory of sets which implies that the CBD is not a discrete phenomenon but is a zone of interaction and cannot be entirely divorced from the city as a whole.

Each zone could be characterised in terms of its land use at various floor levels and the patterns which they described were replicated by D. H. Davies in Cape Town and by D. R. Diamond in Glasgow.[16] Studies following the procedures developed by Murphy and Vance have essentially used intensity of land use, the CBI, as a second dimension to the basic land use patterns. Zones based on 100-yard intervals are arbitarily defined by similar gradations of land use from the centre and typical clusters of activities appear to be generic to the western industrial city.

Other studies have related land use to different centrality measures. W. W. Olsson's Shop Rent Index was only applicable to retail trade but could be used to distinguish sectors of varying centrality within the retail district;[17] D. T. Herbert's Rate Index had similar though more general application. Pedestrian flow, although liable to distortion, has been used in South Wales to identify points of contrasted centrality within CBDs[18] (Figure 21). One of the most detailed studies of locational qualities of groups of functions and individual activities was that by Peter Scott, of Australian CBDs.[19] Analyses of the internal organisation

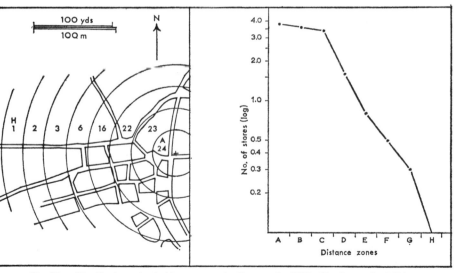

Fig 21. *Distribution of clothing stores in Swansea's CBD:* Numbers of clothing stores are shown in each 150 yard zone outwards from the point of peak pedestrian flow (+). The graph shows the steep decline in numbers of such stores with distance.

of the CBD demonstrate that each sub-district has its own characteristic level of centrality and accessibility (Figure 22). Retail trade occupies the most centrally-located space because it needs centrality and is prepared to bid high prices for it. In practically all cities, certain retail activities will be found on limited areas of land of greatest value. The size of the city under consideration will influence the absolute value.[20] Other districts, such as the office quarters, have less need for pedestrian accessibility and need not bid for the most central sites; whilst specialised functions may find separate nuclei, such as legal offices in the vicinity of a law court. Even within broad clusters of functions, there are distinctive patterns. The 'high-order' elements of retail trades—such as department stores, fashionable clothing and jewellery stores—occupy very central sites whilst 'low-order' stores—such as groceries—are more peripheral. For particular reasons individual functions often have specific locational requirements: furniture stores are often peripherally-located because, although 'high-order' retail trade, they consume large amounts of floor-space; building societies and other finance companies tend to seek central space, though often at upper-floor levels, because they are competitive and need customer accessibility.

The analyses of CBD structure so far described rest essentially upon traditional urban location theory and the economic competition which sifts out land use elements. Non-economic factors must be recognised, such as the ability of tradition and established prestige to maintain particular activities on particular sites. An address on a better canal street carries considerable prestige in Amsterdam; famous specialised districts such as New York's Wall Street have enduring importance; eccentric small units often persist in central parts of British cities through favourable long-term leaseholds. An increasing tendency in recent geographical studies of the CBD has been to state the insufficiency of land use patterns as basic data for study and to stress the importance of understanding linkages and activity patterns. As F. S. Chapin has suggested: 'Land use analysis is incomplete without a concurrent activity analysis.'[21] Chapin's method of approach contained an inventory of both land uses and the linkages which each element of land use possessed (Figure 23). From this basis of activities, linkages and interrelationships, the CBD can be analysed in its proper context as part of the wider urban system. A difficulty with this method is that of data collection and interpretation.

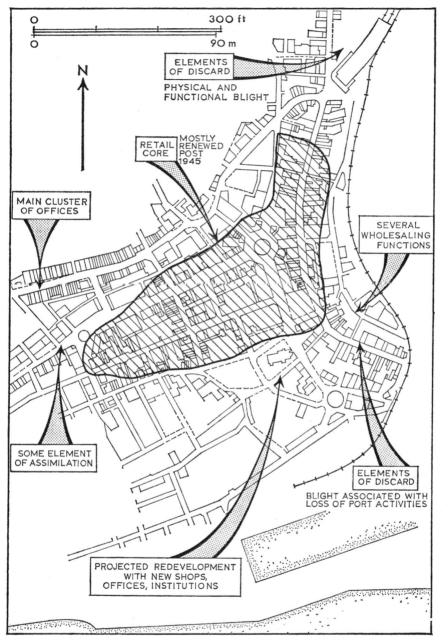

O — 300 ft
O — 90 m

N

ELEMENTS OF DISCARD
PHYSICAL AND FUNCTIONAL BLIGHT

RETAIL CORE
MOSTLY RENEWED POST 1945

MAIN CLUSTER OF OFFICES

SEVERAL WHOLESALING FUNCTIONS

SOME ELEMENT OF ASSIMILATION

ELEMENTS OF DISCARD
BLIGHT ASSOCIATED WITH LOSS OF PORT ACTIVITIES

PROJECTED REDEVELOPMENT WITH NEW SHOPS, OFFICES, INSTITUTIONS

Fig 22. *Generalised zones in central Swansea:* The patterns of functional structure and change which are evident could be identified in most British cities.

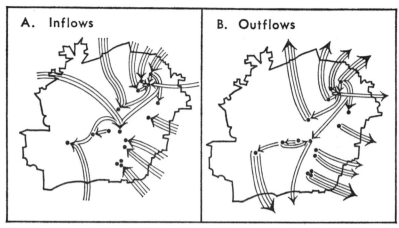

Fig 23. *Schematic view of CBD activity patterns:* F. S. Chapin's framework for the study of retail activity patterns, the main elements of which are to classify activities, to identify the spatial relationships and to depict the nature of interaction.

Some basic information on activity linkages is available, but current research experimentation is with the improvement of data sources by keeping activity diaries and time-budget accounts which record all linkages and interactions for individual activities. Substantive progress towards this kind of analysis is found in F. S. Chapin's work,[22] whilst an example of CBD analysis using interaction data is J. Goddard's study of taxi flows in central London[23] (Figure 24).

TEMPORAL CHANGE

Academic studies of temporal changes in the CBD have been few compared to the literature on delimitation and internal structure. The general expansion of the CBD—both horizontally and vertically—as the city has grown is an obvious fact but there have also been territorial shifts of emphasis and a high level of internal adjustment. R. E. Murphy and J. E. Vance recognised geographical shifts of the American CBD and identified zones of discard and assimilation as typical of American cities.[24] They suggested that the juxtaposition of the point of highest land value and the geographic centre gave the main indication of movement, the latter having slow, steady progress whilst the former lagged

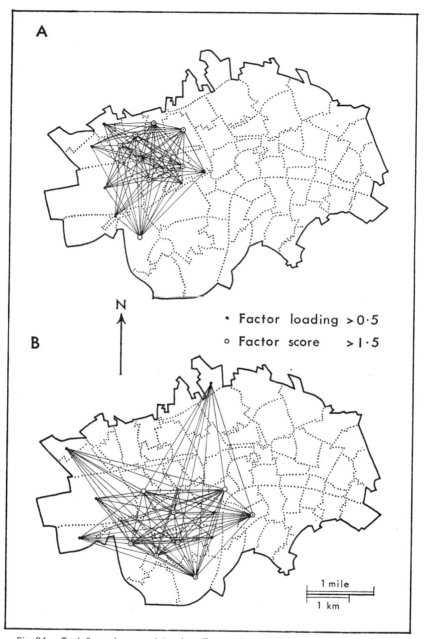

A

N

• Factor loading > 0·5
○ Factor score > 1·5

B

1 mile

1 km

Fig 24. *Taxi flows in central London:* These examples taken from a multi-variate study of taxi flows show: A. The West End cluster of flows; B. The Westminster cluster, (After Goddard, J.B. 'Functional Regions within the City Centre', *I.B.G. Transactions*, 49 1970) 161-82. By permission of the author and the Institute of British Geographers. For definition of factor loading and score, see appendix.

behind and occasionally leap-frogged several blocks. The zone of discard was typified by an assemblage of low-status functions, such as pawnshops, cheap restaurants and cinemas; the zone of assimilation was characterised by new functions such as speciality shops, car showrooms and banks. Availability of data for past periods has hindered study of temporal change but a number of recent studies have provided valuable insights into the dynamism of American cities, largely confirming the generalisations of Murphy and Vance[25] (Figure 25). Outside North America, a series of studies in North Staffordshire by D. T. Herbert showed temporal change over a period of nearly 100 years in six CBDs.[26] There were data problems which meant that accurate patterns could only be identified at two past time-periods, 1865 and 1912, but some indication of CBD expansion and change was possible. Between 1865 and 1912, the CBDs expanded physically and industrial activities were displaced; between 1912 and 1962 there was no further expansion but CBD space was more intensively used and well-defined sub-districts emerged. The North Staffordshire study provided a series of 'snapshot pictures' but not a continuous analysis of land-use change. J. A. Giggs used Valuation Lists (local tax records) in Barry, South Wales, to show detailed change and was able to demonstrate that the incidence of vacancies gradually diminished as the CBD grew but increased at a time of economic depression when the particular section studied became a zone of discard[27] (Figure 26). Other studies of CBD change are limited but P. Schöller's analysis of Japanese cities demonstrated high levels of instability of land use within the CBD.[28] There seemed to be characteristics peculiar to the Japanese case in that cheap real estate (buildings were timber-framed) and a weak transport network in the cities he described did not foster centralisation; a frequent shifting of activities was the result.

Although there is still a comparative paucity of detailed geographical studies of CBD change, there is now some evidence of new perspectives, set in a temporal context, which will allow real insights in the nature and future development of the CBD. Recent emphases upon activity systems and linkages, upon measurement of the changing image of the central city,[29] and upon process rather than form, all belong properly in a temporal context. This together with the recognition of the need to see the CBD in a non-compartmentalised context represents frontiers in CBD research. In this latter context it is clear that central place

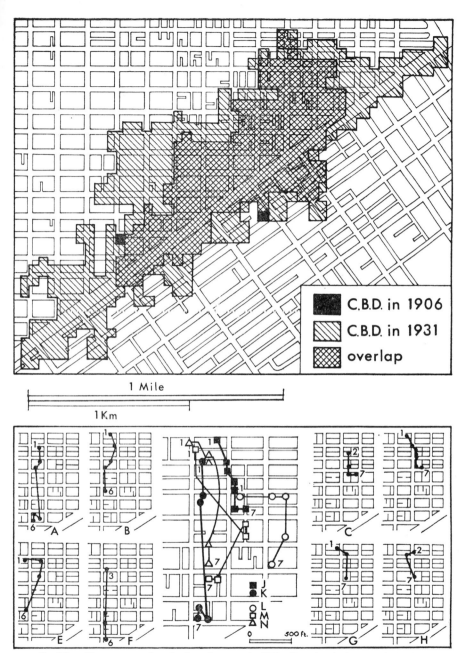

Fig 25. *Change over time in San Francisco's CBD:* Functional change within the central city can be shown both by shifts of the CBD and by movements of individual activities. A. dry goods; B. men's clothing; C. insurance; D. banks; E. jewellers; F. milliners; G. rent estate; H. stockbrokers; I. finance; K. women's clothing; L. garments; M. hotels; N. theatre; 1. 1850; 2. 1854; 3. 1858; 6. 1869; 7. 1875. (Adapted and reprinted with permission from Bowden, M. J., 'Downtown through Time', *Economic Geography*, 47 1971, 121–35.)

Legend within map:
C.B.D. in 1906
C.B.D. in 1931
overlap

1 Mile
1 Km

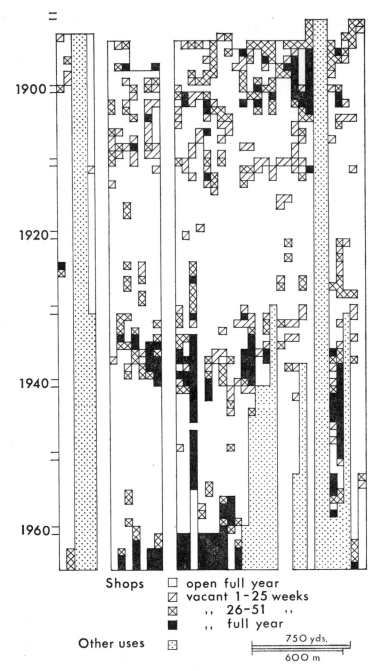

1900

1920

1940

1960

Shops   ☐ open full year
                      ◹ vacant 1-25 weeks
                      ⊠   ,,   26-51   ,,
                      ■   ,,   full year

Other uses   ⊡

750 yds.

600 m

Fig 26. *Functional change in Barry:* Fluctuations in vacancy-rates for retail trade can be related to general variations in a town's economic prosperity. (Davies, W. K. D., Giggs, J. A. and Herbert, D. T., 'Directories, Rate Books and the Commercial Structures of Towns' *Geography*, 53 (1968), 41–54.)

theory, which has still little application at an intra-urban level, must contribute to an academic understanding of the CBD. Geographical studies of the CBD have tended to languish since the mid-1950s but new and important perspectives now seem likely to emerge.

EMPIRICAL TRENDS AND THE WESTERN CBD

In terms of commercialised development, the CBD of the American city is clearly the most advanced form. There is considerable contemporary evidence, however, that it has suffered a comparative decline in status within the American urban system and considerable conjecture exists on its future role. This conjecture is heightened by the fact that the American CBD is often viewed as the prototype towards which CBDs in other parts of the world are progressing as the tenets of urban location theory increasingly dominate their development. There is very little evidence of CBD decline outside the United States but recent American experience would seem to suggest that advancing technology involves a decrease in the importance of the single centre. The heyday of the American CBD was that of an advanced money economy, a society based on capitalism and a highly developed public transport system. As these conditions have changed, particularly the latter, so the monopoly of central space has diminished. Similar arguments have been advanced by J. E. Vance in his depiction of the 'seven lives' of downtown.[30] His process of *extension* involved the break-up of the compact downtown and the emergence of arterial business streets as individual mobility increased; the processes of *replication* and *re-adjustment* involve the outward-movements of CBD units to new sites and the need for the CBD to adjust to far-ranging changes. The impact of changes in transport technology was emphasised by A. Pred who suggested that the urban core was most valid in times of pedestrian movement and electric traction but became questionable in days of automotive transport.[31] Similarly, R. L. Nelson argued that the dominance of the CBD as a retail centre corresponded with a growing dependence on railway tracks and local transport modes of street-cars, elevated railways and subways.[32]

The decline of the CBD in the American city is now generally agreed and the private automobile as a form of transport and the growth of suburbia are seen as the two main forces for change. The process of decentralisation of functions from the central city began with industry but later affected retailing and office activities. Re-centralisation is sometimes preferred as a term because activities relocated around new nuclei at some distance from the city-centre: regional shopping centres have since the late 1940s become the major alternative locations for retail trade and around 9,000 have been constructed in the United States. It had become clear by the 1950s that these regional shopping centres were not merely suburban precincts, servicing the new increments of population growth, but were competing with the CBD in real terms. Some idea of the scale of modern regional shopping centres can be obtained from Yorkdale in Toronto (see Figure 27), which has over 100 stores, including two department stores, and parking space for 6,500 cars. The great attractions of such regional shopping centres are accessibility, space and modernity and they need good locations to be economically viable. Older regional shopping centres which have become engulfed in urban growth are already in decline as their advantages disappear. H. Hoyt, in an analysis of American retail trends,[33] showed that between 1958 and 1963 general merchandise sales outside the CBD had a spectacular rise of 89 per cent compared with 54 per cent during 1954-8. In twenty-eight out of forty-nine metropolitan areas studied, there was an absolute loss in general merchandise sales in the CBD and in all others there was a relative loss. In 1958 general merchandise sales of the CBD dropped for the first time below that of stores outside the CBD and in 1963 it was one-half. Statistics for three major American metropolises showed this shift in emphasis:

Table 3   Comparison of CBD sales for three American cities, 1958–63

| | 1958 (Sales $000s) | | 1963 (Sales $000s) | |
	CBD	outside CBD	CBD	outside CBD
New York	849,801	643,708	908,859	1,197,487
Los Angeles	141,062	773,428	130,951	1,357,667
Chicago	288,011	652,480	288,728	1,038,476

* Figures from Hoyt, H., Urban Land (1966).

Department stores are thought to be particularly good indicators of change and whereas in 1910 (in a study of 116 Metropolitan Areas) at least 90 per cent of total department store sales

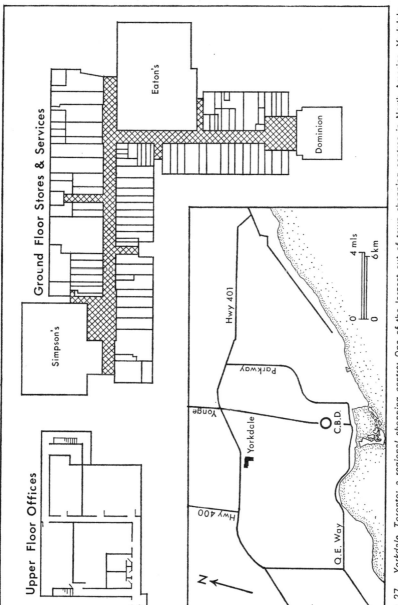

Fig 27. *Yorkdale, Toronto: a regional shopping centre:* One of the largest out of town shopping centres in North America, Yorkdale has over 1¼ million square feet of commercial space, over 100 stores together with theatres and restaurants in an all enclosed area with climate-controlled malls: sited near a major freeway intersection, there is parking for 6,500 vehicles.

were in the CBDs, in 1958 the figure was 57 per cent and in 1963 37 per cent. This decline is due both to new modern department stores opening in regional shopping centres and to firms leaving the CBD. There is a contrast between type of city; in new places such as San Diego, Los Angeles and Houston, dominated by the private automobile, the CBD share of department store sales were 8·4, 9·8 and 15·3 per cent respectively, whereas in older cities with well-developed mass transit systems, such as New York, Philadelphia and Boston, the shares remained high at 41, 42 and 34 per cent.

With such trends very much in evidence in American cities, questions arise on the future of the CBD, and an indifferent optimism of the early 1950s has been replaced by the acceptance of the fact that fundamental changes are occurring. J. E. Vance made the distinction between mass selling and specialty selling and suggested that: 'The CBD has become the mass seller to the inner part of metro, the specialty seller to the geographical city and the office area for the region.'[34] J. Allpass attempted to explain the fundamental processes at work in the need for accessibility.[35] He suggested that the larger a business became, then the more important were its internal as opposed to external transactions. Larger businesses, like departmental stores, had less need of contiguous activities and more of space and regional accessibility, whilst for small specialised businesses, external transaction within the CBD was still important. In American cities, therefore, change is evident; the former monopoly of the CBD, particularly in retail trade, no longer exists and it is adjusting to a more specialised role. The future of the CBD in individual cities generally indicates decline, but the extent is related to a number of factors such as metropolitan trends, mass transit facilities, and the image of the central city. In older American cities with inherited urban fabrics and large amounts of invested capital, a significant future role for the CBD is probably assured but in the newer metropolitan areas more limited importance is likely. A further distinction could be made within the United States but is particularly relevant when comparing American with Canadian cities. The central city may have a more dynamic future in Canada because it does not possess America's intense racial problems and to this extent the future of the CBD is tied to the wider central city and the extent to which it maintains links with the spreading metropolis.

The CBD in European cities shows some comparable trends for

OPPOSITE: The central city: *(above)* A modernising centre: downtown São Paulo, Brazil; *(below)* A British central city: modern retail area: Swansea.

change but has distinctive characteristics which may allow its greater persistence. R. E. Dickinson, commenting upon past trends in European cities, identified a shift of the CBD and public buildings to the wide boulevards erected on the sites of earlier fortifications such as the *Ring* in Vienna and Köln.[36] The equivalents of regional shopping centres are evident in Europe where new urban growth has occurred; for example Main-Taunus near Frankfurt and Ruhr-Park near Bochum. Similar examples can be identified in other European countries such as the South Hampshire centre in Britain and the Frolunda Torg centre in Sweden. The impact of these is not comparable with those in America and the Urban Land Institute of the USA in a European study tour concluded that there was universal action to safeguard the CBD.[37] New planned shopping centres were intended to cater for new suburbs and not to bankrupt existing retail districts. Further, 'The modernisation of the central city is definitely in evidence today with new downtown shopping places and upgrading of housing areas. European citizens continue to go there for their excitement and Sunday promenading.'[38] This last point is important in the promise of a continuing prosperity for the European CBD. It has far less of the violence, tension and superficial gloss of its equivalent in urban America. The attractive image of the CBD as a place of sociability, interest and involvement persists in Europe in CBDs which are often steeped in tradition and historic legacies as well as modernity and innovations. The great qualities of accessibility, availability and prestige of a CBD location persist for firms; for people the image is not tarnished.

THE ZONE-IN-TRANSITION

The term zone-in-transition applies to that part of the central city which is contiguous with the CBD, is characterised by ageing structures and derives many of its features from the fact that it has served as a buffer zone between the CBD and the more stable residential districts of the city. The most explicit characterisation of this zone dates from the concentric zonal model of E. W. Burgess and the features which he attributed to it were essentially those of the American city. The zone exists in other parts of the world in a strongly modified form and once again the main division is between western and non-western cities.

The American zone-in-transition is typified by change and

OPPOSITE: A British central city: *(above)* Office and professional district: Swansea; *(below)* zone of discard: Swansea.

G

instability affecting both the use of land and the resident population. Initially, in the early stages of urban growth, the high income groups occupied space close to the central area within easy access of their place of business. As the city grew, so demand for central space increased and spiralling commercialisation and congestion led to a reduction in the residential attractiveness of inner city locations. A land value gradient became operative in which land was most highly valued at the centre and least on the periphery. Advances in transport technology affected the higher-incomes groups first and these by and large opted for low-density residence in suburban locations where they incurred high transport costs but low per-unit costs for land. Thus began a process which was enacted many times as greater mobility came within the reach of successively lower income groups. The most consistent vacuum appeared in the zone-in-transition, adjacent to the CBD, where obsolescent structures became occupied by low income groups incurring low transport costs but occupying high value land at high densities. Because of their immobility they of all groups were able to exercise least choice.

    This process of change in American cities has been well-documented in Boston where D. Ward has described the evolution of Boston's CBD and its effects upon the adjacent zone-in-transition.[39] (Figure 28.) The CBD developed from a specialised waterfront section and market halls in the early-nineteenth century to a larger CBD with general commercial, financial and insurance functions. The major retail and wholesale complexes came later in the nineteenth century and were closely allied to revolutions in urban transport and the streetcar system. Most manufacturing concerns became entirely displaced from the CBD but other elements, notably wholesaling and ware-housing, were powerful expanders. A net effect was that the CBD edge became an area of considerable instability and although its effects were not uniform the dynamism strongly affected the adjacent areas and led to zone-in-transition features. The Irish, who dominated Boston's immigrant population in the first half of the nineteenth century, first settled in shanty dwellings on the city periphery, in a way reminiscent of modern *favelas*, but later began to infill areas adjacent to the CBD where prestige groups had moved out. Temporary buildings occupied the grounds of formerly elegant houses and the mansions themselves became subdivided into tenements by the speculators who acquired them.

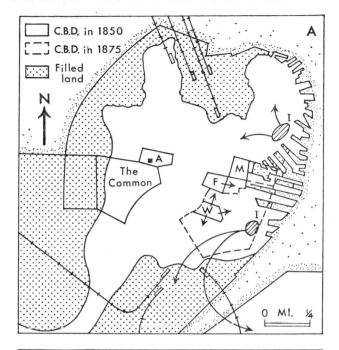

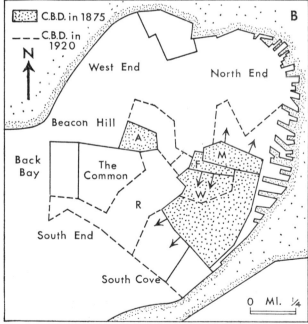

Fig 28. *Expansion of Boston's CBD:* The central city and its immigrant population have been dramatically affected by CBD expansion. Instability has contributed to the formation of the transition-zone whilst the persistence of high status areas at Beacon Hill and Back Bay is related to relative stability of contiguous areas, which include Boston Common. A. administration; M. food markets; F. finance; W. warehouses; R. retail; I. original immigrant quarters. (After Ward, D., 'The Emergence of Central Immigrant Ghettoes in American Cities: 1840–1920; *Annals of the Association of American Geographers*, 58, 1968, 343–59, reproduced with permission of the author and the Association of American Geographers.)

Land values remained high and rents were only manageable through the high density of occupance in over-crowded conditions where maintenance or improvement was minimal. Where the CBD edge was stable, more established communities could develop, but where it was unstable then the worst features of the zone tended to accrue. Ward noted that the Irish destroyed their own enclaves by building the expanding wholesale district. Over time the nature of the resident population changed and as the Irish assimilated into Boston society and filtered towards the suburbs, they were replaced by Italians and later Negroes. A classic cycle of sequent occupance could be traced in Boston's zone-in-transition.

The zone in Boston was not in the early-twentieth century one of blighted properties and poor people, but retained some quality districts. Beacon Hill and Back Bay in particular resisted pressure, for reasons which Ward identified as adjacency to the more stable parts of the CBD edge which were occupied by administrative buildings, parks, and Boston Common. Walter Firey assigned different reasons to the maintenance of these districts, reasons associated with the symbolic and sentimental values of older families who occupied the two districts.[40] The Beacon Hill Residents' Association was organised to resist change for such non-economic reasons and Firey used this example as an argument against mechanistic processes in city growth. The symbolic values, however, served to delay rather than to prevent change and over time the high-status families have gradually abandoned Beacon Hill which has now assumed a somewhat different character.

A further analyst of Boston's zone in transition, H. Gans, identified within the Italian settlements of North End a social order which made them an 'urban village' rather than an 'urban slum'.[41] Other poor residential districts within the zone, such as West End and South Cove, could be more truly described as slums, and their position on an expanding CBD edge seemed crucial. Settled communities could not develop in these conditions of instability, and skid rows found their locale. Modern trends in Boston provide evidence of the full cycle as urban renewal has displaced part of the poor population with only a limited return to the central city of high-income groups. The pattern of this well-documented Boston example was repeated in major cities throughout the United States. Much earlier, E. W. Burgess had identified the zone-in-transition in Chicago,[42] with its constituent parts of Chinatown, the Ghetto, the Slum, Skid Row and Little Sicily, several of which were studied in depth by urban ecologists such as H. W. Zorbaugh[43] and Louis Wirth.[44] But in many ways the zone-in-transition is now a relict form within the American city and has been considerably modified in recent years.

The zone-in-transition in the present-day American city is again strongly influenced by contemporary trends in the CBD. A halt to horizontal expansion of the CBD since the 1920s has given increased stability to the zone-in-transition but a number of factors have combined to delay substantial improvement, not least of which has been the maintenance of land values at an artificially high level. Speculators, unwilling to accept the fact of a permanent decline in demand for central city space, have sought to maintain high land values but remain unwilling to improve real estate. Land continues to be a heavy investment from which returns can be obtained only by its intensive use. The character of the central city has also been affected by social and demographic trends, as growth of suburbs in the present century has substantially lowered the population of the central city and this shift has been accompanied by dramatic changes in the ethnic balance. Between 1940 and 1960, metropolitan populations increased by 55 per cent, 27 per cent in the central city and 102 per cent outside it. Between 1950 and 1960, the white population increased by 5 per cent in the central city and 49 per cent outside it, but the Negro population grew by 50 per cent in the central city and 31 per cent outside. In 1960 more than one-half the metropolitan white population lived outside central cities but 80 per cent of metropolitan Negroes lived within them. Large parts of the zone-in-transition are being abandoned to minority groups, particularly the Negroes, while real estate has progressed through what has been termed a 'neighbourhood cycle'[45] of successive downgrading in a central city which adds a racial problem to its urban blight. R. L. Morrill, in his analysis of the Negro ghetto,[46] found it to be characterised by all the parameters of underprivilege, including sub-standard and overcrowded housing. The ghetto has often established itself spectacularly; for example, the Hough district of Cleveland had a population of 66,000 in 1950, of which 2,500 were Negro, but by 1960 of its 72,000 inhabitants 53,000 were Negro. Morrill suggested that geographers could use simulation techniques to analyse what was effectively a spatial diffusion process in which Negroes were the active agents and whites passive. Whites would accept between 5 and 25 per cent Negro population as a threshold, but above that abandonment of a district would occur. The distinctive ghettos were less clear-cut in new urban areas of America and H. M. Rose in Miami[47] identified a fragmented pattern grouped around places of employment. Perhaps the greatest forces maintaining the Negro ghettoes are poverty, prejudice and the operation of the housing market. Whereas all other minority groups in America have been assimilated over time, Negroes show few signs of doing so. The result will be two spatially segregated societies in which the central city increasingly becomes the domain of the Negro. The central city of Washington is already two-thirds Negro, Newark is one-half and on present trends a great many cities will have Negro majorities by the end of the present century.[48]

The trend involving the Negro population continues a traditional role of the American zone-in-transition as the domicile of under-privileged groups. Other traditional elements remain including ethnic minorities such as the Chinese and Puerto Ricans, although the former have developed commercialised and socially cohesive communities. Skid Rows, the habitat of misfits and dropouts, with death rates eight times the national average and a predominantly male population with high rates of disease and alcoholism[49] remain in many cities. Overall, the continuance of large-scale blight or lack of improvement maintains the unenviable image of the zone-in-transition.

Against these trends, some evidence exists for an attack upon this indictment of the overall American metropolis. Urban renewal in America dates predominantly from the Federal Housing Act of 1949 and has become the main attempt to deal with the zone-in-transition. Urban renewal can now be used to tackle the slums, to improve the image of downtown by aesthetic projects, and to provide space for new and essential items such as car parks and road extensions.[50] A great deal of controversy has surrounded urban renewal. It has been dubbed 'Negro removal' because it mainly affects the Negro areas; it has raised federal/local issues and M. Anderson in his book *The Federal Bulldozer*[51] raised a wide range of criticisms. H. Gans showed that urban renewal had disrupted a cohesive Italian community in Boston,[52] whilst M. Fried found the resultant psychological stress to be prolonged and extreme.[53] These are social costs exaggerated by the fact that demolition has not in the past been accompanied by an obligation to re-house (though recent evidence suggests increased social responsibility) and projects have often meant the shifting of Negroes from one 'legal' city to another, a diminishing supply of low-cost housing and consequent increased overcrowding. Urban renewal does, however, improve the physical and social images of the areas it affects and Anderson has shown that rebuilding on cleared sites is often accompanied by vastly increased rent and a different social class of inhabitant. This changeover is related to the other trend for improvement, the so-called 'return to the central city'.

The return to the central city refers to the tendency for some sections of higher-income groups to move back towards downtown for residence. Many writers have identified this trend which undoubtedly exists and is allied to the increase in apartment living. The question of the extent to which it is occurring is less clear,[54] W. Alonso writing in 1964 judged it to be a short-term trend related to land shortages and the slowness of road-building programmes in the 1950s.[55] There are other factors including the spiralling of land costs which places a house beyond a great many people's budget, such as has occurred in Toronto over the past decade.[56] Most would seem to agree that the return to the central city is selective including young unmarried people, childless couples, and some highly mobile professionals. Circumstances may vary locally and it is clear that in Toronto the range may be wider. Urban renewal by creating new open space has allowed the development of luxury apartments in downtown locations. The return to the central city has also caused the up-grading of some older districts and J. T. Davis noted that although there was a general displacement of middle-class housing outwards from the CBD, stability had been achieved in some cases.[57] An example of improvement was Georgetown in Washington which, although a slum in the 1920s, had become an expensive and attractive neighbourhood by the 1960s and similar trends could be found in New York's Greenwich Village and in older districts of inner Toronto. H. Perloff has tried to give some framework to these trends with his Intown-Newtown concept which postulates the creation of good living areas within the zone-in-transition.[58] For the moment, however, the return to the central city remains a minority preference and the zone-in-transition retains many of its former characteristics. L. S. Bourne has suggested that its blight will not be solved by private enterprise and much rests upon an enlightened urban renewal programme.[59] In America, however, the emphasis for renewal seems to have shifted to the 'middle ring' where rehabilitation of older houses prevents the spread of blight and has fewer political hazards.

The zone-in-transition in American cities is clearly a dynamic and complex area which contains some of the most challenging of all urban problems. Yet geographers have afforded it scant attention and R. E. Murphy identified this void in 1966 when he suggested that: 'The delimitation and study of the zone in transition that borders the CBD presents a challenge to the urban geographer. It is surprising that it has thus far given rise to no published literature.'[60] More recently D. W. Griffin and R. E. Preston have delimited the zone, using procedures comparable to the CBI, and suggested an interpretation and schematic represent-ation of its contemporary structure.[61] They identified a number of sectors based upon land-use and current processes of growth (Figure 29). L. S. Bourne was critical of the transition zone concept formulated by Griffin and Preston on the grounds that it was a compartmentalised view and emphasised land use rather than process.[62] His own analyses of the central city, particularly in Toronto, have placed the emphasis upon process, decision-making, investment procedures and the influence of existing real estate.[63] In part of this at least, Bourne is in accord with J. Rannels who viewed the central city as a consequence both of the chang-ing contemporary processes of urban growth and of partial inheritances bequeathed by each system of activity to its succes-sor.[64] Bourne's view that private investment in the core of the Canadian city was insufficient and that major projects, such as the Toronto City Hall, would only come from public funds is disputed by others who argue that the absence of a racial problem gives continued attraction to the central city.

The zone-in-transition is a particularly North American phenomenon and although it has equivalents in European cities the characteristics are never so pronounced. British cities have a similar type of zone, sometimes referred to as a zone of decay or deterioration, which contains the oldest and most substandard parts of the city and often other features of its American counter-part. I. M. Castle and E. Gittus noted that in Liverpool there was an inner zone, formerly occupied by wealthy merchants, which had now fallen into disrepair and was taken over by Irish and

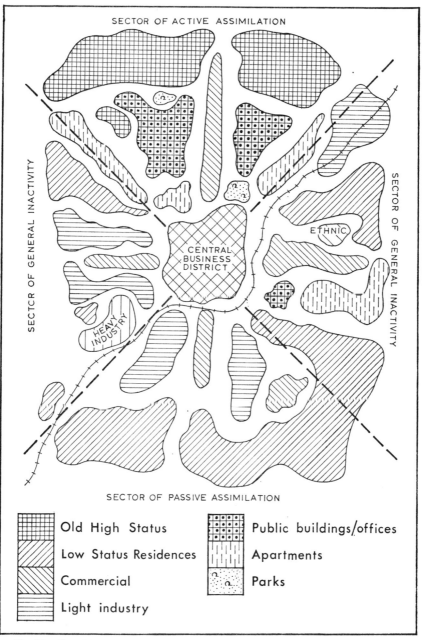

Fig 29. *Transition-zone concept: a schematic pattern of land use for the American city:* (After Griffin, D. W. and Preston, R. E. 'A Restatement of the Transition Zone Concept' *AAAG*, 56, 1966, 339–50, reproduced with permission of the authors and the Association of American Geographers.)

Commonwealth immigrants.[65] During the 1950s, the influx of Commonwealth immigrants into the inner areas of many British cities consolidated the similarities. Detailed studies of London and Birmingham have shown that coloured minorities are segregated in these inner city areas but the numbers involved are not great and nothing resembling the Negro ghettoes of American cities has yet emerged.[66] Coloured immigrants are always in minorities, less than one-third of total populations, in substandard districts which they share with British lower-income groups. Peter Hall, in a description of inner London,[67] identifies a pattern of sequent occupance which closely resembles American experience and in many other aspects of land use, activities and the problems of substandardness, zone-in-transition features exist. In many ways it is the substandardness which typifies the zone in British cities and John Rex has suggested that 'The zone-in-transition is that area of the city where the least privileged housing classes live'.[68] Instability is present but the image of the zone is somewhat better than in American cities; wider powers for planners have resulted in the gradual removal of the worst slums, the relief of overcrowding, and rehousing in more peripheral locations.

Other European cities bear similar resemblances to the American pattern and Chombart de Lauwe's 'zone of acculturisation' in Paris was characterised by deteriorating physical structures and a disorganised social structure.[69] This zone included distinctive quarters such as Montparnasse and Montmartre, occupied by artists and entertainers; the literary and scientific groups of the Latin Quarter and St Germain des Pres; and the ethnic areas such as the Chinese at Gard de Nord and the Bretons at Montparnasse. Substandardness, resulting from old and often unimproved structures, typifies the zone-in-transition of Paris and other European cities, though traditional values often persist in the historic inner city and the presence of what John Rex has called romantics, deviants, and intellectuals provides an extra quality. The continuing vitality and ethos of the central city in Europe has meant an avoidance of some American problems and some of the worst elements of the zone-in-transition have never appeared. Analogies to sequent occupance and assimilation appear in European cities though the scale and diversity of in-migration rarely approaches American experience. European central cities have experienced a consistent population loss since the latter part of the nineteenth century as overcrowding has decreased, as suburban homes have become available and as business functions have displaced residential use of land.

In its highest expression the zone-in-transition is particular to American cities where it emerged and has persisted with the aid of a number of special conditions. The more general factors which lead to a zone-in-transition, a dynamic CBD and ageing structures, are present in European cities and some zone-in-transition qualities result. More than any other section of the western city, the zone-in-transition is the product of complex interaction of societal forces and defies attempts at rigid compartmentalisation. It is, by definition, a locale of change and this characterises all its associated elements, its real estate, its land use, and its population. In the past it has provided essential functions, such as available cheap housing in central locations and a point of assimilation for new migrants, within the western city. Over time wider-ranging innovations have rendered these functions largely redundant and the zone has become more relict than essential.

THE NON-WESTERN CENTRAL CITY

The two characteristic zones of the western central city, the CBD and the zone-in-transition, have emerged and have taken their contemporary form because of a specific and reasonably general set of forces which are operative in western urban society. The process of centralisation as part of an overall pattern of urban growth created a highly commercialised CBD within which land values were high and economic competition for land was intense. Dispersal and a reaction against over-congestion have since diminished the significance of the CBD but in western cities it remains a dominant element of urban structure. The zone-in-transition is closely related to the past dynamic nature of the CBD from which it derives its features of instability, is typified by blighted physical structures and is occupied by those sections of the population who are 'at the back of the queue' for housing. To the extent that these forces and conditions are absent in the great majority of non-western cities, the two characteristic zones are not clearly developed. For many writers the trends for change are obvious and adjustments already occurring will lead the non-western central city to a form which more closely resembles that of the west. Contemporarily, however, the typical non-western central city retains many features which distinguish it quite clearly from the western counterpart.

The CBD is only found in a modified and weakly developed form in many non-western cities and from recent evidence retains a resemblance to the prototype of the pre-industrial city. Indian cities have been described as multi-nucleated and possessing only a modest development of the CBD. R. Mukerjee provided valuable empirical information both upon western/non-western contrasts and upon the differences imposed by scale in India.[70] The CBD in the small Indian town is, from his description, still in the traditional form. 'Temple, court, money-lender's business platform, retail shop and rich man's mansion may jostle one another in the same district, usually at the centre where communications intersect and focus.'[71] With urban growth, however, new patterns emerge in the larger cities. 'There is at first congestion in the retail shopping area which expands on all sides, encroaches upon the central square with its temple, tank and garden.'[72] The traditional structure was also an African feature described by A. L. Mabogunje for the Yoruba towns.[73] The central palace occupied an extensive area of land, whilst opposite it was the most important market of the city and the principal mosque. Mabogunje was also able to show that larger cities such as Ibadan and Lagos tended to combine traditional with modern elements of structure (Figure 30). Within Ibadan, a system of twin centres had emerged, comprising the traditional centre of the Iba Market, serving not only economic but also social and political functions and acting as a focal point within the city, and the newer Gbagi business district containing shops, offices, banks and stores and displaying western features of space competition and areal differentiation. Lagos possessed a modern CBD at the Marina, already formed into specialised quarters, but the traditional markets of the city retained a considerable importance in the daily rhythm of life. There is similar evidence from other non-western countries to suggest that CBDs are emergent rather than established and that traditional elements remain important. T. Caplow in his description of middle-American cities in the 1940s suggested that the shift towards a highly dynamic structure based upon economic centralisation was far from complete.[74] In his study of Guatamala City, he identified a very large territorial CBD but one lacking a clearly defined central point or any clear segregation of functions. Contemporarily, the larger cities of

Latin America contain well-developed CBDs, the product of improved functional bases and transport systems and increased capital investment, often from external sources. Less developed was the CBD of Lourenço Marques, Mozambique, which was described as possessing limited office space and retail frontage in some blocks which was only 30 to 40 per cent of that available.[75] The overall functional structure of the CBD was strongly affected by the traditional and plural nature of the economy.

That part of the central city which surrounds the CBD in non-western countries cannot be closely compared with the western zone-in-transition. One major reason for contrast is that the single-centred urban form around which a definable zone might develop is uncommon in non-western cities; another is that CBD expansion and its concomitant effects on adjacent parts of the city are little developed. A common feature of the central city is that it does contain the oldest parts of the urban fabric, often now substandard and in need of renewal, but also frequently includes traditional parts of the urban fabric. A United Nations report on new building in Old Lagos stated: 'Unfortunately every demolition implies the sacrifice of interests which may be very worthy of respect . . . it is the very essence of traditional

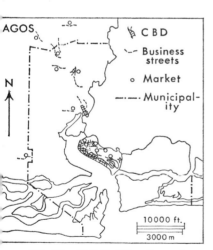
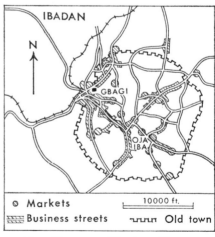

Fig 30. *Commercial patterns in non-western cities:* These two Nigerian cities demonstrate the importance of the traditional markets. (After Mabogunje, A. L., *Urbanisation in Nigeria*, 1968, with permission of the author and the University of London Press.)

life that is affected . . . the palaces of the chiefs . . . and the homes of their subjects, which were arranged around the palaces in closed circles rather than streets.'[76] The gradual depopulation of the central city, evident throughout this century in western society, is not a feature in the non-western world and central densities increase as cities grow. A result of this trend is the existence of incredibly high population densities, fed by high birth rates and the inflow of rural migrants, and of overcrowding in some of the worst slum conditions of the world. C. Abrams has documented the conditions of living in the central areas of many non-western cities,[77] such as Hong Kong and Singapore; A. L. Mabogunje described densities of 600 per acre in parts of Lagos. The urban poor, crowded into the insanitary districts of the non-western central city, live in conditions more extreme than the worst slums of early-nineteenth-century England. Because these central city slums are the only refuge for large parts of the population they are not comparable with zone-in-transition traits. As Mabogunje stated for Ibadan, 'Unlike in many developed countries, the slum areas are, however, not coincident with areas of moral and social deviance, criminality and delinquency . . . life in the slum area is particularly integrated.'[78] Oscar Lewis painted a similar picture in his studies of the central *vecindades* of Mexico City where the 'culture of poverty' was accompanied by a high measure of social cohesion and traditional values.[79] J. F. C. Turner, however, in a survey of shanty-towns in non-western cities,[80] distinguished between the centrally located 'provisional squatter' settlements which were comparable to the western slum and the peripherally-located and progressive 'semi-squatter' settlement which were comparable to the western suburb. Evidence for change was also found by Mabogunje at Ibadan where he described a 'growth by fission' in the central areas of the city.[81] The process involved social change, in the shift of emphasis from an extended to nuclear family, and physical change as the traditional compound gave way to independent housing units (Figure 31).

The central city in non-western countries clearly has many particular qualities which make it distinctive from its western equivalent. These particular qualities result in the most part from the traditional elements of the central city, the symbolic rather than economic users of land, the multi-nucleated overall structure and the contrast between these older fabrics and modern trends.

Most writers would identify modern trends as forces which will eventually lead to closer resemblances between western and non-western cities and there is ample empirical evidence, particularly in relation to the CBD, that this is taking place. There are also grounds for suggesting, however, that the process will be prolonged and similarities may never be close. The western 'model' presupposes wealth from which investment is forthcoming both to promote the activities of the CBD and to provide the necessary urban infrastructure upon which they might grow. Wealth is a commodity in which non-western societies are singularly lacking. Again the plural nature of society and traditional elements of structure may serve to keep distinctive facets

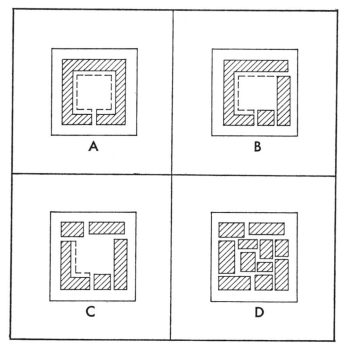

Fig 31. *Growth by fission: a concept of socio-spatial change in the non-western central city:* A. L. Mabogunje has demonstrated modern trends towards individualism in Nigerian cities: A. traditional compound based on extended family; B. one member breaks away from agriculture and from kinship system; C. others follow this trend; D. change over to individual homes and nuclear family. Reproduced by permission of the author and the University of London Press.

in the non-western central city. The tendency to generalise can, however, be misleading and there will doubtless be considerable diversities within non-western countries and between those societies which are comprehensively controlled and planned and others which are less so. At current levels of urban population growth and overcrowding, large parts of the central city are likely to be taken over by the underprivileged mass of the urban poor. In these circumstances, even without the instability promoted by an expanding CBD, much of the central city may bear some resemblance to a zone-in-transition. There have been many generalised and empirical descriptions of the processes of change affecting the non-western central city but very few attempts at systematic measurement. In this context the study of inner Tokyo by R. L. Meier and I. Hoshino[82] is of interest, even though Japanese cities are often regarded as transitional between western and non-western. Activity in a particular district for the mid-1960s was compared with that recorded in 1965 and it was found that life had become steadily more cosmopolitan. Using measurement based upon visual appearance, it was found that 88 per cent of the images observed in 1951 had been modernised whilst those that remained in their traditional form were less frequently encountered. Without many more detailed studies of this kind in a non-western context, and indeed in the absence of more basic data, it is difficult to assess the pace and nature of change in the non-western central city. From the evidence of past experience, the commercialised city centres are likely to be in the vanguard of more general innovative processes. R. L. Meier sees communication, mass-media and mass marketing as key factors and has suggested that geographers have missed out in the past by neglecting to study the dissemination of knowledge and the fusion of culture traits.[83] Some of these processes may be intangible and difficult to measure but they must at some point enter an analysis of the central city.

CHAPTER FIVE

The Residential Structure of Cities: Natural Areas and Social Areas

THE residential districts of the city occupy a large part of the overall urban area and present a number of basic patterns in terms of their social geography. A recent feature of the analysis of these patterns has been a more quantitative approach and the application of multivariate techniques*, the latter in recognition of the increasing complexities of urban structure—based upon a myriad of elements and inter-relationships—which require multivariate solutions. More important, however, than the *operational* procedures has been the increasing acceptance that the more traditional terms of reference need to be widened and, in particular, that social organisation must form part of any spatial model. This shift towards an interest in social organisation and behaviour is reflected in recent statements by geographers. For example, N. Ginsberg,[1] commenting in a wider geographical context, suggested that the new emphases are being placed on the organisation of an area and on the social behaviour that underlies that organisation. The study of the residential structure of towns has

* See Appendix for a brief description of these techniques.

H

reflected this broadening of terms of reference as much as any other aspect of human geography. Anne Buttimer posed some of the challenges for the geographer concerned with residential areas: 'How does the silent language of time and space influence mankind's cultural variations? Geographers ask themselves, should we be satisfied with drafting an opaque, objective map of social patterns in space, or must we supplement this with the subjective or inside view?'[2] Such concern with social space is reminiscent of that of David Harvey for the involvement of the sociological with the geographical imagination.[3] The French concept of social space already possessed a geographical context and proposed a hierarchy of spaces within which groups live, move and interact. The more common usage of the term social space, however, is derived from E. Durkheim's *substrat social* which had no geographical context but was differentiated in terms of socio-cultural attributes such as status, religion or ethnicity[4] (Figure 32). Philip Rees, for example, used a definition of social space which was based upon socio-economic status and stage in the life cycle[5] and it is the latter definition of social space which will be used in the following two chapters, although Chombart de Lauwe's perspective is relevant to the contexts of neighbourhood and mobility.[6]

If social space and the sociological imagination are to be involved, the geographer's tasks in the study of residential areas become more explicit. Order and patterning can be readily identified but the relationship of these to underlying dimensions of social organisation needs to be understood. A social geography must emphasise the relationship of spatial dimensions to urban-social structure, but must also involve other dimensions. Those studies aimed at the definition of urban sub-areas will illustrate the progress towards identifying and understanding patterns in terms of formative processes and will also demonstrate the constraints upon a geographical analysis. Such constraints are related to the level of generalisation at which analysis can proceed. The geographer, like the urban ecologist, operates at a meso-level of analysis, studying areal characteristics and aggregate phenomena. The concern is with the group rather than with the individual and theories rest upon a probabilistic framework. The group or aggregate is itself an amalgam of individual characteristics and individual decisions but as P. Rees has suggested: 'An orderly social geography results as like individuals make like choices, in response to regularities in the operation of land and housing markets.'[7] The value of such a level of generalisation remains for some a matter of academic debate but it is the level at which much geographical analysis is carried out. In academic terms, the debate on the ecological as opposed to the individual correlation is the relevant context; some would question whether observations made upon group data, such as census tracts, have reliable meaning because they might cloak individual diversity.[8]

Geographical approaches to the definition of urban sub-areas have evolved from a position where social organisation was virtually ignored to one where it has become central. The concept of the urban sub-area suggests that, within the overall residential structure of the city, there exist comparatively homogeneous sub-divisions which are characterised by an internal consistency and by a personality which distinguishes them from other parts of the city. Such sub-areas are the natural neighbourhoods or quarters of the city which emerge as distinctive districts over time and, within the overall urban structure, form a mosaic of

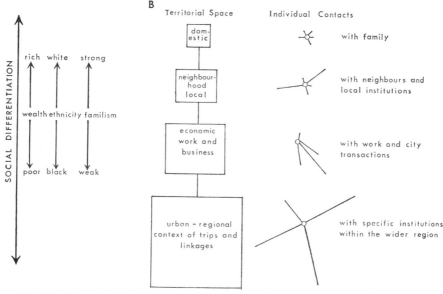

Fig 32. *Concepts of social space:* A. non-geographical social space is analogous to Durkheim's *substrat social;* B. social-geographical space involves territories of various dimensions within which contacts occur. Each scale of territory reflects a social context and is analogous to de Lauwe's social space and Webber's urban realms.

definable but inter-related segments. Any large city has sub-areas of this kind and the larger the city, the more numerous and well-defined are the sub-areas. The problem of definition, of identifying boundaries and of characterising the sub-area, can be likened in many ways to the broader methodology of regionalisation in geography.[9] The city is the universe within which there are sub-regions to be identified, the qualities of which will be determined by the delimiting criterion which is adopted. Regional unity may be expressed in terms of a single criterion or on the basis of several criteria.

MORPHOLOGICAL SUB-AREAS

The urban morphologists provide a useful starting point in a review of approaches to the definition of urban sub-areas (see Chapter 3). Their attempts to define such morphological sub-areas were based upon physical aspects of urban structure and were usually related to historical aspects of growth. Townscape analyses were based upon observation and field study, and derived sub-regions using morphological elements as delimiting criteria as, for example, in the schematic representation of British townscape presented by A. E. Smailes[10] (see Figure 12). H. S. Thurston, in his study of St Albans, employed only morphological criteria but derived a composite measurement technique (which he described as fractional notation) based on land use, roofing material, wall material, number of storeys and age.[11] Street units were first classified in terms of these variables and then aggregated to form sub-areas. A much more detailed morphological analysis was that developed by M. R. G. Conzen in an attempt to explain the individual components of the contemporary town plan by reference to periods and modes of development.[12] The detailed nature of this town plan analysis can be shown by the fact that Conzen's typology for Alnwick, population 7,365 in 1951, contained thirteen major types and forty-nine sub-types.

Although studies in urban morphology occasionally examine decision-making processes which have led to sub-area patterns and normally relate contemporary patterns to growth, they have rarely been concerned with other kinds of relationships. Assumptions have sometimes been implicit, for example that a particular class of housing is occupied by a particular type of people, but these relationships have not been rigorously tested. More recently, however, attempts have been made to examine the relationship between morphology and other urban characteristics and S. T. Openshaw, in a statistical study of South Shields,[13] used two sets of variables to investigate the inter-relationship between morphology and socio-economic structure. The results suggested reasonably clear relationships between social structure and building fabric, exemplified by the correspondence between inter-war housing and high status population groups and that between recent municipal housing and young families. Although these findings confirm associations suggested by qualitative assessment, the careful quantitative analysis provides a much sounder basis for assumptions on correspondence than previously existed. In another quantitative morphological analysis R. J. Johnston proposed a number of conceptual models of townscape development for Melbourne (Figure 33) and employed 114 measures of building fabric.[14] Johnston qualified the use of morphological variables in his assumption that housing types only reflected the social status of the residents for whom they were constructed; a qualification which must of necessity apply to studies of sub-areas based upon morphological indices. Evidence of this necessity may be obtained from P. Amato's analysis of Bogota in which he identified three house-types, Colonial, European and American, particularly identified with high status groups.[15] The locations of these house-types identified clusterings of the upper classes at successive stages of the city's growth, but the house-type as a diagnostic variable was only valid in terms of the original group for whom it was built. From this initiation stage, the house-type might progress through a relatively ordered sequent-occupance: larger houses sub-divide into apartments and pass to lower-income groups; structures age and their attractiveness declines and at each stage the correspondence of morphology with a particular social group is less clear. This fluidity of relation-ship between house-type and social structure is demonstrated very clearly in the inner parts of large western cities, as suburban dispersal and the occupation of older residential property by other population groups occur. In British towns there is no shortage of examples of distinctive morphological units formed for one population group at one point in time many of which remain closely allied to a particular segment of society despite economic change. Philip Jones provided a useful example in South Wales of the uniformity of plan and house-type in colliery

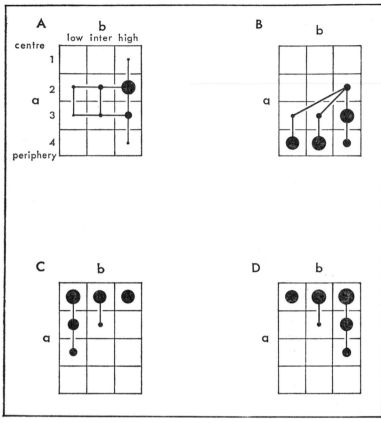

Fig 33. *Diffusion of house type: a morphological model:* The four models have a framework of distance zones from centre to periphery of the city, (a) each of which contains three sectors of high, intermediate and low status, (b) Dates of construction are earliest near centre. A. house-type particular to one sector at one point in time: limited diffusion spatially and temporally; B. house-type initiated in high status sector: maximum expression there in Zone 3 with subsequent decline but later adoption in other sectors; C. house-type universally adopted in Zone 1 but carried forward in inverse proportion to status of sector; D. house-type universally adopted in Zone 1 and maintained as high status feature. Size of circles proportional to significance of type. (After Johnston, R. J. 'Towards an Analytical Study of Townscape' *Geografiska Annaler*, 51 B 1969, 20–32, with permission of the author and Geografiska Annaler.)

settlements.[16] Modern governmental policies occasionally have the effect of linking a particular morphological type to a particular social group, such as municipal housing in Britain which is allocated to lower-paid workers with larger families, or in Prague where a close relationship between morphology and population structure reflects a housing policy which allocates new houses to young families with children and leaves older people in the inner and older parts of the city.[17]

A morphological approach can therefore be used to identify urban sub-areas and as such contributes to what might be termed a set of diagnostic variables for the analysis of intra-urban structure. It is only in recent years that any serious attempts have been made to link morphological sub-areas to social structure in a systematic way and, although good correspondence may be obtained in many cases, the consistent hazard is that it becomes blurred as time and changes in society make associations more complex and generalisations more contentious. The central issue is the relationship between form and function, the exact nature of which can never be lightly assumed although it always exists. Despite these qualifications, there is truth in the assertion that recent quantitative studies have given scant attention to morphological aspects of town structure. The building fabric is one part of the overall urban structure and needs to be carefully incorporated into more comprehensive analyses.

NATURAL AREAS

An alternative set of approaches to the problem of defining urban sub-areas is that which has developed from the natural area concept of R. E. Park and other ecologists of the Chicago school.[18] The natural area was conceived as a geographical unit, distinguished both by its physical individuality and by the social, economic, and cultural characteristics of its population: in contrast to the morphological unit, the natural area was thus envisaged as an area of social unity as well as of physical uniformity. This view—that the urban habitat was necessarily related to the society which occupied it—was clearly related to the broader ecological theory of the Chicago school. Park stated these relationships explicitly in his theoretical arguments but it was the monographs of the Chicago school which provided empirical studies of natural areas[19] and of these the best known were Harvey Zorbaugh's *The Gold Coast and The Slum*[20] and Louis Wirth's *The Ghetto*.[21]

The natural areas identified by Zorbaugh were delimited by the *de facto* boundaries of the urban environment: roads, railways, parks, lakes and rivers. The physical individuality of the natural area was accurately reflected by land values and rent, but Zorbaugh was at pains to stress that the natural area was not necessarily co-terminous with community, as it was the result of economic rather than cultural processes. The attractiveness of Zorbaugh's study, however, lies less in any attempted justification of ecological theory than in his vivid portrayal of life in Chicago's near North Side, a district of some 90,000 people close to the city centre. The near North Side was an area of diversity, the main contrast being between the high-prestige district of the Gold Coast along Lake Shore Drive and the low status district west of State Street (Figure 34). The latter district was itself a mosaic, containing the rooming-house district, hobohemia, Little Sicily and other ethnic quarters, and the Slum. The personalities of these sections of the city were partly derived from the physical structure of which they were composed, but much more from their distinctive populations and ways of life. Zorbaugh emphasised the dynamic qualities which these districts possessed and described the territorial shifts as the invasion succession process took place. Always regarded as less bounded by ecological theory, Wirth's attitude was reflected in his preface to *The Ghetto*: 'Having started with the study of a geographical area, I found myself, quite unwittingly, examining the natural history of an institution and the psychology of a people.'[22] Wirth studied the evolution of Jewish ghettoes in many European cities and described them as communities of interest, motivated by the need to preserve a religion and based upon the inner solidarity of strong family ties. His identification of the Chicago ghetto as a physical entity approached the concept of the natural area as closely as his ecological contemporaries. He identified the Chicago ghetto as a territory demarcated from adjacent parts of the city by environmental barriers such as street-car lines and railway tracks. Within this territory, the natural area was a socially-cohesive community with a distinctive personality. The natural areas which Zorbaugh and Wirth described were identified and defined intuitively from an intimate knowledge of the city, rather than by the use of statistical procedures. Some of the natural areas,

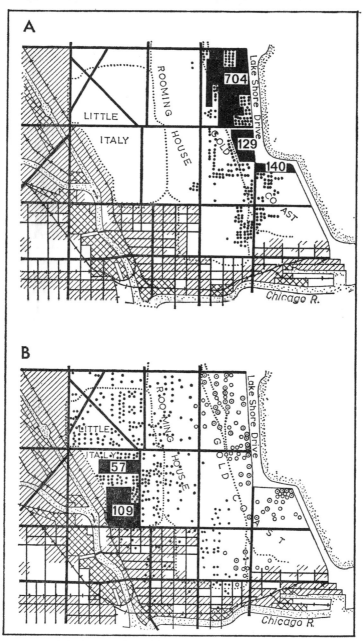

Fig 34. *The Gold Coast and the Slum:* H. W. Zorbaugh, in his famous study of Chicago, was able to identify distinctive territories in the Near North-side. A. each dot represents a person in the social register with some block totals shown; B. each enclosed dot shows a family receiving welfare, with block totals; circles show contributors. The shaded areas are industrial or transport land-uses. (After Zorbaugh, H. W., *The Gold Coast and the Slum*, Chicago 1929. reproduced with permission; copyright 1929 by University of Chicago.)

particularly the ethnic quarters, were close-knit communities; yet others were scarcely communities at all and a feature of the Gold Coast was that 'one does not know one's neighbours'.

The original concept of the natural area was questioned along with other aspects of urban ecology in the 1930s and an explicit reformulation was offered by P. Hatt in his study of Seattle.[23] Hatt suggested that the natural area concept as developed by the ecologists had two interpretations: on the one hand the natural area could be regarded as a spatial unit, limited by natural boundaries and enclosing a homogeneous population with a characteristic moral order; on the other it was regarded as a spatial unit united on the basis of a set of relationships analogous to the biological world. Hatt concluded that this latter interpretation should be rejected but that natural areas could be accepted as logical statistical constructs offering an excellent framework for further analysis. The eventual map of natural areas in Seattle was based upon a diagnostic variable, that of rental values, rather than upon the intuitive approach of ecologists (see Figure 35). Though Zorbaugh and others had certainly been aware of their possibilities, Hatt explicitly used rental values as delimiting criteria for the first time, suggesting that one variable could be used to characterise different parts of the city.

The potentialities of such diagnostic variables of urban structure are now well recognised and their use has extended over a considerable range of problems. In a wider context there are studies using land values, notably by Richard Hurd[24] and Homer Hoyt[25] which pre-date Hatt's study of Seattle, while more recently, statistical analyses of the determinants and correlates of land values have been completed. In the context of defining urban sub-areas, a number of more straightforward British studies have adopted measures of monetary value as diagnostic variables. One problem in studying British cities has been the fact that land values and rental values are difficult to obtain in a consistent form. Therefore rateable values (a form of local taxation), based on the physical characteristics of a property and its general location, have been used instead of land values or rents. The author's study of Newcastle-under-Lyme was fairly typical of this approach towards the definition of sub-areas in a British town.[26] Four categories of rateable value were mapped to produce sub-areas (Figure 36), with the initial hypothesis that the categories within this diagnostic variable would reflect differences in urban social

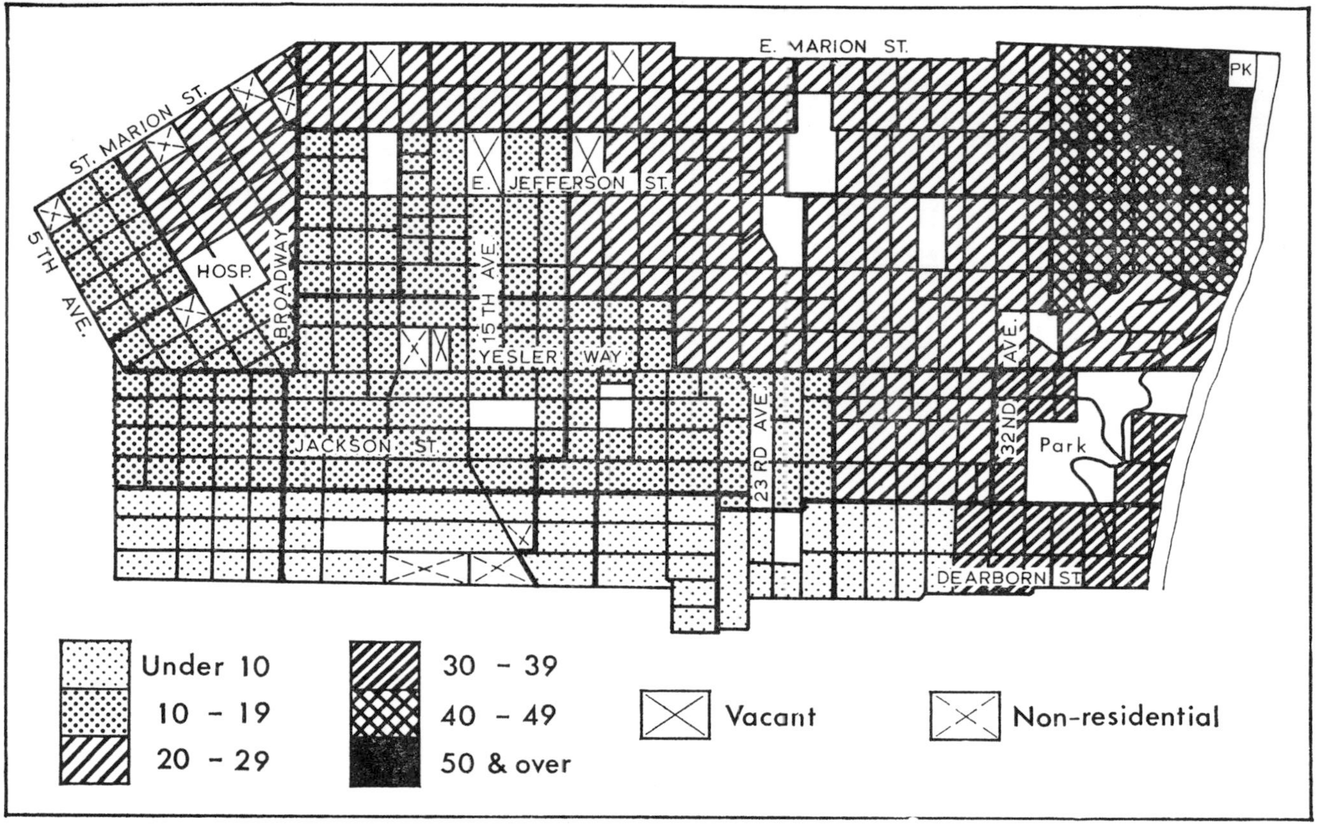
E. MARION ST.
PK
ST. MARION ST.
5 TH AVE.
HOSP.
BROADWAY
E. JEFFERSON ST.
15 TH AVE.
YESLER WAY
JACKSON ST.
23 RD AVE.
32ND AVE.
Park
DEARBORN ST.
Under 10
10 - 19
20 - 29
30 - 39
40 - 49
50 & over
Vacant
Non-residential

Fig 35. *Natural areas in Seattle:* Sub-areas are based upon mean rental value in dollars. (After Hatt, P., 'The Concept of the Natural Area,' *American Sociological Review*, II, 1946, 423–7, with permission from the American Sociological Association.)

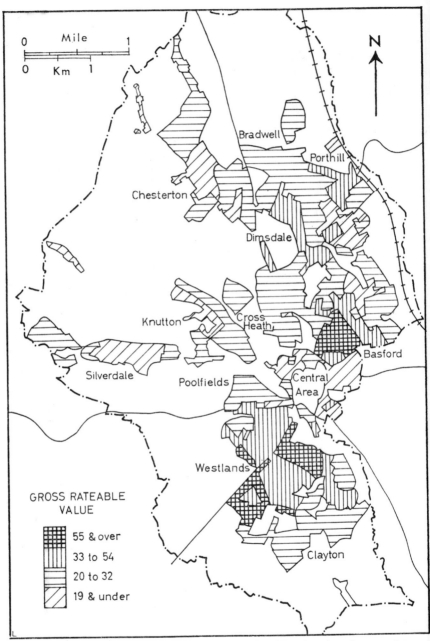

GROSS RATEABLE
VALUE

55 & over
33 to 54
20 to 32
19 & under

Fig 36. *Natural areas in Newcastle-under-Lyme:* Rateable values have been used to identify natural areas in British cities.

structure. These assumptions were tested in a number of ways. First, a field survey of house types showed a close correspondence between morphology and the sub-areas: the lowest-valued category corresponded with the terraced-row districts, the highest-valued category with the large private detached houses. Other tests included the mapping of other variables, such as the locations of homes of professional workers, private telephone sub-scribers and users of welfare services, and measurement of their degree of correspondence with the pattern of sub-areas. In Newcastle-under-Lyme, therefore, the utility of rateable values as a diagnostic variable could be demonstrated. Similar use of this particular criterion have been made by R. Jones in a study of Hereford,[27] by B. T. Robson in Sunderland,[28] and by Emrys Jones (who used Poor Law Valuations) in Belfast.[29] Robson showed the incidence of cholera in low-valued, substandard parts of the town in the mid-nineteenth century, but found that rate-able values in the modern city had lost much of their usefulness because of the considerable amount of municipal housing, which could not be reliably correlated to a particular level of rateable value. His conclusion that municipal housing had seriously detracted from the use of rateable values as a diagnostic variable has considerable validity.

There exists, therefore, a wide range of diagnostic variables which can be used to identify and characterise urban sub-areas. Sub-areas defined by one variable are often assumed to have more general homogeneity and such assumptions can be tested, as in the Newcastle-under-Lyme study. The necessity of such testing was demonstrated in a study of Lansing, Michigan,[30] where three approaches, termed ecological, demographic and social, were used to define comparative sub-areas (see Figure 37). The ecological areas were based upon traditional criteria of natural barriers, land use, land values and racial segregation; the demographic areas were based upon measures of population structure; the social areas upon measures of neighbourhood cohesion derived from field survey data. The study revealed that there was no clear relation-ship between areas identified from the three different criteria and that every kind of ecological barrier was violated when demographic and social indices were used to locate boundaries. This analysis clearly warns against the use of diagnostic variables consistent only in terms of the initial delimiting criterion: any assumptions which are made, whether they concern related

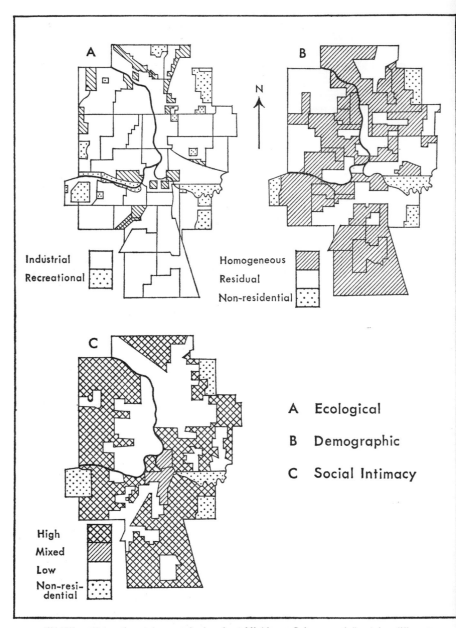

Fig 37. *Alternative sub-areas in Lansing, Michigan:* Sub-areas defined by different criteria possessed few common features. *Ecological areas* were based on natural barriers, land use, land values and race; *demographic areas* on population uniformity; and *socially intimate areas* on levels of local interaction. (After Form, W. H. *et al.* 'Alternative Approaches to the Delimitation of Urban Sub-areas' *American Sociological Review,* 19 1954, 434–40, with permission from the American Sociological Association.)

morphological structures or patterns of social behaviour, must be
tested before they can be incorporated into the analysis.

The range of approaches to the definition of sub-areas in urban
residential structure has been widened considerably by the availability of better census data for cities, both in the range of
recorded information and their publication for small territorial
units, census tracts in North America, enumeration districts in
the United Kingdom, with equivalents in many other parts of the
world. D. McElrath, for example, has used *gruppi di sezione* in
a study of Rome[31] and B. J. L. Berry and P. H. Rees have used
wards in an analysis of Calcutta.[32] Small census areas of this type
must be sufficiently small for a high level of internal consistency
to be assumed, so that when scores are allocated they are the
equivalents of point distributions which may be aggregated to
form areal patterns. To a considerable extent, small census areas
possess these qualities, but there are qualifications. The population
size can vary considerably within one city; the range of census
tracts in North American cities is from under 1,000 to over 10,000
and of enumeration districts in British cities (which are smaller)
from under 100 to over 1,500. The areas are correspondingly
divergent in size, although this is related to density, and the
statistical question emerges of weighting procedures, as used by
B. T. Robson.[33] A more fundamental question concerns the real
internal consistency of small census units. Some censuses have
defined boundaries only with reference to the needs of census-
taking: in the British census, for example, the enumeration
district is arbitrarily defined on mainly topographic criteria. The
Canadian census believes that census tracts are designed to be
relatively uniform in area and population, and such that each is
fairly homogeneous with respect to economic status and living
conditions,[34] and this view is in step with what is required of
census tracts for research purposes. In a wider context, the use of
small census areas as the basic data units has raised many issues
concerning the value of aggregate as opposed to individual
measures.

Census data for enumeration districts have been used fairly
extensively in Britain, more usually to analyse individual variables
than to form composite sub-areas. Emrys Jones in his Belfast
study, however, used enumeration district data to delineate social
regions on the basis of population density, social status and
religious affiliations: the resultant map was judged to provide

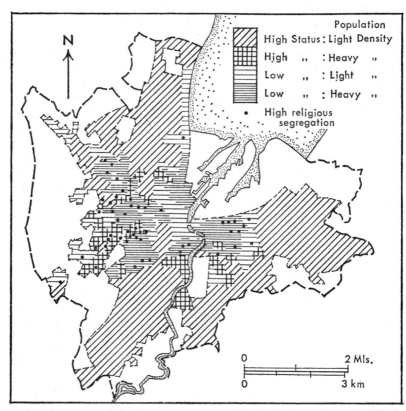

Fig 38. *Social regions in Belfast:* Emrys Jones's map of Belfast is an early attempt to combine several variables into a classificatory measure. (After Jones, E., *The Social Geography of Belfast,* 1960, with permission of the author and Oxford University Press.)

meaningful sub-areas of the city (Figure 38) from which 'The main social regions of Belfast are easily recognisable and compact and sum up features both of the landscape and human geography'.[35] The approach had self-imposed limitations, but it provides a useful link between the natural area concept and subsequent procedures which have made increasing use of census data.

OPPOSITE: *(above)* Sequent occupance in the central city: Former residence near central Los Angeles; *(below)* The North American zone-in-transition: New York's Bowery.

SOCIAL AREA ANALYSIS

Social area analysis was initially developed by the American sociologists E. Shevky, M. Williams and W. Bell.[36] It was evolved as a theory of social differentiation but a major application has been derived from its ability to classify sub-areas within a city: indeed some commentators have described it as a classificatory device, though this is a much more limited function than its originators would propose or accept. The social area analysts have been contrasted with urban ecologists in that they begin with a theory of social differentiation, identifying variations in social space which are then translated into geographical space. By contrast, urban ecologists have always sought initially to identify natural areas as geographical territories and to study them in terms of their social characteristics. Shevky and Bell viewed the city as a part of society as a whole and suggested that change over time would be mirrored in the city. They suggested that such change had three main expressions which could be described collectively as *increasing scale*, implying a continuum of change from a traditional primitive to a more modern civilised style of life (Figure 39). The three expressions of this *increasing scale* they summarised as constructs, each of which was a dominant temporal trend in social organisation. *Social rank* (economic status) described the tendency for society to become more precisely ordered into strata based on specialisation and social prestige. *Urbanisation* (family status) described a weakening of the traditional organisation of the family as the society became more urbanised. *Segregation* (ethnic status) suggested that over time the population group would tend to form distinctive clusters based primarily upon ethnicity. The alternative names for the constructs were proposed and used by Bell,[37] the only difference in computational procedure being that high scores on urbanisation were the equivalents of low scores on family status. Having derived these constructs, regarded as being diagnostic of change, Shevky and Bell sought to measure them from the available census data. *Social rank* was measured by ratios of *occupation*, described as the total number of operatives, craftsmen and labourers per 1,000 employed persons, and of *education*, described as the number of persons who had completed no more than grade school (eight years or less of schooling) per 1,000 persons aged twenty-five years and over. *Urbanisation* was based upon three ratios:

OPPOSITE: *(above)* The North American zone-in-transition: Rooming houses in Vancouver, Canada; *(below)* Activities in the central city: Wall Street, New York.

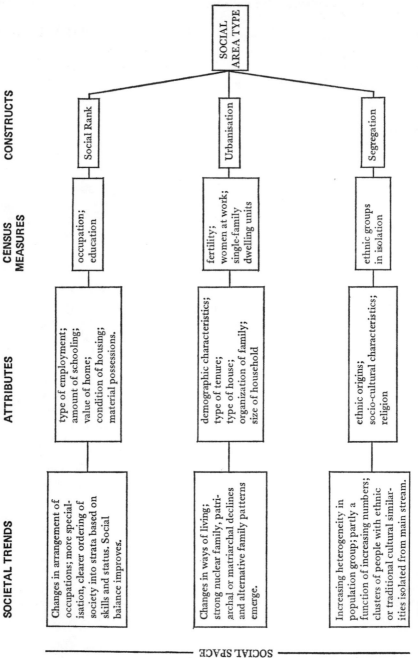

Fig 39. *Increasing scale and the derivation of social areas:* Three societal trends are proposed as expressions of increasing scale; those trends can be characterised by a number of measurable attributes and used to position any census tract in social space. (After Shevky, E. and Bell, W. *Social Area Analysis*, 1955)

fertility measured by the number of children aged 0 to 4 years per 1,000 women aged 15 to 44; *women at work* measured by the number of females employed in relation to the total number of females aged 15 years and over; and *single-family detached dwelling units,* measured by the number of single-family homes (a term which has a specific meaning in North American censuses) as a proportion of all dwelling units. Social rank and urbanisation were the main constructs of social area analysis and a large part of the computational procedure was concerned with their derivation. The third construct, *segregation,* was obtained as a simple percentage of the numbers in specified alien groups (mainly coloureds and all those of ethnic origins outside north-west Europe) as a proportion of the total population.

These constructs and their component ratios were thus identified from social space but were obtained as statistical expressions from the available census data and combined in stipulated ways to form criteria for the definition of urban sub-areas. The operational procedure which leads to the eventual social areas can be briefly summarised:

1. The scores on the individual ratios are initially simple proportions, but Shevky and Bell specify the additional step of transforming the ratios into standardised scores so that for each ratio there is a value of zero and a value of one hundred. The main purpose of this standardisation procedure was to make comparisons more valid.
2. The construct scores are obtained by finding the average of the ratio scores.
3. The social rank and urbanisation scores are each given a four-fold division which in combination provides sixteen possible social area types.
4. Segregation is added to this framework where the proportion of a census tract's total population which is in specified alien groups is above the average for the city as a whole.

The first applications of social area analysis, using data for small census areas, were to Los Angeles and San Francisco,[38] and both provided some confirmation of the utility of the approach. It has become customary to regard a social area as a contiguous territorial unit, though its initial usage was to describe a cluster of scores in social rather than in geographical space. A typical set of results from an application of social area analysis to a North American city can be described from the author's study of Winnipeg, Canada.

The metropolitan area of Winnipeg had a population in 1961 of 475,989, and was divided into eighty-six census tracts with an average population of 5,500; over half the census tracts were between 3,000 and 6,000, with only three with less than 1,000 and five with more than 10,000. The social space diagram for Winnipeg (Figure 40) illustrates the classification of census tracts which was obtained. Each point on the diagram represents a census tract,

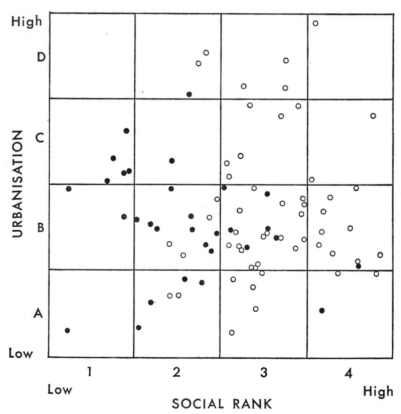

Fig 40. *Social space diagram for Winnipeg:* Each circle shows the position of a census tract in social space with shaded circles marking those tracts which are segregated.

the position of which is determined by its scores on social rank and urbanisation, with a separate symbol for segregated tracts. In this diagram, therefore, the position of each census tract is affected by its scores on the six component variables of the typology: occupation, education, fertility, women at work, single-family dwellings and ethnicity. The census tract in 4D, for example, has high social rank, with few people employed in manual occupations and few without advanced education. It is also high-scoring in terms of urbanisation, with few children, high numbers of women in employment and a comparative absence of single-family homes. The census tract contains few members of specified ethnic groups and is in fact part of a fairly high prestige residential district, predominantly of rented apartments, in a central city location. Besides allowing the interpretation of individual tracts, this diagram also provides an overall impression of the social structure of the city. 63 per cent of the census tracts are within the two higher social rank categories and 25 per cent are in the two higher urbanisation categories; of the 31 tracts which are classed as segregated, only 8 qualify as higher social rank. The analysis has so far allowed an insight into the social structure of Winnipeg by classifying the census tracts in social space.

Social area analysis, as a theory, specifies a set of relationships among its constructs and ratios which must exist if the procedure is to be valid in any case study. The theoretical rationale of these relationships has been questioned but the actual measurements can be tested by statistical techniques, the most straightforward of which is Spearman's rank order correlation co-efficient.* The results of these tests in Winnipeg are shown in Table 4, along with the set of relationships which the theory postulates.

The specified set of relationships shown overleaf requires that the ratios which make up the respective constructs should be independent. This requires high correlations between occupation and education and also among the three ratios which comprise urbanisation. The women at work ratio is held to have an inverse relationship with both fertility and single-family homes. The results for Winnipeg confirm the existence of the specified set of relationships in a way which has been typical of North American studies. An exception in the Winnipeg results, not without precedent in North America, is that the occupation and

* See Appendix.

Table 4 Correlation Scores for Winnipeg

Ratios	Occupation	Education	Fertility	Women at work
Education	+0·84+			
Fertility	+0·53+	+0·34		
Women at work	+0·03	+0·23	−0·53+	
Single-family dwellings	−0·07	−0·33	+0·45+	−0·68+

+ Significant at the 0·1 per cent level (see Appendix)

Specified Set

	Occupation	Education	Fertility	Women at work
Education	+			
Fertility	o	o		
Women at work	o	o	—	
Single-family dwellings	o	o	+	—

fertility ratios have a much higher correlation and the constructs are thus less independent than the hypotheses of social area analysis suggest. The analysis of ten American cities by M. D. Van Arsdol, S. F. Camilleri and C. F. Schmid showed a similar lack of disassociation among the constructs.[39] In general terms, however, the correlational testing confirms the usefulness of the analysis in Winnipeg.

The social space classification forms the basis for the derivation of social areas in geographical space. Contiguous census tracts with scores in the same categories may be aggregated to form social areas in the sixteen-class typology, with the additional segregation categorisation. Figure 41 provides geographical patterns which can be interpreted in terms of the six component variables. Generalised patterns are most easily identified from the separate constructs and the high social rank scores: for example, the southern and western parts of the city indicate the high-prestige residential areas. The more central parts of the city and the northern and eastern districts, which include the central slums and tenements and low-cost suburbs, are characterised by low scores. Urbanisation scores distinguish between the central city districts of low family status and the outer suburbs of strong family life; segregation indices demarcate the Ukrainian districts

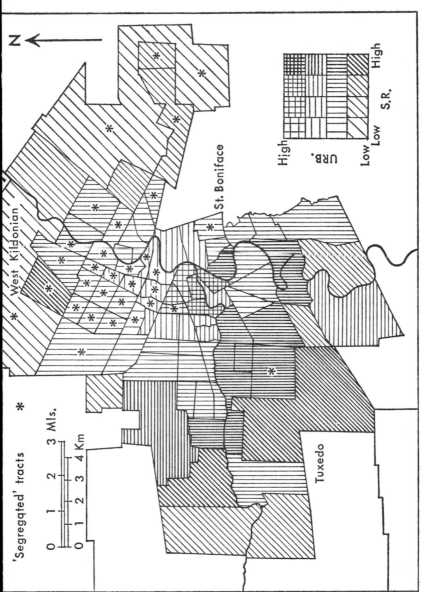

Fig 41. Social areas in Winnipeg, 1961.

extending north along Main Street. The Winnipeg study has served to demonstrate what might be termed a successful application of social area analysis. Reference can now be made to applications outside North America.

In England, social area analysis has been applied to the town of Newcastle-under-Lyme, Staffordshire,[40] which had a population in 1961 of 76,483, much smaller than the North American cities for which this type of investigation has been attempted. The enumeration districts of the British census are much smaller in population size than census tracts; in 1961 Newcastle-under-Lyme had 101 districts with a range of 296 to 1,404 and an interquartile range of 604 to 860. The procedure was carried out using four of the variables suggested by Shevky and Bell, since the single-family dwellings variable is not available in the English census and there were negligible numbers in the specified ethnic groups from which to derive segregation scores. The pattern of relationships among the four variables showed some significant differences from the hypothesised set and from results described for Winnipeg:

Table 5   Correlation Scores for Newcastle-under-Lyme

	Occupation	*Education*	*Fertility*
Education	+0·81[+]		
Fertility	+0·41	+0·32	
Women at work	+0·27	+0·30	+0·08

[+] Significant at the 0·1 per cent level

The relationships within the social rank construct are clearly highly significant, but several correlations show departures from the hypothesised pattern. Occupation and fertility ratios are significantly correlated, showing that the two constructs are not independent. More interesting in this case, however, is the fact that the two variables forming the urbanisation construct have no relationship at all, effectively negating the procedure as a valid analytical tool in this particular study. There have been comparatively few applications of social area analysis in Britain but they seem to confirm the results obtained in Newcastle-under-Lyme.[41] Both the social space diagram and the map of social areas for Newcastle-under-Lyme can only be reliably interpreted in terms of social rank, as the urbanisation scores are crude averages over a wide range of possi-

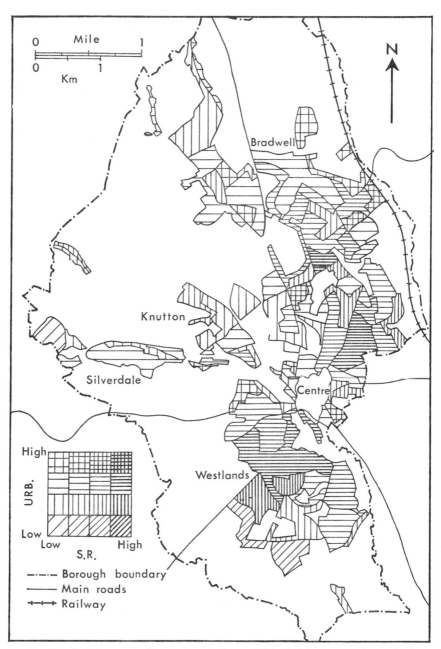

Fig 42. *Social areas in Newcastle-under-Lyme,* 1961: Social areas can be derived from British data but lack the correct statistical relationships among variables.

bilities. Independent plots of the social rank scores distinguished between districts of varying residential prestige, but the ratios of fertility and women at work had to be shown separately to produce meaningful patterns. The fertility ratios were high for peripheral estates and low for older parts of the inner area; women at work ratio scores had a more complex distribution which threw some light on the fallibility of the overall procedure in Britain. The number of women at work was low on some municipal estates where fertility was high, the expected pattern in social area analysis. It was also high, however, in some districts of low fertility where, owing to demographic and social class structure, there is little necessity for women to work. This influence of social class and the stage in the life cycle of the family seemed well illustrated in the Westlands district of New-castle-under-Lyme, where the husbands held well-paid professional jobs, lessening the need for a second income, and the population formed a mature and established community. A further factor may be the limited amount of available female employment. The usefulness of the Newcastle-under-Lyme study is that it provides an empirical test of social area analysis outside North America and indicates some of the limitations of the system.

Other European applications, of which the best known is D. McElrath's study of Rome,[42] have found less marked departures from the hypotheses of Shevky and Bell. McElrath found that whereas most of the necessary variables could be derived from the Italian census in terms of *gruppi di sezione*, which had average populations of 4,324, he had to substitute a literacy ratio for the education ratio and could calculate neither the single-family dwelling ratio nor the segregation construct. McElrath's correlational testing showed that the postulated relationships existed within the constructs, but that social rank and urbanisation were not independent. He nevertheless concluded that his findings strongly supported the broad theoretical and analytic utility of the Shevky and Bell approach.

The problem of forming adequate generalisations concerning the geographical patterns obtained from social area studies has been aided considerably by the work of T. R. Anderson and J. A. Egeland[43] who suggested the use of analysis of variance techniques.* Earlier studies, in particular the broader ecological models of urban structure, had suggested concentric zonal and sectoral

* See Appendix.

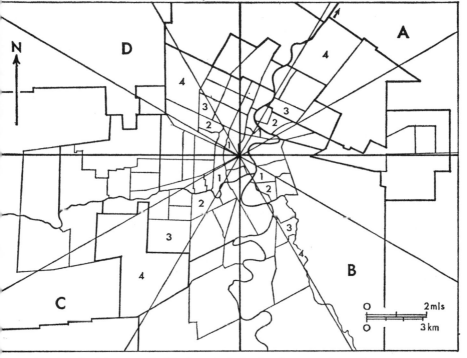

Fig 43. *Spatial patterns in Winnipeg:* Analysis of variance may be used to measure spatial patterns formed by economic status and family status scores: A, B, C, D are four sectors within each of which four census tracts are selected in a regular progression from centre to periphery forming zones 1, 2, 3 and 4.

Actual scores for economic status (E) and family status (F) were:

	1		2		3		4	
	E	F	E	F	E	F	E	F
A	22	54	39	29	46	32	38	18
B	56	58	59	50	62	35	60	26
C	69	87	89	50	91	26	96	25
D	23	54	22	40	30	38	49	30

The technique showed economic status and family status scores to be respectively sectoral and zonal.

patterns as possible generalisations. Anderson and Egeland used these two forms as hypotheses which could be tested by analysis of variance, a technique which shows whether any specific grouping of values or scores is significantly different from that which might arise by chance by comparing the amount of variance between each sample (between sample differences) with the variance within each sample (within sample differences). The sample design can be so arranged that the existence of sectoral patterns for social rank scores and of zonal patterns for urbanisation scores are tested. If these patterns exist, then the expectation is that between-sample differences will be much greater than within-sample differences and the arrangement of values shown by the sample could not have arisen by chance. Statistical comparisons of the between-sample and within-sample variances can be made by a test of significance, usually the Snedecor's F-test.* The procedure suggested by Anderson and Egeland involved the identification of a central point within the city and the marking-off of twelve sectors at 30° intervals around it. A sample of four equally-spaced sectors is usually taken, though this is influenced by the size and shape of the city, and within each sector four census tracts are chosen so that one lies near the central point, another is on the periphery and the others are spaced between; again the number may vary. Figure 43 illustrates the application of this procedure to Winnipeg, where the central point was taken as the junction of Main Street and Portage Avenue with the central business district. For the test of sectoral patterning of social rank scores in Winnipeg a Snedecor's F value of 33 was obtained, easily significant at the 0·1 per cent level, while the test of zonal patterning of urbanisation scores gave a value of 10·9, again significant at the 0·1 per cent level. The results for Winnipeg show social rank to have a sectoral geographical expression and urbanisation to have a zonal geographical expression, results paralleled in the four American cities of Akron, Dayton, Indianapolis and Syracuse, which were examined by Anderson and Egeland.

AN ASSESSMENT OF SOCIAL AREA ANALYSIS

Although social area analysis has been eclipsed in recent years by the development of multivariate procedures,* the theory and

* See Appendix.

its application have stimulated a good deal of academic discussion. The concept of increasing scale, always controversial, has been questioned on several grounds. In a well-known review, A. H. Hawley and O. D. Duncan went so far as to suggest that the theory was an *ex post facto* rationalisation for the choice of indices;[44] F. L. Jones suggested that the use of societal scale was derivative and largely descriptive;[45] J. R. Udry made empirical tests and found that trends suggested were not consistent over time.[46] Urbanisation is a suspect construct, and Bell has recently suggested that Shevky's original concept was not adequately measured by the ratios employed. Bell, who always preferred family status as a description, also accepted the interpretation of T. R. Anderson and L. L. Bean that there were two distinct elements which should be known as familism and urbanism.[47] The related point that the relationship between fertility and women at work could not be assumed but was in fact a complex research problem, was substantiated by British experience. Other points of criticism on the theory relate to the social rank construct, which, though empirically viable, had not been rigorously tested as a theory of social stratification. Critics such as Hawley and Duncan would see little justification for social area analysis except as a classificatory device. More sympathetic writers, of whom J. M. Beshers is a representative,[48] although admitting no theoretical basis for urbanisation, regard social rank and segregation as well-established indices of social stratification. This is a fair assessment and, as recent writings by L. Reissman[49] and R. N. Morris[50] seem to suggest, the constructs are significant as measures of social change, though they are not fully adequate in themselves.

A further controversy of direct relevance to social geography concerns the link between the deductive theory of social differentiation and the classification of sub-areas within a city. The criticism, well expressed by J. R. Udry,[51] is that social area analysis is not one theory but two and that there is no basis for translating a theory of societal change into a typology. Wendell Bell's response to this line of criticism used an analogy of white balls gradually turning black and providing a mosaic at any one point in time.[52] This analogue process, however, has vital points of difference from the link between change in societies over time and its expression within one city at one point in time. A city population at one time is the product of the same technological age, particularly in western society. There are real patterns in social space and in geographical space but they are not necessarily related to a concept of societal change over a long period of time. The differences between a downtown apartment district and a suburb are related to stages in the life cycles of individual families and to prestige levels, but these are not differentiated along axes of societal change of the kind contained in the theory of Shevky and Bell.[53] A more convincing case might exist for the non-western city where there are real cultural differences between the urban poor and urban rich, of the kind analysed by Oscar Lewis and others.[54] A similar unwillingness to accept the translation of social change into sub-areas was expressed by Anderson and Bean[55] who preferred the terms prestige-value, urbanism and familism because they were meaningful in geographical as opposed to social space. A rejoinder to this last point might well be that social space was the primary concern, but most applications have in fact been aimed at identifying territorial patterns. However tenuous the theory, empirical tests in North America and elsewhere have supported the validity of the statistical procedure,[56] and it seems likely that a theoretical explanation must exist. The emphasis in empirical applications and in the search for theory, however, has shifted from social area analysis to a set of more sophisticated statistical methods which can be summarised as multivariate analyses.

CHAPTER SIX

The Residential Structure of Cities: Factorial Ecology

THE use of multi-variate approaches in the study of residential areas is the result of several contemporary trends, including a wider interest in quantitative methods, the availability of high-speed computational facilities, and an increasing awareness that these techniques offer realistic tools in the complex problems of urban analysis. Factor analysis, itself a set of approaches, has been the most generally adopted multivariate technique in geographical studies.* The term factorial ecology is of recent origin and has been used to describe those analyses of urban-spatial structure which employ factor analysis as a technique.[1] By most urban geographers, factor analysis is now the preferred approach to problems of defining sub-areas within the city and of identifying the main social dimensions of urban structure. Advantages of such approaches include considerable objectivity and ability to handle large amounts of data. Factor analysis can be described as a summarising device which operates in terms of the inter-relationships among the set of input variables and identifies, in the order of their significance, a series of factors which are diagnostic of the input and which account for measurable amounts of the

* See Appendix for a more detailed explanation of statistical terms and procedures.

initial variance. These qualities can perhaps be made clearer by drawing an analogy with social area analysis which, through deductive reasoning, identifies changes in society, transforms these into constructs and selects census variables or ratios with which to characterise them. Factor analysis, by contrast, derives factors which can be regarded as equivalents of constructs, by an objective statistical procedure (Figure 44). These factors are derived statistically from an input of variables designed to cover as wide a range of urban characteristics as possible. The nature of each factor can be identified from its associations with the original variables, expressed through measures known as loadings. Factor scores are calculated for each of the original measurement units (small census areas) and these allow spatial patterns to be identified. The general qualities of factor analysis and its application to the analysis of residential areas can be demonstrated, again using Winnipeg as a case-study. The input was 34 variables (see Table 6) obtained from the 1961 Canadian census and calculated for each of 86 census tracts in Winnipeg.[2]

Table 6   Variables used in Analysis of Winnipeg

Population Structure
% under age of 5 years
% under age of 15 years
% over age of 65 years
fertility ratio
sex ratio
single persons as % of adult population

Tenure
median value of dwelling
average contract rent

% owner occupiers

% tenant occupiers
% occupancy 2 years or less
% occupancy 10 years or more

Socio-cultural Characteristics
% immigrant 1946 to 1961
% British origins
% French origins
% Other European, Italian, Asian

Household Characteristics
% single person households
% 2 to 5 person households
% 6 or more person households
% single-family dwellings
% apartments or flats
persons per room
crowded dwellings

Labour Force
% women at work
% males in managerial, professional, technical employment
% males in primary, craftsmen, labourers
% males salary $1,999 or less
% males salary $6,000 or more
average wage and salary income

% Ukrainian
% English language only
% Roman Catholic
% Elementary school only
% High school or university

OPPOSITE: *(above)* Activities in the central city: Street market in Lahore, West Pakistan; *(below)* Ethnic areas in American cities: Chinatown, San Francisco.

This particular study used a Varimax Rotation programme, although there are several options in terms of procedure.* The first output for Winnipeg shows the factors in decreasing order of importance and also indicates the proportion of initial variance which is accounted for by each:

Table 7   Winnipeg: eigen values of factors

Factors	Eigen Values	% Variance	Cumulative %
I	10·9	32·2	32·2
II	8·1	23·8	56·0
III	2·9	8·6	64·6
IV	2·3	6·7	71·3
V	1·9	5·7	77·0
VI	1·6	4·6	81·6
VII	1·1	3·1	84·7
VIII	1·0	2·9	87·6

The eigen values (column 2) indicate the relative strengths of the factors (column 1) and can be expressed as proportions of the total variance (column 3). The term total variance can be taken to mean the total variability, almost the overall complexity, of the initial data: what factor analysis has achieved has been to reduce this variability to a small number of summarising factors or dimensions. The results for Winnipeg are typical of sub-area studies: the first factor accounts for almost one-third of the total variance, the first two factors for over one-half (column 4) and the first eight for nearly 90 per cent.

Table 8 shows the loadings which identify the nature of each factor; each original variable has a loading with each factor and the three or four highest loadings are shown for the first three factors. The input data, selected to cover as wide a range as possible of urban characteristics, has been reduced to a small number of dimensions. From the evidence of the loadings, factor I is described as a measure of housing style, related to family characteristics; factor II is described as a social prestige measure; and factor III is an ethnic measure. The leading three factors are clearly reminiscent of the constructs of social area analysis and the great majority of North American analyses have produced similar results.

* See Appendix.

OPPOSITE: *(above)* Ethnic areas in American cities: Mexican district. Olvera Street, Los Angeles; *(below)* Residential patterns: Port Credit: suburban Canada.

K

MORPHOLOGICAL SUB-AREAS

1. Concept of townscape typology or morphological plan units related to phases of urban growth.

Measures based upon physical attributes: housing style, materials, age etc.

2. Sub-areas of morphological unity

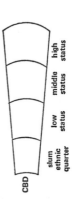

historic core

tenements   terraces   villas

3. Relationship between growth and morphology

Relationship between form and function constraint of relict fabric.

Cycles of morphological development.

NATURAL AREAS

1. Concept of 'real neighbourhoods' within the city.

2. Define sub-areas: intuitively using natural boundaries — parks, roads, rivers etc.

Objectively using a diagnostic variable — rent, rates.

3. Sub-areas of physical unity: socio-economic characteristics, moral order

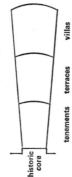

CBD

slum   low   middle   high
ethnic   status   status   status
quarter

4. Interrelationship between built environment and patterns of behaviour.

Ecological concepts of community, segregation, invasion and succession.

SOCIAL AREAS

1. Deductive identification of main dimensions of non-geographic social space. Main constructs of economic, family and ethnic status are derived from census variables.

2. Scores from constructs form typology
a) Census Tracts classified in social space

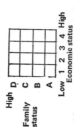

High D
Family   C
status   B
           A
      Low 1 2 3 4 High
              Economic status

b) Census Tracts have a spatial location: sub-areas can be designated in social geographical space

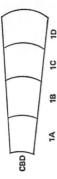

CBD

1A   1B   1C   1D

3. Sampling framework
Comparative studies
Basis for generalised spatial patterns

1. Input of available variables, mainly from Census. No initial theory but could be hypothesis-testing.

2. Technique produces main dimensions in decreasing order of significance.

Proportion of total variance accounted for by each Factor is stated.

3. a) Factors are dimensions of social space Census Tracts can be placed in non-geographic social space.

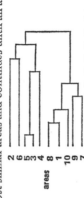

b) Census Tracts have spatial location: factor scores classify sub-areas

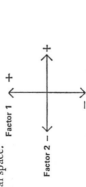

4. Informational base for theory-formation sampling framework for detailed studies. Bases for generalised spatial models.

1. Input of available variables, mainly from Census. Input sometimes reduced by Factor Analysis to more manageable dimensions. No initial theory.

2. Technique aggregates Census Tracts on the basis of their proximity in 'n'-dimensional space. n-dimensional space defined by number of variables x-number of observations.

3. Linkage tree (dendogram) proceeds stepwise; links two most similar areas and continues until all are aggregated.

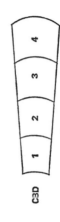

4. Spatial classification obtained by taking cut-off points on the dendogram where natural breaks occur. No precise social dimensions is also used.

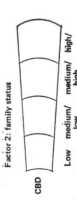

5. Typology provides comparative framework. Allows study and assessment of particular areas. Bases for generalised structure.

Fig 44. Approaches to urban sub-areas

A

High

Low

2 mls
3 kms

B

High

Low

N

C

Ukrainian

French

Fig 45. *Factorial ecology in Winnipeg:* The maps, based upon factor scores, identify A. stage in life cycle differences between city centre and suburbs (where low scores identify high family status); B. social status sectors; C. ethnic districts.

Table 8   Winnipeg: nature of factors

Factor I (housing style)		Factor II (social status)	
Variables	Loadings	Variables	Loadings
% single family dwellings	+0.91	% high school or university	+0.93
% single person households	−0.89	% males in managerial, professional, technical employment	+0.92
% owner-occupied households	+0.89	% males primary, craftsmen, labourers	−0.91
% tenant-occupied households	−0.87	% males salaries $6,000 or more	+0.88

Factor III (ethnicity)	
Variables	Loadings
% French origins	+0.98
% English language only	−0.97
% Roman Catholic	+0.89

The last output from the analysis is that of scores, which are recorded for each factor for each census tract and allow patterns to be identified in geographical space. The spatial patterns of scores are shown in Figure 45: Factor I scores (A) distinguish between the central city and the family suburbs; Factor II scores (B) between the high prestige districts of south and west and the low prestige districts of north and east; Factor III (C) identifies the French district of St Boniface. Social geographical patterns could be described as zonal for Factor I, sectoral for Factor II and clusters for Factor III; patterns which conform with those identified by analysis of variance for social area scores and with the model suggested by R. A. Murdie for Toronto.[3] A further expression of the spatial patterning of scores was obtained by a grouping procedure (see Figure 46), which classifies census tracts on the basis of their similarity of scores for the first six factors. The grouping procedure is described in the appendix, and the diagrams, Figure 47, demonstrate the way in which it achieves a typology of sub-areas in Winnipeg.

The Winnipeg case-study provides an example of the use of factor analytic procedures and produces a set of results which are typical of North American applications. Both those studies which have been designed as direct tests of the Shevky-Bell hypotheses and those which evolved as independent investigations of the

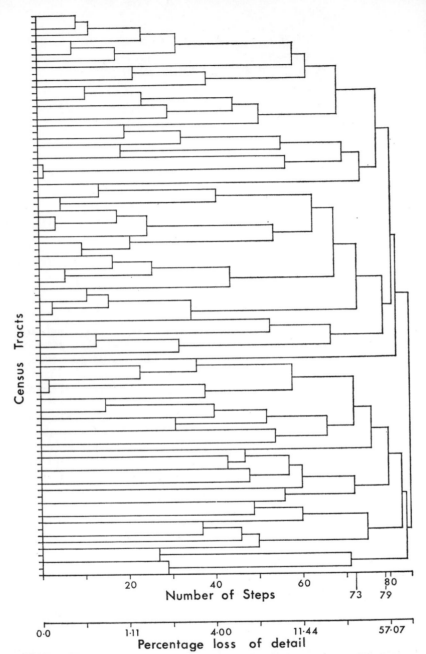

Fig 46. *Cluster analysis dendogram: Winnipeg:* This diagram shows graphically the combination of individual census tracts into clusters of the greatest internal consistency. The 86 initial tracts are combined in a step-wise manner until they form one group.

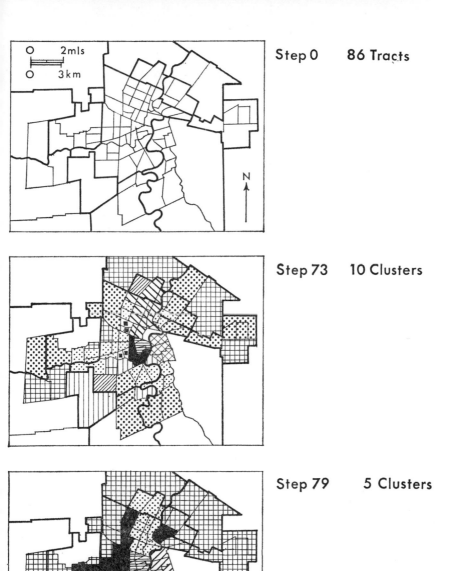

Step 0   86 Tracts

Step 73   10 Clusters

Step 79   5 Clusters

Fig 47.   *Sub-areas from cluster analysis: Winnipeg:* At step 0 all census tracts are separate; at step 73 the tracts have been aggregated to ten clusters with a 27 per cent loss of original detail; at step 79 there are five clusters with a 50 per cent loss of detail.

dimensions of urban-social space, have tended to confirm the existence of the three main constructs of economic, family and ethnic status. Another recent example was the study of Chicago by Philip Rees in which three factors were identified which he described as socio-economic status, stage in life-cycle and race/ resources[4] (Figure 48). Studies concerned with central cities have tended to stress ethnic dimensions, for example by Rees, who varied the scale of his analysis in Chicago and by C. G. Janson in a study of Newark, New Jersey.[5] Attempts to incorporate a temporal dimension in North American analyses have revealed the persistent importance of social area analysis constructs, though some variations do occur. R. A. Murdie's comparative study in factorial ecology of Toronto between 1951 and 1961 provided an example of change.[6]

Table 9   *Factors in Toronto 1951 and 1961*

| Dimension | Rank of Factor | |
	1951	1961
Economic status	I	I
Family status	II	IV
Ethnic status	III	—
Italian	—	II
Jewish	—	V
Recent growth	IV	VI
Service employment	V	—
Household characteristics	VI	III

(after R. A. Murdie)

The social area analysis constructs were the main dimensions at both points in time, with a separate Italian ethnic dimension crystallising in 1961 and reflecting the large-scale migration of Italians into Toronto during the 1960s. The main characteristics of change between the two time periods were described by Murdie as suburbanisation, ethnic change and urbanisation. Another example of change over time was provided by L. E. Brown and F. E. Horton at Chicago, though their emphasis was upon changing spatial patterns.[7] They described their main change characteristics between 1950 and 1960 as 'occupational polarisation' or an increase in the proportion of renters; 'income profile' or salary increases; 'life cycle profile' or increasing proportion of households in the middle life cycle; and 'ethnic composition' or

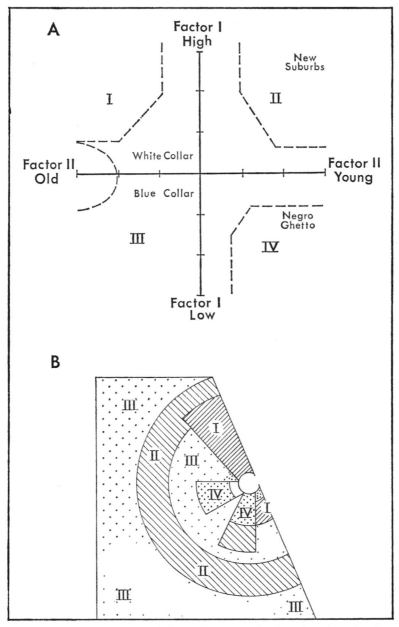

Fig 48. *A factorial model for Chicago*: The two main dimensions from American experience, socio-economic status (Factor 1) and stage in life cycle (Factor 2) are identified in Chicago. A. The two factors are used to locate tracts in social space. B. A generalised spatial model could be formed for Chicago. (After Rees, P. H. 'Concepts of Social Space', in Berry, B. J. L. and Horton, F. E., *Geographic Perspectives on Urban Systems*, New Jersey. 1970, with permission from the author and Prentice-Hall, Inc. Englewood Cliff, New Jersey.)

an increase in the number of Negro households. With the first two dimensions of change in particular a concentric zonal pattern could be discerned; downgrading of occupations and change to rented accommodation were typical of the central city and the inverse of peripheral areas.

FACTORIAL ECOLOGIES AND EUROPEAN CITIES

European cities which have been studied through factor analysis have produced results broadly similar to those in North America, but usually with some significant differences of detail. P. O. Pedersen used 14 socio-economic variables for 76 urban zones of Copenhagen and identified both in 1950 and 1960 three main factors which he named family status, socio-economic status and population change.[8] The first two displayed zonal and sectoral characteristics respectively, in accordance with North American experience, though the central city of Copenhagen was of uniformly low status. F. L. Sweetser attempted a comparative study of Helsinki, Finland, and Boston, using twenty common variables for 441 census tracts in Boston and 70 statistical areas in Helsinki.[9] Part of Sweetser's objective was to test the value of factor analysis in the differentiation of residential areas and he considered the value proven from his results. His main factors for Helsinki were socio-economic status, family status (progeniture) and urbanism. These studies of Copenhagen and Helsinki both reproduce the two main North American dimensions of socio-economic status and familism/urbanism, but not the ethnic dimension. This latter omission is a point of societal difference as European cities do not, for the most part, possess the substantial, under-privileged ethnic minorities which are so typical of American cities. The existence of the other two dimensions, however, does offer considerable support to their value as general dimensions for western cities, upon which classifications of residential areas may be based.

British studies, however, showed marked divergence from the results so far described. These differences may be related to the available data, but also seem to reflect differences in the structure of society and, in particular, the role of local authorities in the housing market. A number of studies of British cities using principal components analysis* have been made which display

* See Appendix.

a considerable degree of consistency in results.[10] The way in which the leading components have repeatedly emerged as measures of occupance and tenure and of housing conditions has been most impressive. The single census variable of persons per room, a measure of the density of occupance, has appeared in most studies as being highly correlated with the first component. Although variations in input must clearly play a part, housing has proved a highly diagnostic variable in British cities. Analyses have been completed of Cardiff and Swansea in South Wales, using a common list of 26 variables (see Table 10) for 334 and 221 enumeration districts respectively, and these are used as examples of British studies.[11]

Table 10   Variables used in Cardiff and Swansea

1. % of persons aged 0–4 years
2. % of persons aged 0–14 years
3. % of persons aged 65 years and over
4. Overall sex ratio
5. Single as % of total adult population
6. % women aged 20 to 24 ever married.
7. % single persons per household
8. % households sharing a dwelling
9. % households without exclusive use of WC
10. persons per room
11. % households at over 1·5 persons per room
12. % households owning their accommodation
13. % households renting from Local Authority
14. % households renting private unfurnished
15. % households renting private furnished
16. % born in British Caribbean Territories
17. % born in British Africa (except South Africa)
18. % born in India, Pakistan, Ceylon
19. % born in Cyprus
20. % born in Malta
21. % born in Ireland
22. % born outside England and Wales
23. % in professional, managerial, executive occupations
24. % in manual occupations
25. % with terminal education age under 16 years
26. % moving into area in previous year

The output from Cardiff and Swansea analysed in Table 11 is limited to the first two components in each city: these accounted for 50·9 per cent of the total variable in Cardiff and 41·3 per cent in Swansea.

The two leading components, closely similar for Cardiff and Swansea, are typical of results for comparable British studies. The first component could be described as a dimension of housing occupance and tenure, whilst the second component identifies

Table 11   Nature of Components in Cardiff and Swansea

Principal Component I

Variable	Loading	Variable	Loading
persons per room	+0·91	persons per room	+0·56
% aged 0–14 years	+0·87	% aged 65 years and over	−0·85
% renting municipal		% aged 0–14 years	+0·80
housing	+0·86	% renting municipal	
% aged 65 years and over	−0·85	housing	+0·79

Principal Component II

Variable	Loading	Variable	Loading
% foreign-born	+0·70	% without exclusive	
% without exclusive use		use WC	−0·75
of WC	+0·69	% renting private	
% at over 1½ persons		unfurnished	−0·74
per room	+0·67	% sharing dwellings	−0·62
% renting private		% left school before 16	
unfurnished	+0·66	years	−0·56

different conditions of housing. The contrasts which these components identify can be seen most clearly from the spatial patterns derived from the mapping of scores for enumeration districts (Figure 49). Component I distinguishes between the public and private sectors in housing, with high positive scores delimiting municipal estates which occupy large districts such as Ely and Llanrumney in Cardiff. Other residential areas similarly categorised by this component include smaller pockets of urban redevelopment and some districts where small-size and low-price private housing possesses qualities similar to those found on municipal estates. The high negative scores on Component I identify those housing districts which are in most marked contrast to the public housing sector: these include high prestige areas of Llandaff, Roath and Cyncoed and also some older districts of terraced housing with small families and a low density of occupance. This leading dimension illustrates the influence of the public sector in British cities: in Cardiff, for example, just below 30 per cent of all housing is owned by the municipality. Component II is a measure of substandardness and of overcrowded housing conditions, the high positive scores for Cardiff identifying the poorer housing of the central city which was the product of the second half of the nineteenth century; these are areas which lack basic facilities and are generally in need of rehabilitation and renewal. The high negative scores on this second component identify newer housing, both publicly- and privately-owned, which has been constructed to modern standards of urban design, space and amenity. The overall spatial pattern of this second component could be generalised in terms of zones of progressively ageing urban fabric towards the centre of the city.

Although the social area analysis dimensions of socio-economic status and family status are indirectly involved in the main dimensions of British cities, housing characteristics are the direct measures. To a considerable extent the incidence of public housing would appear to be a distinguishing feature of British cities and a brief point of comparison may be made with evidence from

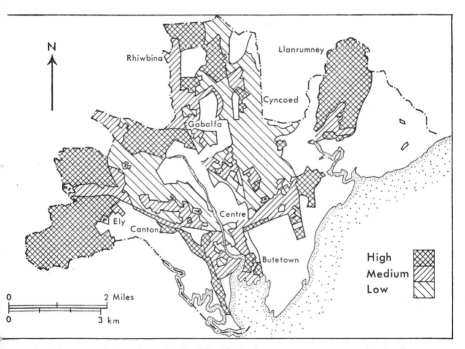

Fig 49. *Factorial ecology in Cardiff, 1961:* Component scores on the leading component, marked high, medium and low in the key, distinguish between public and private sector housing. Social status is indirectly measured with a high status sector north of the city centre; high component scores identify local authority tenancy and lower social status.

Prague, though this was not obtained from factor analysis.[12] In Prague, the pre-Communist structure was not unlike that of North American cities, but now the private enterprise market has been dismantled and all housing is publicly owned. The result is that although the dimension of familism appears of some significance, socio-economic status has no importance in spatial terms. The wider implications of these departures from the private enterprise model and the effects on social geography are discussed below.

Melbourne, Australia, provides a non-European example of a city where North American findings appear to be replicated. A factor analysis study, using 70 variables for its 611 districts, was arranged as a test of the social area analysis dimensions and the results confirmed their existence.[13] The organisation of the study, however, conditioned the results and some tests showed the three dimensions to be less than independent. The utility of this study is limited, however, in that as the product of a westernised society correspondence with results obtained in North America could reasonably be expected. Of much more significance are two studies of two fundamentally different non-western cities, Calcutta[14] and Cairo,[15] in which one might rationally expect differences between the western and non-western worlds to be reflected in urban ecological structure.

NON-WESTERN FACTORIAL ECOLOGIES

The Calcutta study adopted a factor analysis procedure with varimax rotation to analyse a data matrix of 37 census variables recorded for each of the 80 wards of the city. The data are less reliable than those used in most analyses of western cities and many of the wards must have had extremely large populations for this type of procedure. The nature of the factors obtained in Calcutta is shown in Table 12.

Factor I is strongly reminiscent of the original social area analysis construct of urbanisation and appears in a much 'truer' sense in this Indian city, where the process of urbanisation really is at work, than was originally suggested for cities in California. Urbanisation seems likely to be much more identifiable as a process and to be more accurately reflected in urban-spatial structure in a contemporary non-western city where change is still gathering momentum, than it is in American cities where society is already effectively urbanised. The contrasts revealed within Cal-

Table 12   Calcutta : nature of factors

Factor I (land use and familism)		Factor II (Muslim)		Factor III (literacy)	
Variable	Loading	Variable	Loading	Variable	Loading
% solely dwellings	+0·89	% females employed	+0·88	% females literate	+0·92
% females over 15 years	+0·82	% in service employment	+0·85	% males literate	+0·81
population size	+0·76	% in construction employment	+0·81		
% married women	+0·75				
% business and offices	−0·83	% in transport employment	+0·78		
% living in institutions	−0·81				

cutta, for example, are between the central city, with its many recent in-migrants and single-male street sleepers, and the established families of the peripheries: also between the mixed land uses of more central districts and the peripheries where increasing functional differentiation of land use occurs. Factor II could be identified as a Muslim dimension, mainly in terms of the comparatively high proportion of female employment, the latter being a characteristic of Muslim population in contrast to other religious groups in which females do not take employment. The factor thus identifies an important ethnic distinction in Calcutta and the high scores for wards pick out those parts of the city in which there are concentrations of middle and upper class Muslims. Factor III, a measure of literacy with strong inverse relationships with proportions of the population in Scheduled Castes, could effectively be identified as a socio-economic status dimension. Berry and Rees concluded that the leading factors could be related to broad patterns in geographical space: 'A broadly concentric pattern of familism, an axial arrangement of areas according to degrees of literacy, and both substantial and increasing functional differentiation in land use.'[16] (See Figure 50.) These simplified geographical expressions, however, were complicated by the considerable ethnic variability within the city; ethnic factors were instrumental in the decision on where to live. Berry and Rees, from the evidence of their study, saw Calcutta at a stage of transition between the pre-industrial and the industrial city. Elements of change were present, such as an increasing specialisation in land use, but many traditional features remained.

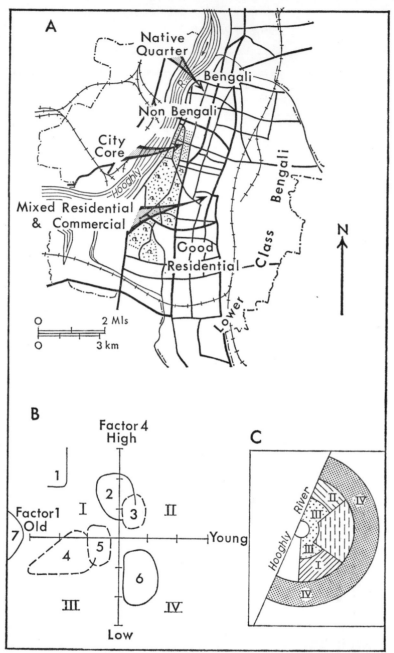

Fig 50. *A factorial model for Calcutta:* A. Generalised spatial structure. B. Social space defined by Factor 1 (familism) and Factor 4 (substantial residential areas); including 1. exclusive residential areas on Maidan; 2. superior residences; 3. native quarters; 4. commercial; 5. mixed use; 6. bustees; 7. city core. C. generalised model. (After Berry, B. J. L. and Rees, P. H., 'Factorial Ecology of Calcutta', *American Journal of Sociology,* 74, 1969, 445–91, with permission of the authors: copyright 1969 by the University of Chicago.)

The analysis of Cairo by Janet Abu Lughod provides a second example of factorial ecology in a non-western city.[17] The problem of data comparability remains, as only thirteen variables were used in an analysis of the 216 census tracts of the city. A factor analysis procedure was followed for both 1947 and 1960 and in each instance the first four factors accounted for more than three-quarters of the total variance. The results for 1947 and 1960 were substantially the same and the nature of the leading three factors for 1960 is shown in Table 13.

Table 13   Cairo : nature of factors

Factor I (socio-economic status)		Factor II (transients)		Factor III (social disorganisation)	
Variable	Loading	Variable	Loading	Variable	Loading
% never mar- ried females	+0·95	Sex ratio Never married	+0·97	population density	+0·72
% female literacy	+0·92	males	+0·49	% Muslim % females	+0·55
fertility ratio	−0·89			divorced	+0·41
% females employed	+0·85				
% male literacy	+0·81				

Using literacy as the main indicator, Factor I could be interpreted as a socio-economic status dimension, though it was also highly associated with variables related to family life style. The high-scoring census tracts on this factor were characterised by commodious housing, a literate population, and resident domestic servants. These are of course high-prestige qualities associated with which were indicators of Cairo's modern (as opposed to traditional) life styles such as female education, delayed age of marriage and lower fertility. By contrast, the low-scoring census tracts on this factor identified low-prestige districts with over-crowding and illiteracy and traditional life-styles, such as female exclusion from education and early marriage. Factor II, mainly associated with an excess of males, picked out central districts and institutional areas where unattached migrant males had gathered. Factor III was described by Abu Lughod as a measure of social disorganisation and its high scores identified the central slums where the physically-handicapped, the unemployed, and the

L

divorced women formed a large part of the population; the low scores were recorded by peripheral areas with stable families. Although Abu Lughod made little attempt to generalise about the spatial patterns produced by these first three factors for Cairo, the main contrasts appeared to be between the central and peripheral parts of the city. The emphasis upon the process of modernisation and change is reminiscent of findings by Berry and Rees in Calcutta, and Cairo seems similarly representative of cities in transition towards a form which will more closely approximate the western industrial city.

TOWARDS GENERALISED MODELS FROM THE EVIDENCE OF FACTORIAL ECOLOGIES

Any comparison of results from studies in factorial ecology from various parts of the world rests upon the assumption that findings from varying inputs are representative of societal contrasts and their expression in the spatial structure of cities. But their validity depends upon the quality of the original data and the fallibilities of the technique.* Perhaps the most impressive single feature of the results of factorial ecologies has been the confirmation in North America of the constructs proposed by Shevky and Bell: confirmation which has also been forthcoming in some European studies. The greatest consistency has been in terms of the dimensions of socio-economic status and of family status, the latter interpreted as stages of the life cycle. The precise form of the original urbanisation construct has been less readily confirmed, nor has ethnic status, a clearly separate dimension in North America, appeared as decisively elsewhere. The ethnic status dimension is *always* present in North American studies though its precise form varies with local conditions; in Winnipeg, French and Ukrainian minorities were demarcated; in Toronto, Italians and Jews; in most American cities, Negroes. Many factorial ecologies, however, have not conformed with the patterns suggested by Shevky and Bell and in Europe, British studies in particular revealed differences. The evidence from non-western cities is extremely limited, but the two major studies described reveal some basic points of contrast. The uniformity of results in much of the western world and, perhaps, more signi-

* See Appendix.

ficantly, the divergences which have been observed, require explanation in terms of an overall theory, and Janet Abu Lughod has provided an extremely useful basis for such understanding.[18] Abu Lughod focused her attempt at explanation upon the two main dimensions of socio-economic status and familism, arguing that it is only in terms of these that sufficiently reliable evidence for generalisation has been forthcoming. These two dimensions have appeared consistently in analyses of American cities and Abu Lughod tried to stipulate the conditions for their existence and for their independence. Her reasoning was that an independent socio-economic status dimension would occur where there was an effective ranking system in the society, distinguishing population groups according to their status or prestige and where that ranking system was matched by corresponding sub-divisions of the housing market (each prestige group lived in a particular type of residential area). Similarly, a familism dimension would occur where family types could be linked to specific stages of the life cycle and where each stage was paralleled by available residential sub-areas. Socio-economic status and familism dimensions might be associated in social space but could still appear as geographically separate where a comprehensive housing market could cater for all life cycle stages within each socio-economic status level. The necessary conditions for the two leading dimensions are, therefore, ranking by socio-economic status, clear stages of the life cycle, a housing market structured to cater for each possible combination of these characteristics in distinctive sub-areas, and a population consisting of independent households mobile enough to use the possibilities. A factorial ecology in which the two dimensions failed to emerge could be explained in terms of the absence or limited expression of these necessary conditions. Abu Lughod did not include ethnic status in her interpretation, but Philip Rees views the dimension in the American context as a limited microcosm of the city as a whole.[19] His argument was that there are constraints which limit minority groups, such as Negroes, to particular sections of the city and that within these sections the relevant range of socio-economic status levels and life-cycle stages had to be incorporated. With reference to his Chicago study, Rees was able to identify this range within ethnic districts but owing to constraints of other kinds, mainly mis-allocation of resources between white and coloured people, it was never fully represented. These necessary conditions described by

Abu Lughod are fulfilled most completely in contemporary North American cities and to a lesser extent in other parts of the world where cities are the product of western industrial society. The general milieu in which these conditions exist might be described as a free enterprise, pre-welfare state stage of capitalism, with the additional attributes of an advanced economic and technological development and what might be crudely summarised as a non-traditional cultural context.*

Janet Abu Lughod's argument, as outlined above, is a valuable basis for an explanation of the main factorial dimensions identified in Western cities. Accepting its general validity, deviant results from individual studies can be explained in terms of the hypothesised necessary conditions. A common deviant situation is the failure of socio-economic status and familism to be independent or disassociated, *even though they are recognisable as dimensions*. Most individual studies exhibiting this lack of disassociation record significant relationships between measures of socio-economic status and that of fertility.[20] The results recorded for Winnipeg (Table 4) showed this tendency, as did those for four Southern cities in the United States and for Rome.[21] In each of these studies, socio-economic status existed as a ranking system in social space and was matched geographically by residential segregations. Family size, however, was not independent of socio-economic status and the housing market did not seem to cater for a sufficient range of life-cycle stages in an orderly way. The four Southern cities in the United States all had relatively high proportions of Negroes: 'The range of family forms in these cities, as described by the fertility measure, has not yet become disassociated from social rank.'[22] The presence of the Negro population, with its distinctive characteristics of low status and high fertility, together with imposed constraints upon mobility and a limited housing market, diminishes the likelihood of family status emerging as a separate and independent dimension for the city as a whole. The evidence from Rome was such as to suggest that high fertility was significantly related to low socio-economic status and that the housing market did not provide a sufficient range of residential districts to cater for successive stages of the family cycle. The implication of these various studies was that

* Interpreted as a modern society in which economic and functional forces dominate the more traditional socio-cultural forces such as family and religion.

they would cease to be deviant cases over time as family status became independent of socio-economic status and as a more mobile population was catered for by an improved and more specialised housing market. This kind of change, however, is likely to be inhibited in some American cities where residential constraints on non-white population are real and persistent.

The deviances noted above were even more clearly present in the two studies of non-western cities, Cairo and Calcutta, which have already been described. Abu Lughod found that in Cairo a clear ranking system based on socio-economic status was not evident and that an independent family status dimension did not emerge. The leading factor in the Cairo study (Table 13) combined socio-economic status and family status and the conditions for their separate emergence were far from being satisfied. Residential segregations in socio-economic terms could be identified but these retained related familism characteristics. Similarly in Calcutta, B. J. L. Berry and P. Rees found that the necessary conditions for the emergence of the separate dimensions were largely absent and that ethnicity had a powerful influence. In both the Cairo and Calcutta studies, a process of change was emphasised which might take the urban ecology further towards the form identified in developed countries, though some cultural variations could prevail. Abu Lughod talked of modernisation and westernisation in Cairo, while Berry and Rees thought that the ethnic bases of communities in Calcutta were being replaced by functional determinants. Berry and Rees were prepared to conclude that there was a separate family status dimension but that socio-economic status and 'minority-group' membership were linked. It was this latter feature which was most likely to be affected by change: 'As the transitional process continues, however, and as caste transforms into class, one might reasonably expect the socio-economic and ethnic bases of differentiation to separate.'[23]

The steps towards a general theory in this aspect of urban-spatial structure suggested by Abu Lughod imply that cities at various stages of development—summarised perhaps by her modernisation process in Cairo—are moving towards the identified western model in which the conditions for the emergence of socio-economic status and family status as separate dimensions exist. This principle is supported by Berry and Rees who suggested a number of ways in which the three basic dimensions of socio-economic status, family status and ethnicity might be combined to typify different societies: 'The expectation is, therefore, that different urban ecologies related to different factor combinations can be arranged along a scale of urban development from pre- to post-industrial forms.'[24] A similar attempt to form a typology of urban dimensions has been made by D. W. G. Timms[25] (see Figure 51).

The evidence available of non-western cities is limited but the analyses of Cairo and Calcutta, together with findings of other geographical studies of non-western cities,[26] provide some basis for understanding, although carefully-designed comparative

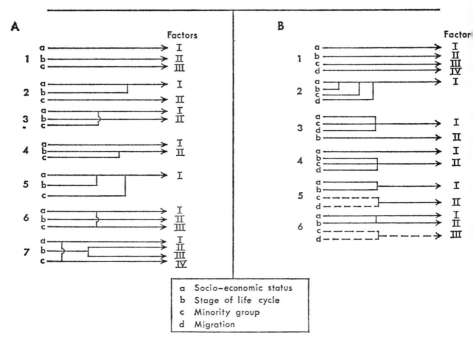

Fig 51. *Generalisations from factorial ecology:* This diagram summarises two attempts at identifying alternative models from the evidence of factorial ecology. A (P. H. Rees's factor combinations) describe 1. social area analysis; 2. Cairo result; 3. American southern cities; 4. Miami result; 5. single-dimension; 6. Chicago result (Rees); 7. Toledo result. B (D. Timms's item constructs) describe; 1. modern city; 2. feudal city; 3. colonial city; 4. immigrant city; 5. pre-industrial city; 6. industrialising city.

studies of the spatial structures of cities in Africa, Asia and Latin America are an essential prerequisite for definitive theory (see Figures 52 and 53).

The results from factorial ecologies of British cities, whilst based on different input data from those used in North America, show sufficient uniformity to suggest a different kind of deviance.

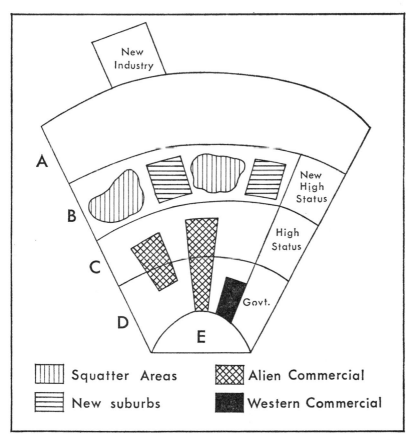

Fig 52. *Generalised spatial structure of a large South-east Asian city:* A. market gardening zone; B. zone of new suburbs and shanty-towns; C. middle density residential zones; D. mixed land-use; E. port zone. Only port and market gardening zones are constant; the rest of the city is characterised by mixing of land use. (After McGee, T., *The South-east Asian city,* 1967, with permission of the author and G. Bell and Sons Ltd.)

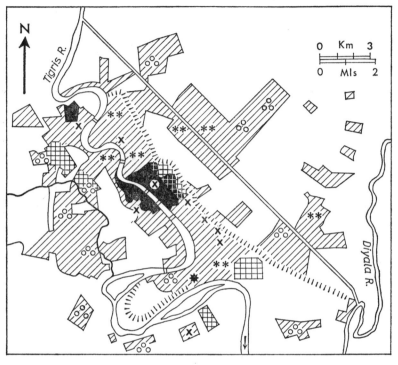

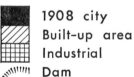

	1908 city		☀	Upper Class
	Built-up area		✳✳	Middle Class
	Industrial		°₀	Workers
	Dam		x	Ethnic/Religious quarters

Fig 53. *Spatial patterns in a non-western city: Baghdad:* The spatial order of American cities is not present in the non-western world and distinctive ethnic/ religious quarters remain a feature. (Adapted from Gulick, J. 'Baghdad: Portrait of a City in Physical and Cultural Change', *Journal of the American Institute of Planners,* 1967, and reprinted with permission.)

Britain is in a post-welfare-state stage and some of the differences observed from the North American model may be explicable in these terms. Similarities to American cities and to other European cities are evident: there is a ranking system for socio-economic status which is matched by residential segregation; the life cycle stages are also important but these are only reflected to a limited extent in residential areas because of comparatively low residential mobility and the inadequacies of the housing market. The effect of public sector interference in housing is complex, but can in some ways be said to maintain the dimensions of differentiation. Socio-economic status is maintained because part of the criteria by which municipal housing is allocated to tenants is based on income and occupation: it is, by and large, the lower-income and lower-status groups which are housed. Family status differences are also maintained because the system of allocating municipal housing gives priority to larger families, particularly those living in shared or over-crowded dwellings. These systems of priorities would seem to demarcate more clearly in geographical space, the various status groups and the various stages of the life cycle. Other characteristics of British municipal housing policy, however, must be weighed against these factors. There are frequent attempts, for example, to rehouse the total populations from comprehensive redevelopment schemes and to plan demographically balanced neighbourhoods. Again, the lack of variety and the immobility of tenants has allowed demographic and family status character-istics to change *in situ*, as a neighbourhood ages from one generation to another. Municipal householders tend to be immobilised because their right to that style of housing is not transferable from one municipality to another. The impact of this public sector housing on the ecological structures of British cities is best seen in its spatial expression. Municipal housing, often accounting for one-third or more of the total housing stock, is located both centrally and peripherally within the city and in virtually all sectors. The municipal governments have been powerful agents in the housing market, particularly since 1920, and have acquired and developed land on a comprehensive scale. The decision-making processes leading to the location of public housing are affected by a myriad of considerations which include the availability of public utilities and services, 'diplomatic balance' amongst the wards of the city, and established patterns of local preference. The spatial patterns which emerge have few repetitive qualities upon which generalisations could be formed. Outside the public sector in housing, the private residential patterns are broadly analogous to those found in North America and for these a spatial model probably could be formulated (Figure 54) though even here there are significant differences related to the more limited range of house-types, the lesser mobility and the greater amount of inherited urban fabric.

The present limited emergence of a separate ethnic dimension in British cities, in common with the majority of European studies, is likely to be largely a function of limited numbers. There are several British cities in which there is evidence of incipient ethnic segregation which bears some resemblance to American patterns.[27] Although the scale of these developments is very different to American experience, characteristics similar to those described by P. Rees in Chicago, such as societal constraints, discrimination and misallocation of resources, do exist. Differences between British and North American results, as reflected in both factorial ecology and social area analysis, are influenced by comparability of data but also represent differences in society. To some extent British results conform with those obtained from other European cities in which the basic American dimensions are identifiable but less specific, although it must be emphasised that more good comparable analyses of European cities are needed before generalisations can be attempted: there are clearly differences of considerable significance within Europe. In other ways, British cities serve as examples of post-welfare-state societies with features mirrored in a more exaggerated way in socialistically organised countries: the descriptive analysis of Prague referred to earlier contains some confirmation of this latter hypothesis,[28] as does a recent statement on the spatial structure of Warsaw[29] (see Figure 55).

This discussion of factorial ecology has concentrated upon multivariate approaches, factor analysis in particular, and their general validity in this context is central to the argument. The fallibilities of the techniques are discussed in the Appendix, but practitioners have been content to regard factor analysis as a rigorous technique which gives valid interpretations of urban structure and the comments of F. L. Sweetser in this context are pertinent: 'Modern factor analysis, using factor structure as a model for ecological structure, is the method *par excellence* for comparing cross-nationally (and intra-nationally) the ecological

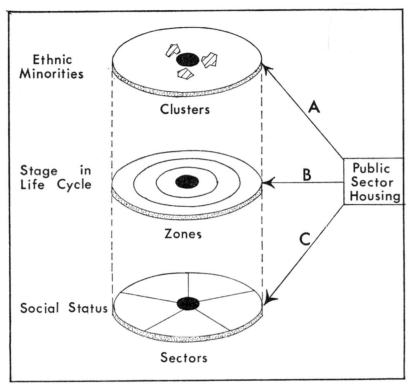

Ethnic Minorities

Clusters

Stage in Life Cycle

Zones

Social Status

Sectors

A

B

C

Public Sector Housing

Fig 54. *A spatial model for the British city:* One can see in the British city general elements which are common to North America, but public sector housing provides significant distortions. A. Ethnic minorities, particularly West Indians, Indians and Pakistanis, found in some British cities are small numerically but generally clustered in central city districts of sub-standard housing. Public housing policy should serve to disperse the clusters but does in fact often consolidate them. B. Life cycle stages are generally represented in spatial terms though the zonal form is tentative. Public sector housing may reinforce zones by placing young families with children on the periphery of the city. C. A few definable status sectors often exist but public housing modifies these by relocating low income groups in high status sectors.

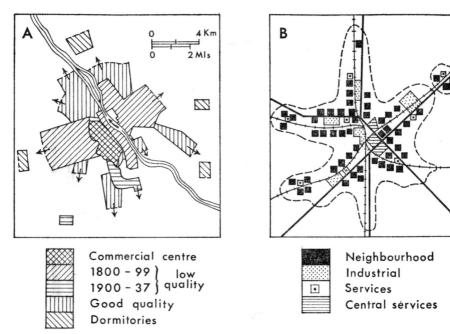

Commercial centre
1800 – 99 } low
1900 – 37 } quality
Good quality
Dormitories

Neighbourhood
Industrial
Services
Central services

Fig 55. *Model of a socialist city: Warsaw:* A. Growth of Warsaw to 1937; B. Model hypothesised for future Socialist cities. (After Dawson, A. H., 'Warsaw: an example of city structure in free market and planned socialist environments', *Tijdschrift voor Economische en Sociale Geografie,* 1971, with permission of the author and *Tijdschrift voor Economische en Sociale Geografie.*)

differentiation of residential areas in urban and metropolitan communities.'[30] Factor analytic procedure is in fact analogous to social area analysis rather than to ecological approaches to the residential structure of cities. The two former procedures first identify dimensions within social space, factor analysis by an objective statistical procedure and social area analysis by deductive reasoning, before using those dimensions as criteria for the definition of sub-areas (see Figure 44). Ecological and geographical approaches, by contrast, have first defined the distinctive territory and then proceeded to identify its characteristic life styles. Close links exist, however, among all the approaches and each has contributed to the identification of residential sub-areas and the comprehension of the social geographical patterns which they form.

The emphasis in this discussion has been placed upon problems of defining sub-areas within cities: the assumption throughout has been that residential areas are related to social structure and this theme will be elaborated in subsequent chapters. The other assumption is that the residential area is a meaningful unit of analysis, depending as it does upon the validity of the aggregate level of study. Geographers have consistently argued that this aggregate scale, though it is by no means the only scale with which they are concerned, continues to be valuable and productive. A specific discussion on the validity of the residential area has recently been provided by J. M. Beshers in his study of urban social structure.[31] Beshers argued that if social structure exists as an aggregate, its effects must be revealed in residential areas and that because residence is such an important item in life styles, the residential area must act as a symbol of social position. Using the example of decision-making on residential locations Beshers suggested that idiosyncracies will exist but that the great majority of people will behave in accordance with rational and similarly based evaluation of alternatives and that aggregate behaviour will give ordered choices on where to live, thus producing real sub-areas through the decision making processes. Geographers, using a probabilistic framework, would similarly argue that there are empirical regularities in individual behaviour, affecting factors such as the proportion of household income spent on housing* and the preferences of individuals, which produce an orderly social geography. The spatial patterning of residential areas and the characteristics by which they are distinguished form, therefore, a valuable insight into the structure of the city. P. H. Rees provided a succinct statement of geographical interpretation with his assessment of the dimensions which he identified in Chicago: 'They showed that, within the limits of the technology and resources at their command, people choose to minimise, through living apart from those unlike themselves, the possibilities of conflict because of class, generational, racial, and religious or national differences.'[32] An acceptance of the validity of an aggregate approach and of the residential area as a unit does not

* White-collar workers are likely to spend high proportions of their income on housing because of the greater priority which they give to residential status.

of course imply that they are always sufficient. The suggestion is that the approaches to the definition of residential sub-areas are valuable in themselves and that they form useful bases for more detailed analyses in social geography, as the following chapter will attempt to demonstrate.

CHAPTER SEVEN

Social Patterns
Within The City

SOCIAL geographers have developed a whole series of approaches to the problems of defining urban sub-areas and of analysing urban-spatial structure. Some of these approaches are merely aimed at descriptive classifications but most form part of a wider methodology with theory-building as a point of emphasis. One hypothesis proposed is that the residential area in itself is a meaningful unit of city structure which has significance in social as well as in geographical space: a further set of hypotheses concerns the relevance of spatial location in general and residential location in particular to the understanding of patterns of behaviour, activities and attitudes within the city. Sub-areas can be shown to possess high levels of formal uniformity; the question is one of whether there is similar uniformity in terms of the life-styles of their inhabitants and, also, of identifying the roles of location and urban environment as determinants of those uniformities.

Many studies illustrate a relationship between geographical space and social activity. J. M. Beshers,[1] for example, referred to studies of the development of social relationships in a housing project and also to several investigations of marriage patterns in order to demonstrate that location, through its influence on amount of contact, was a factor of considerable importance. The exact nature of the relationship between location and behaviour is thus crucial to the social geographer. It is a relationship which is complex and likely to be extremely variable between situations in which the geographical referent is virtually all-important to others in which it has only minor significance. In the interpretation of this relationship geographers, along with all other social scientists, face the recurrent problems of establishing causality. Statistical techniques can be used to measure associations in precise terms but they do not necessarily establish relationships in terms of cause and effects. Hirschi and Selvin have examined the dangers of assumed causality from statistical association: 'After measuring the association, the analyst must demonstrate that his independent variable is causally prior to his dependent variable . . . the third criterion of causality is to demonstrate lack of spuriousness in the relationship.'[2] The warnings of Hirschi and Selvin should loom large as social geographers seek to demonstrate how they can, with their particular expertise on location and area, contribute to a better understanding of social patterns within the city. Misinterpretation can blur the extent to which location is a causal factor or merely an intermediary between true cause and effect. An attempt to show a particularly bad urban environment as a cause of poor physique among children, for example, might be to understate the true causes which might be found in social class terms.[3] Again, individual cause and effect relationships are often not directly studied in a scale of analysis which is primarily concerned with the aggregate or group. A geographer's explanation would be based on the probability that sufficient uniformities exist for generalisations to be valid and J. M. Beshers again offers a pertinent comment: 'Given the great variation among human beings, it is likely that any given condition either recognised or unrecognised, will not elicit a monolithic, uniform response. Nevertheless, one type of response may be so widespread that we may speak of a high probability that it will occur.'[4]

MEDICAL GEOGRAPHY OF THE CITY

Health indices form a useful initial example because their association with particular city environments can often be readily seen, even in causal terms. The evidence from British industrial cities in the nineteenth century often suggests a localisation of ill-health by substandard housing where pollution was particularly high. The best-known empirical case was the discovery of the correspond-

OPPOSITE: Residential patterns: *(above)* A high-status residence: Toronto, Canada; *(below)* African shanty, Nigeria.

ence between contaminated water supply and the 1854 outbreak of cholera in London:[5] an association which was identified by plotting the incidence of cholera cases (Figure 56). A study of York, which demonstrated that districts of low-quality housing were breeding grounds for disease, could have been replicated for virtually any contemporary British city. B. S. Rowntree's description of schoolchildren and Army conscripts from districts of York, whose poor physiques were the product of poverty and malnutrition, was not untypical.[6] The slums were the locus of poverty; ill-health and substandard housing and sanitation were some of its concomitant effects in a series of causal relationships which are not difficult to comprehend. The overall effect was to give distinctive spatial concentrations of ill-health: sub-areas within cities where high incidence of disease and infant mortality accompanied bad living conditions. These characteristics have weakened through time with advances in medical science and with general improvement in living conditions, but in some areas of some cities they persist. A recent study of the St Ann's district of Nottingham identified conditions not that dissimilar from those of the last century: 'Children from this depressed area are generally in a poor state of physical development. For their age, they are noticeably smaller and less well-developed than children from middle-class residential areas.'[7] Although comprehensive evidence is not easily accessible for non-western cities, close correlations between ill-health, disease and those poorer districts in which water supplies and sanitation are minimal must be extremely prevalent. S. N. De's description of life in Calcutta's *bustees* or shanty-towns, which house a high proportion of the population of that city, gives a clue: 'Within the *bustees* there is but one water tap for every twenty-five persons and no means of disposing of sewage. Cholera is endemic. Life is often brief and brutal.'[8] Within Calcutta, as in European cities some decades ago, the causes of this situation are many, mainly associated with poverty, but the effect is a spatial concentration and the neighbourhood itself becomes an accentuating force.

A recent and comprehensive analysis of medical geography within the city has been provided by G. F. Pyle.[9] Using a number of measures, such as income, education, housing conditions, and unemployment, Pyle identified 'poverty areas' in Chicago and used factor analysis on nineteen health indices to derive a number of 'syndromes' (Figure 57). His first factor, the poverty

OPPOSITE: Residential patterns: *(above)* Marina Towers: high cost apartments in central Chicago; *(below)* Habitat 67: futuristic apartment living in Montreal, Canada.

M

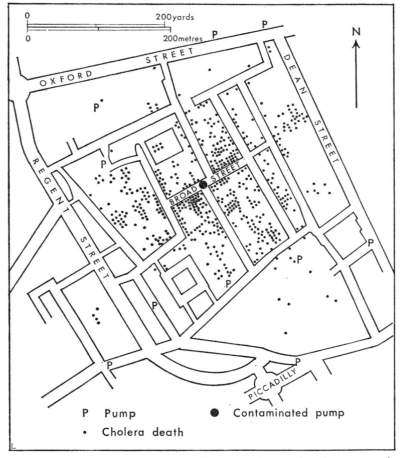

Fig 56. *A map of cholera deaths in London, 1840s:* A contaminated water pump in Broad Street proved the source for the spread of cholera. (Drawn by Dr John Snow about 1854; shown in Stamp, L. D., *A Geography of Life and Death* 1964.)

syndrome, showed a close correspondence between such health indices, the incidence of tuberculosis, syphilis, and infant mortality and the poorest neighbourhoods in the densely-populated central city. Pyle's second factor, a density syndrome, had associations with three childhood diseases, mumps, whooping cough and chicken-pox, thus again being linked with the poor neighbour-hoods. Although the third and fourth factors—upper respiratory

and rubella syndromes—showed no clear geographical pattern,
the fifth, a water syndrome, isolated infectious hepatitis and
identified a definite relationship between high scores on this
factor and stretches of open water. Pyle's study demonstrated
how health indices could be analysed for a city quantitatively
and his findings illustrate the increasingly complex inter-
relationships between health and city structure. His poverty
syndrome was a relict of the older city in which some diseases are

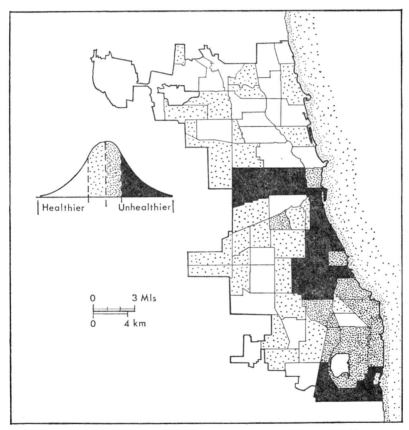

Fig 57. *Poverty areas in Chicago:* Factor analysis was used to identify poverty
areas in Chicago and to correlate these with health indices. (After Pyle, G. F. *Some
Examples of Urban-Medical Geography* (University of Chicago M.A. thesis, 1968
and with the author's permission.)

localised into neighbourhoods of poverty and substandardness. A less simple pattern was evident in the rubella syndrome which had no obvious spatial concentration but seemed to be affected by the high mobility of suburban populations. The difficulty which Pyle encountered in identifying clear spatial patterns for several health indices is symptomatic of the improvement in western cities which has eliminated the basic causes of disease: it is only in limited areas of under-privilege that the concentrations persist.

Indices of mental health have provided urban ecologists with challenging problems which in many cases appear to be associated with the urban milieu. Mental health is a general term and it has been obvious for a considerable time that detailed study of specific forms are essential for meaningful analysis. A classic study by H. W. Dunham of Chicago[10] analysed the incidence of schizophrenia and manic depression. His sample of schizophrenics consisted of 7,253 cases, recorded in terms of the 120 community areas of Chicago which provided the spatial framework, and incidence rates were found to vary from 111 per 100,000 population on the city periphery to 1,195 near the centre. The community areas with high incidence rates were all found in the central city and corresponded with districts such as hobohemia, the rooming-house district, and the ethnic quarters (Figure 58). A regular gradient, with scores decreasing from centre towards periphery, was found to exist even when race was held constant and three Negro districts extending southwards from the centre had rates of 772, 470 and 410 respectively. The same consistency was maintained when the sexes were distinguished and when different types of schizophrenia were mapped separately. Dunham also analysed the incidence of manic depression using two samples, the largest of which consisted of 2,311 cases, and failed to identify a spatial distribution which could be described as other than random. Whereas, therefore, schizophrenia bore strong relationships to ecological structure, being concentrated in under-privileged and substandard parts of Chicago, manic depression had no such simple geographical pattern and appeared more related to personality and psychological factors than to the urban environment. The Dunham study was carried out in the 1930s. A more recent analysis of the same indices in an American city by N. L. Mintz and D. T. Schwarz[11] initially established a framework of sub-areas, diffentiated by their scores

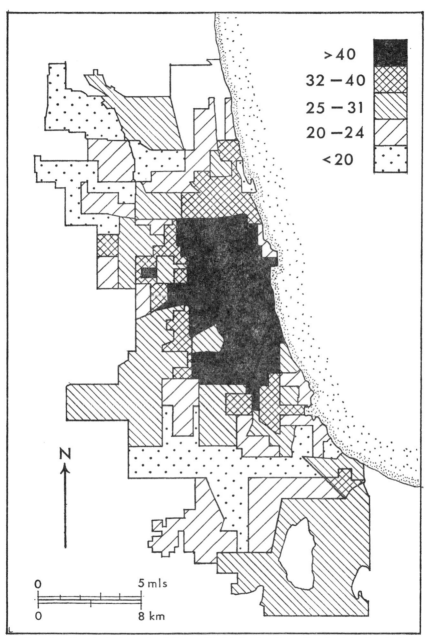

Fig 58. *Mental deviance in Chicago:* H. W. Dunham's study of schizophrenia in
Chicago identified a clear spatial association between it and urban ecological structure.
(After Dunham, H. W., 'The ecology of functional psychoses in Chicago', *American
Sociological Review,* 2, 1937, 467–79, with permission from the American Socio-
logical Association.)

on an eleven-point scale of stability: area type one, for example, was composed of single family dwellings with high average rents, while area type eleven was a district of deteriorating rooming houses. Their general finding provided some confirmation of Dunham's earlier study in that a high association existed between the stability of a neighbourhood and the incidence of schizophrenia, but manic depression once again showed a random pattern. Studies of American cities over time, therefore, demonstrate that at least one form of mental disorder is consistently associated with particular types of neighbourhood within the city.

An example of a similar study in a British city was provided by I. M. Castle and E. Gittus in Liverpool.[12] Their findings substantiated the spatial patterns found in American cities with concentrations of mental illness in residential wards adjacent to Liverpool's industrial areas and commercial core (Figure 59). In a more recent study, Elizabeth Gittus has noted similar concentrations of social defect (measured by indices including mental illness) in the Rye Hill area of Newcastle-upon-Tyne and Manchester's Moss-side.[13] D. Timms studied several kinds of mental illness in Luton[14] and schizophrenia again emerged with the clearest patterns of spatial segregation, with concentrations in substandard neighbourhoods and what he termed the rooming-house district. Another type of area with high incidence of mental illness, identified in Luton and several other British cities, has been the older municipal housing estates. Timms in Luton found that although schizophrenia showed clear spatial patterns, it was not possible to generalise upon mental illness as a whole and that some specific indices, notably neuroses, had a random distribution. A more recent study by John Giggs in Nottingham was concerned only with schizophrenia and he identified a strong spatial clustering in parts of the central city.[15] (Figure 60.)

Several points emerge from this brief discussion of medical geography within cities, the main one being that distinctive geographical patterns exist, particularly the high incidence of illness in specific neighbourhoods. Each type of illness must be individually analysed in its specific context, but with proper qualifications some generalisations can be formed. There are instances where the location or territory itself is a direct cause of the high incidence of illness, such as cholera in nineteenth-century European cities or in the modern *bustees* of Calcutta;

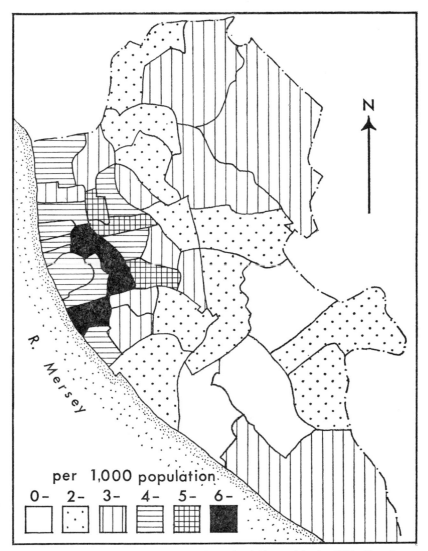

per 1,000 population

| 0- | 2- | 3- | 4- | 5- | 6- |

Fig 59. *Social defects in Liverpool:* This study of Liverpool in the 1950s (based on ward data) found some confirmation for spatial patterns identified in American cities. (After Castle, I. M. and Gittus, E., 'The Distribution of Social Defects in Liverpool', *Sociological Review,* 5, 1957, 43–64, with permission from Miss Gittus and the *Sociological Review.*)

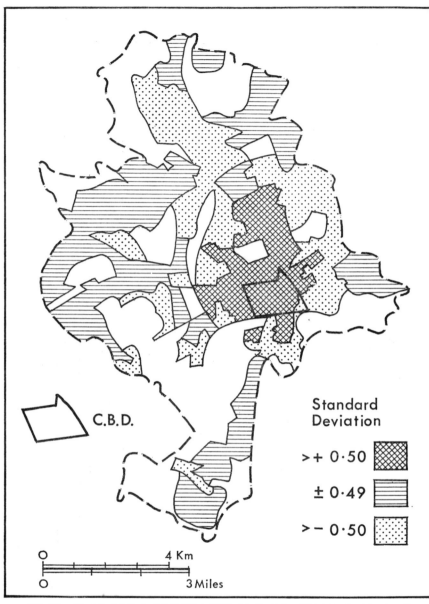

C.B.D.

Standard Deviation

> + 0·50

± 0·49

> − 0·50

4 Km

3 Miles

Fig 60. *Mental defect in Nottingham 1963–69:* Spatial patterning of schizophrenia in Nottingham still reveals the classic clustering near the city centre. This map is based on factor analysis and schizophrenia is strongly associated with characteristics such as a transient population and rented private unfurnished housing, indicative of urban environments which are socially and physically substandard. (After Giggs, J. A., 'The Spatial Distribution of Schizophrenia in Nottingham 1963–69. Unpublished MS. 1971, with the author's permission.)

there are instances where the territory may have an aggravating effect but the basic cause is poverty or bad life-styles of the population, such as high rates of infant mortality; there are also instances where the neighbourhood is causal not just as territory but as an urban-social milieu and some forms of mental illness may be explicable in these terms. The whole question of explanation is complex and will be raised in more detail when other forms of social defect have been discussed. For the moment it is sufficient to demonstrate that many health indices have spatial distributions within the city which are far from random and social geography has a contribution to make at least in their representation and probably in their explanation.

DELINQUENCY, CRIME, AND SOCIAL GEOGRAPHY

The characteristics of schizophrenia as a geographical phenomenon are closely similar to those observed in many studies of delinquency and crime within cities; indices of mental illness have in fact frequently been combined with delinquency indices to form composite measures of social defect or social malaise. The fact that delinquency and crime rates tend to be particularly high in the older and substandard parts of the central city has been recognised at least since the early part of the nineteenth century when it was described as a matter of common observation.[16] Contemporary writers were able to comment on this feature in graphical terms and Henry Mayhew,[17] in the mid-nineteenth century, made a more statistical study of the incidence of crime in England and Wales. He was able to show that on a regional scale crime was most frequent in those parts of the country in which industrial and urban growth were most developed, whilst within the city of London there were distinctive clusters of crime, and of the seven police districts, two contained two-thirds of all juvenile offenders. Mayhew's findings in England were paralleled by a number of contemporary studies in other parts of Europe.[18] London proved a fruitful area for study and when Burt mapped high rates of delinquency in the 1920s,[19] he demarcated districts similar to those described by Mayhew and to those recognised by Booth as the neighbourhoods of greatest poverty.[20]

Chicago and urban ecology again provided substantial advances in the study of crime and delinquency and Clifford Shaw and Henry McKay were especially associated with these.[21] Their first major work was the Illinois Crime Survey of 1929 in which they developed techniques for the mapping of delinquency and for the calculation of delinquency rates which, applied to Chicago, provided a framework for analysing the distribution of delinquency and crime within the city. The delinquency areas which they identified were concentrated around the Loop (Chicago's business centre) and were adjacent to the industrial districts near the Chicago river, the Union Stockyards, Calumet Lake and South Chicago. Rates of delinquency showed striking gradations from city centre to city periphery in ways conforming with a gradient principle. Shaw and McKay extended their analyses to cover twenty American cities in the Wickersham Report which was published in 1931. Using a standard format of concentric zones and generalised gradients to test distributions, they found their Chicago pattern to be replicated in the other cities. Always interested in explanation as well as representation, Shaw and McKay noted that in the cities which they studied there were recurrent correlates of crime. Most commonly these were substandard housing, poverty, foreign-born population and mobility. The broad contrasts which Shaw and McKay observed were between the central districts of poverty and physical deterioration, whose inhabitants were mobile and possessed confused cultural standards, and the stable family suburbs where delinquency was invariably low. Their theory of social disorganisation summarised the conditions of life within delinquency areas and remains a credible proposition; variations within the central city could be related to the extent to which particular districts were socially disorganised. Shaw and McKay, in common with most others who have analysed the ecology of crime, realised the limitations to their contribution: 'While these maps and statistical data are useful in locating different types of areas . . . they do not furnish an explanation of delinquency conduct. This explanation, it is assumed, must be sought in the field of more subtle human relationships and social values.'[22] Delinquency area research from Chicago was a major contribution: related contemporary studies, often finding similar patterns, were concerned with vice and mental illness.[23]

A remarkable persistence over time of the basic urban geography of delinquency and crime in American cities was revealed by C. F. Schmid's recent study of Seattle.[24] Schmid collected data on 35,000 cases known to the police and on 30,000 arrests and was able to record twenty categories of crime for ninety-three census tracts in the city. In order to relate crime to social structure, he also included eighteen socio-economic variables and used factor analytic techniques* to interpret his information. The spatial patterns of crime in Seattle were basically those of the 1920s; central districts had high concentrations of crime whilst the suburbs had characteristically low rates. When specific categories of crime were studied individually, separate patterns could be observed. The central business district was the locale of crimes such as cheque fraud and shop-lifting; Skid Row had the highest rates of vagrancy, disorderly conduct and drunkenness, both of these examples having obvious explanations for the associations. A factor analysis of the thirty-eight variables was used to identify the relationships between types of crime and socio-economic characteristics. Factor I (low social cohesion and low family status) picked out the older, declining neighbourhoods of low status in which family life was weak and a few crimes, including car-theft and shop-lifting, were particularly associated with these areas. Factor II (low social cohesion and low occupational status) picked out population groups with relatively high proportions of unskilled labourers, unemployed, and Negroes and associated these with fighting, robbery, non-residential burglary and disorderly conduct. Factor III (low family status and low economic status) had high scores in census tracts containing large numbers of unmarried and unemployed men and was regarded by Schmid as the crime dimension *par excellence*, being highly associated with a wide range of crime indices. Mapping of scores by census tracts showed that the central city which contained thirteen census tracts, 10·8 per cent of the area and 15·5 per cent of the population of Seattle, also contained 47 per cent of its crime. Gradient techniques showed that for most categories of crime there were regular declines in incidence from city centre to periphery. The study by Schmid replicated, after a gap of thirty years, the patterns found by Shaw and McKay. (For another modern American example, see Figure 61.) It also showed the same general correlates of crime, though Schmid again emphasised the constraints of this scale of analysis: 'Any conclusions that might be derived directly from the analysis logically pertain to areas and not to individuals . . . although one may be strongly tempted to infer causality, the results of factor analysis

* See Appendix.

merely measure the degree of concomitance and community structures and characteristics.'[25]

What could be termed the traditional spatial patterning of delinquency and crime rates in American cities has also been identified in a number of European studies. I. M. Castle and Elizabeth Gittus analysed several delinquency variables in their study of Liverpool[26] and the distributions which they recognised were reminiscent of American experience with the highest concentrations in the central dockland area and its immediate environs; other British studies have obtained similar results. A European example is provided by the inter-war study of Budapest[27] in which elements of the American ecological structure existed, although they were modified by the structure of the

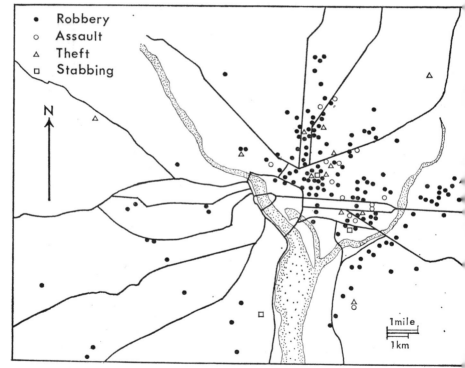

Fig 61.   *Crime patterns in Washington:* Crimes committed in Washington during one week in 1971 display a familiar ecological pattern. (Data from *Sunday Times Magazine*, June 1971.)

historic city (Figure 62). This type of modification, an inertia element induced by traditional fabrics and population groups in long-established cities, has general importance outside North America. Yet the resemblances are clearly evident and the slums were located centrally around Budapest's commercial district and a worst slum appropriately named Chicago: 'Chicago is the home of the very poorest of our people. Dregs of humanity congregate there as the sediments of wine go to the bottom. It is the home of cut-throats and brigands, pickpockets and beggars.'[28] Outside Europe, the ecology of crime follows established patterns where the western city has been transplanted to other societies. Peter Scott described a delinquency core area in Hobart, Tasmania, which existed before 1954:[29] A. W. Lind, in a 1930 study of Honolulu, showed that juvenile delinquency, dependency, suicides and common vice were concentrated in Palama and Kakaato, both located immediately adjacent to the central business district. Although reliable delinquency area studies outside the United States are comparatively few, it seems reasonable to suggest that the social geographical patterns identified in America have had some general application to the western industrial city as it appears in Europe and other parts of the world. Three points of qualification are necessary: first, that the present-day persistence of these spatial patterns has only been demonstrated for one American city and temporal modifications have yet to be fully discussed; secondly, to recognise that historic structures in European cities may imply modifications; and, thirdly, to emphasise that the meaning of the patterns and their internal consistency have not been explored. Neither have any of the examples described so far been non-western cities which, because of their marked structural contrasts, might be expected to reveal a different social geography of delinquency and crime from that established for the western industrial cities. Before attempting to remedy these deficiencies, it is pertinent to consider the various theories for delinquency and crime, developed in relation to the western 'model', and examine their relationships to spatial patterns.

THEORIES OF DELINQUENCY AND CRIME

Most analyses of the spatial patterning of delinquency and crime have contained some attempt at explanation. This often

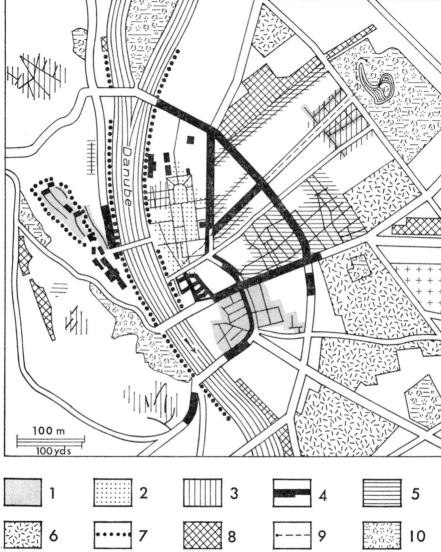

Fig 62. *Spatial patterns in central Budapest (pre 1939):* Budapest at this point in time combines elements of the historic city and a pre-socialist form. High status areas are centrally located whilst the locations of slums and vice areas are reminiscent of the American model. 1. upper class residence; 2. finance; 3. high status; 4. shopping; 5. vice areas; 6. slums; 7. promenades; 8. railway station; 9. subway; 10. parks. (After Beynon, E. D., 'Budapest: An Ecological Study' *Geographical Review*, 33, 1943, 256–75, copyright by the American Geographical Society of New York.)

took the form of a theory based upon the observed correlates; Shaw and McKay[30] followed this line of reasoning and earlier correlative hypotheses of this kind have often been developed into more rigorous theories. A continuing difficulty in the study of delinquency is that a consistent and testable theory has failed to emerge and something of the frustration was reflected by G. Trasler: 'It is fair to assume that if there had been a clear-cut pattern in the data, we should have discovered it by now.'[31] E. W. Burgess and D. J. Bogue,[32] in an assessment of theories of delinquency, identified seven separate approaches: social biology, social disorganisation, anomie and deviant sub-culture, social psychiatry, social definition and social interaction. Three of these approaches, social disorganisation, anomie and deviant sub-culture, are particularly relevant to social geography in that their emphasis is upon the aggregate scale of analysis and the role of the neighbourhood: the individual is seen primarily as the product of an urban-social milieu. This is a particularly useful interpretation for a geographer; other social scientists might emphasise different aspects and the originators of some of the theories doubtless saw them in a wider societal context rather than the specifically urban.

Social disorganisation is the most general theory and has many ecological qualities relating to its origins and to the work of Shaw and McKay. The correlations which were consistently observed between crime, delinquency and a host of other variables, such as mobility, substandard housing and particular ethnic groups, led to the suggestion that these were manifestations of a common factor which could be termed social disorganisation. The concept suggests that it is the absence of a stable society with legalistically based behaviour codes and established norms and values which promotes a situation of social disorganisation. Shaw and McKay described their delinquency areas as the typically unstable parts of the central city, which lacked social cohesion and organisation and were characterised by physical and social deterioration. The theory is best understood in the context of the American cities of the interwar period which were assimilating successive waves of immigrants unadjusted to a new set of societal codes and definitions: it does, however, have generality and remains a valid explanation of spatial patterns of crime. Although Shaw and McKay were associated with the Chicago school, they were never fully committed to ecological theory and were at pains to emphasise the modifying effects of social structure. Some of their best-known works were case-studies of individuals. Social disorganisation offered a comprehensive theory and this quality has in fact been a point of criticism. Judged by the normal indices, there were large parts of the inner city which had the attributes of social disorganisation and yet delinquency was not general. J. B. Mays[33] has followed this line of criticism and suggested that within parts of the slum there was order and that the theory failed to account for the evidence of social cohesion which existed among deviant groups. That stable societies existed within the zone of substandard housing is undisputed and the socially cohesive Chinatowns of modern North American cities are useful examples. Shaw and McKay, however, were aware of the fact that diversity existed and that even in those neighbourhoods which were socially-disorganised, not all adolescents became criminals. Their overall explanation incorporated an awareness of the influence of factors other than neighbourhood, such as the individual quality of family life, the school, the playgroup and particular companions during the adolescent years. Many individual hypotheses contained within the writings of Shaw and McKay have since been developed and articulated as separate theories of delinquency.

The theory of anomie is closely aligned to some of the main principles of social disorganisation and has been associated more recently with the work of B. Lander[34] who followed the original concept of Emile Durkheim. A general definition was offered by Burgess and Bogue: 'In an urban setting many cultures are brought into contact with each other, with the result that old and established customs and definitions cease to command adherence and to exercise social control. Persons become familiar with two or more value systems, and feel loyalty and obligation to no one system. The result is comparative normlessness and ego-centred and highly diverse behaviour.'[35] This definition suggests the similarity between anomie and the more general theory of social disorganisation. Bernard Lander's study of Baltimore[36] was an early example of the employment of multivariate techniques in the analysis of delinquency patterns: his main thesis was that anomie was a causal correlate of crime. Those districts of Baltimore which had high rates of crime were the areas of anomie; other districts, such as the Jewish and Chinese quarters, although similar in terms of substandardness and over-

OPPOSITE: Residential patterns: *(above)* the dispersing city: Hollywood Bowl in Hollywood, California; *(below)* the compact city: a residential compound in Lahore, West Pakistan.

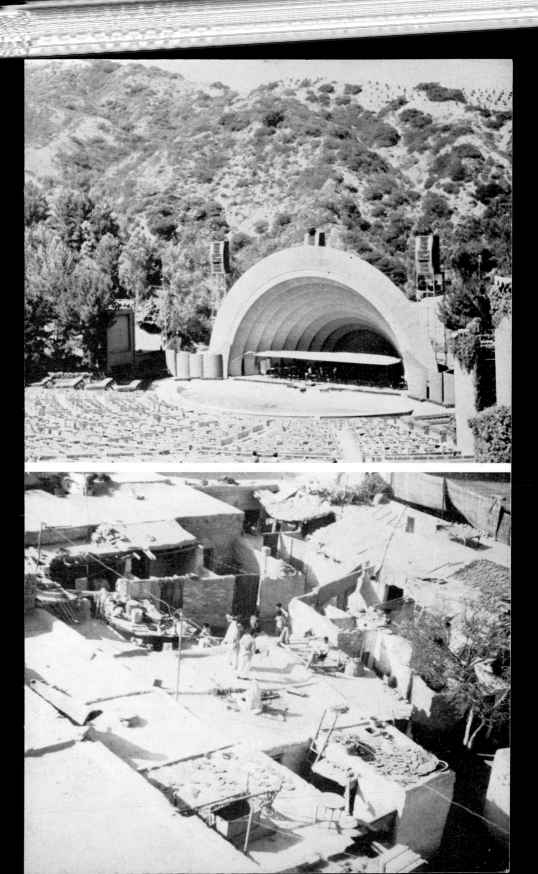

crowding, had low rates of crime because they were stable and cohesive communities. The particular indicators of anomie chosen by Lander were non-owner occupiers and non-white population; others have questioned both the choice of indicators and their interpretation in Baltimore. R. J. Chilton,[37] in particular, analysed the sets of data for three cities, Baltimore, Indianapolis, and Detroit, and showed that results from each city were ambiguous in relation to the hypothesis that delinquency was closely related to a condition of anomie. Although Chilton could not support this hypothesis, the comparability allowed by the procedure recommended an ecological type of approach. The failure of Lander and the others to establish anomie as a statistical correlate of crime does not invalidate the concept and a recurrent weakness has been to use one or two variables as indicators of anomie. A more sophisticated attempt was that by L. Srole who assembled a fifteen-point scale of measurement.[38]

The deviant sub-culture approach can again be related to social disorganisation, but it has been developed as a separate theory. The basis of the theory is that among the populations of particular parts of the city there are accepted norms of behaviour which are at odds with those of society as a whole. Deviancy and delinquency are not regarded as products of socially-disorganised groups but as typical of organised social groups acting in conformity with a set of values by which they are acceptable. An allied interpretation could be the fact that deviance is legally-defined and that definition might have little meaning to some sections of society. The notion of deviant sub-cultures was used by J. B. Mays in his researches on Merseyside gangs[39] but was more fully articulated by Albert Cohen in his work on delinquent boys.[40] Even before these definitive studies, however, the earlier literature of delinquency showed that the sub-culture type of effect was being recognised. Henry Mayhew described the nineteenth century 'rookeries' of London, where crime was learned and practised as a trade or profession.[41] Clifford Shaw and Henry McKay identified similar processes: 'Delinquency frequently becomes an established social tradition in certain gangs and is transmitted from older members to the younger.'[42] Frederick Thrasher found similar evidence in his study of Chicago gangs[43] and the concept is also in accord with E. Sutherland's differential association theory: 'If there is a preponderance of criminal influence in the environment, the likelihood of any individual

OPPOSITE: Residential patterns: *(above)* pressure on land in Rio de Janeiro, Brazil, with apartment blocks, shanties and cemetery; *(below)* housing contrasts in Rio de Janeiro: shanties and mansion.

N

becoming an offender is accordingly increased and vice-versa.'[44] The deviant sub-culture phenomenon was identified, therefore, but Cohen's work gave it separate status. His interpretation of sub-cultural delinquents as low-status boys reacting against middle-class normative society, however, has been questioned by others who view low-status delinquency as an established tradition of that segment of society.

The sub-culture line of explanation received a considerable boost through the writings of R. A. Cloward and L. E. Ohlin who developed it in terms of individual aspirations and opportunities.[45] An initial observation was that sub-culture, along with other ecological theories of delinquency, could only be a partial explanation: not all youths in a particular district or even members of a specific gang would develop in a delinquent way. Cloward and Ohlin argued that the situation in which any individual had to react was multi-faceted. They argued that discontent and alienation might develop from restricted access to normal and legal avenues of progress, whilst the likelihood of actual delinquent behaviour was related to the availability of illegal opportunities. An attempted explanation of delinquency should thus take into account not only the constraints upon legitimate progress but also the frequency of non-legitimate paths. Cloward and Ohlin hypothesised three levels of reaction, termed criminal, aggressive and retreatist, in a sub-culture situation. E. B. Palmore and P. E. Hammond operationalised these ideas by defining legitimate and illegitimate opportunities and choosing variables to represent them.[46] Variables of race, sex and school achievement were taken to represent legitimate opportunities and variables of family deviance and neighbourhood deviance to represent illegitimate opportunities. Cloward and Ohlin have been criticised on the grounds that their assumption that low-status groups aspire towards middle-class norms is not proven and Palmore and Hammond on the grounds that they have not formed adequate measures, but an attraction of this theory is that whereas it can be formulated in terms of groups, any one of the attributes, such as family conditions, may vary and so account for individual variation within areas and groups: 'Each individual occupies a position in both legitimate and illegitimate opportunity structures and the likelihood that he will pursue a deviant path is the product of his position in both structures.'[47] Some of the difficulties of broader ecological theories, including social disorganisation and more general statements on deviant sub-culture in explaining a partial occurrence of delinquency in potentially deviant areas, are thus avoided. The problem of operationalising the concepts remains and the experience of Barbara Wootton, who described the part which casual acquaintances appeared to play in diverting individuals into delinquent acts, suggests that even chance factors may need to be incorporated.[48]

Many studies, although not attempting to form general theories of delinquency, have demonstrated the utility of individual variables or small groups of variables as correlates of crime and delinquency. Population mobility is one such variable and T. E. Sullenger, in his study of Omaha,[49] suggested a direct and positive relationship. R. Freedman looked at mobility as an index of delinquency in Chicago,[50] where he identified migrant-zones and compared migrants with non-migrants. Unable to identify consistent patterns, Freedman advanced the hypothesis that it was not only physical mobility which distinguished disorganised from stable neighbourhoods but also mental mobility, or the extent to which the population had adapted to the fact of movement. Physical mobility was a disorganising factor where the population group was not accustomed to movement.

Race or ethnicity is another variable frequently used in analyses of delinquency. A major theme in American cities has been that some ethnic groups, particularly the Negroes, tend to have delinquency and crime rates far above average. Evidence relating to Negro populations tends to be contradictory. Bernard Lander, for example, originally picked out non-white population as an important correlate in Baltimore, but this was not really confirmed in either Detroit or Indianapolis. C. V. Willie and A. Gerschenovitz classified the districts of Washington into white, non-white, and mixed, in order to test Lander's hypothesis that delinquency rates were highest in mixed neighbourhoods.[51] Their calculations (for youths aged ten to seventeen years) showed an average rate of 13·2 per 1,000 in white districts, 29·7 in mixed districts and 37·0 in non-white districts. Limiting their analysis to districts of similar socio-economic status, they found that in every instance the delinquency rates were highest in mixed areas. Differences in delinquency rates on a racial basis were emphasised much more at the lower socio-economic status levels, with rates in mixed areas 125 per cent higher than in white areas. The overview on relationships between Negroes and crime in the United

States is one which sees the relationship stemming from the social disadvantages of the Negro population rather than from any racial or ethnic factor *per se*.

Socio-economic status variables have frequently occurred independently as correlates of delinquency and crime. Most studies would suggest that low socio-economic status implies a high incidence of social deviance, whilst admitting to the fact that white-collar crime and middle-class crime exist. Middle-class crime is of low recorded incidence and spatial patterns do not readily emerge. J. B. Mays suggested that crime was closely associated with low status neighbourhoods but that middle-class crime was not locally based.[52] More recent tests of socio-economic status as a correlate of crime have come from studies concerned with analysing delinquency rates in terms of social area analysis. C. V. Willie found that both economic and family status correlated with juvenile delinquency,[53] R. Quinney formed a composite index of delinquency and crime which showed some correlation with economic status,[54] whilst C. F. Schmid found a correspondence between low economic status and his crime dimension.[55]

The individual variables described above, together with others such as overcrowding, substandardness and broken homes, have been widely used as correlates of delinquency but inconsistencies remain and an efficient theory seems as elusive as ever. One of the great difficulties has been that of establishing causality among the correlational analysis and have shown that, in many past studies, Hirschi and Selvin have carefully spelt out the dangers in correlational analysis and have shown that in many past studies, causality has been inferred where it has been spurious and that the necessity for careful testing before assuming a relationship has been ignored. Hirschi and Selvin espouse a multi-factor approach: 'There is wide acceptance in the field of delinquency of an eclectic, multiple-factor approach which assumes that there are many causes of delinquency, crime is assignable to no single universal source, nor yet to two or three, it springs from a wide variety and usually a multiplicity of alternative and converging influences. It is no accident that the results of delinquency research have been inconclusive and inconsistent—yet these are probably the facts and properties of an eventual explanation.'[56] L. T. Wilkins has made similar observations,[57] describing multiple-causation as the most vigorous modern theory with such a breadth of reference that it may be impossible to disprove. The same breadth of reference is potentially a weakness of the multi-factor explanation: its generality is so great that any specific causality is difficult to identify and its solution would be so lacking in clarity that it offered little advance in terms of understanding. If multiple causes are accepted, however, then multivariate techniques seem the obvious means of reducing the large number of possibilities to a few summarising dimensions. Factor analytic procedures offer one form of solution, though Hirschi and Selvin see multiple regression as a potentially better approach because of its ability to distinguish between dependent and independent variables, and P. McNaughton Smith has demonstrated the possibilities of predictive attribute analysis.*[58] This brief summary of theories has done scant justice to a vast literature but some awareness of the theories and their critics is essential to an adequate social geography of social deviance in cities. Equally essential is an acknowledgement of the problems of definition and data reliability.

PROBLEMS OF DATA AND DEFINITION

A recurrent problem in the social sciences is that which concerns the adequacy of data, and studies of delinquency and crime are particularly vulnerable in this respect. A basic necessity is that of distinguishing between data on residence, where criminals live, and on commission or where crime is committed. The two sets of statistics do not, of course, coincide; the central business district, for example, although a locus of crime commission, is often non-residential. Most researchers have maintained an awareness of this distinction and S. L. Boggs has constructed crime occurrence rates related to the environmental opportunities for particular types of crime.[59] Boggs has argued that valid crime occurrence rates should be probabilistic and based upon the risk of specific forms of crime in particular areas of the city: the crime occurrence rates in the central business district are high in absolute terms, but less so when related to the number of opportunities which exist for many types of crime. An empirical study of St Louis showed that there was no consistent relationship between crime occurrence and crime commission: both rates were high in the central city where there was a high measure of

* See Appendix.

familiarity between the offenders and their targets; but occurrence rates only were high in prestige residential areas,
where rewards and opportunities for offenders were greater than
could be found in their home districts. A further caveat in relation
to delinquency and crime residence statistics is that data are
obtained from police records which refer only to detected crime,
a minority in fact of offences which occur. Information on crime
commission is much more comprehensive than that on crime
residence. A more serious bias in statistics probably occurs in that
recorded crime is likely to be higher for certain sections of
society. This bias may arise for several reasons. Middle-class
offences are frequently settled out of court and without recourse
to police action; low-status groups may make more general use
of the police for a wider range of petty offences. J. B. Mays has
suggested that middle-class youngsters commit offences similar
to lower-class children but they tend in the main to be treated
as miscreants rather than delinquents.[60] Middle-class crime is of
a different quality to crime in general and only the likelihood of
major returns justifies the amount of risk involved. J. B. Mays
concluded: 'Any research, therefore, which is mainly based on
court cases will miss the complex subtleties of criminal behaviour
and tend, however unwittingly, to perpetuate the widely held
view that delinquency is predominantly a lower-class phenomenon.'[61] There are clearly fallibilities involved in the use of
available data on delinquency and crime and these should be
recognised, but in the absence of alternatives this data must form
the bases for analysis and theory-formation. A careful methodology and an acknowledgement of the constraints upon interpretation can allow credible conclusions.

A final point on data is that ecological studies adopt an
aggregate scale of analysis with its attendant difficulties. The
delinquency area level of analysis can offer little guidance to
individual cases: in a situation, for example, where some children
are delinquent and others in the same family are not, then
explanation may be in terms of aspirations and opportunities as
described by R. A. Cloward and L. Ohlin or even in terms of
different psychological development. The argument for an
aggregate level of analysis is that individuals are parts of groups
and neighbourhoods and their life-styles must be seen in those
contexts. Marshall Clinard, with reference to less-developed
countries, has stressed the importance in delinquency studies of

specifying the scale of analysis: 'The researcher should analyse and present his data so as to avoid suggesting that the relations he observes are stronger than they actually are. One way of avoiding such suggestions is to distinguish carefully between properties of individuals and properties of the distribution of individual traits over a group or class.'[62]

CROSS-CULTURAL SPATIAL PATTERNS OF DELINQUENCY AND CRIME

The delinquency studies described so far have presented spatial patterns which are simple and repetitive; more recent evidence, however, suggests that more complex patterns may be an accompaniment of changing urban structure. The apparent consistency of delinquency patterns in American cities over time has been demonstrated by a comparison of the classic studies of Shaw and McKay with those of C. F. Schmid. There is some evidence, however, that even in American cities some shifts of emphasis are occurring and that whilst crime residence remains concentrated in the central city, crime occurrence has increased in suburban areas. Many American writers, such as Jane Jacobs,[63] have documented the increase in crime in their cities and the fear of violence is a dimension of urban life. Jane Jacobs suggested that indiscriminate urban renewal and unimaginative housing projects were aggravating factors, but the basic causes seem related to the under-privilege of large population groups and in some less tangible way to modern societal forces. The central city retains the main problem areas but increasing crime occurrence in suburbs is related to the greater opportunities for crime which they present and to the increasing mobility of offenders. Middle-class crime is largely a hidden dimension which is relevant to specialised forms of delinquency.

Recent studies of British cities suggest that the traditional spatial patterns of delinquency have been more drastically modified. The main factor influencing these modifications has been the intervention of the public sector in housing redevelopment in the twentieth century. Terence Morris found a high incidence of delinquency in Croydon,[64] not only in the older central districts, but also in newer peripheral estates built by the municipality. Morris suggested that the organisation of the social group was more important than the physical environment and

explained the high incidence of delinquency in inter-war municipal estates as a result of transfers of population groups who
maintained their patterns of living: 'One can say that legally-
defined delinquency is a social characteristic of working classes
in general and of the family of the unskilled worker in particular.'[65] Morris saw merit in deviant sub-culture as an explanation
and explained variations within estates in terms of the groupings
of satisfactory and unsatisfactory tenants. Duncan Timms found
a similar pattern in Luton,[66] where he suggested that the inter-war
municipal estates had emerged as problem areas because they had
served as repositories for less desirable tenants. John Giggs, in his
study of Barry, Glamorgan,[67] found similar departures from the
American prototype of delinquency residence patterns, but had
different explanations and, indeed, varying patterns. The social
geography of deviance in Barry included high rates in both
central and peripheral districts but with no regular relationships
to physical structure. Giggs used the varying levels of mobility
to explain the patterns which he had justified. It was in those parts
of the central area which combined low-status and substandardness with high mobility that delinquency was common; more
stable parts of the same inner area had low defect rates. The older
municipal housing estates had become stable communities but
were characterised by high defect rates; newer municipal estates
had high rates of defect associated with their instability and the
increased financial burdens incurred with recent moves. Private
housing estates, even of recent origin, tended to have low social
defect rates. Hypotheses have been formulated on the potential
roles of mobility as both a stabilising and a disruptive force on
social relationships. Geographical mobility when accompanied by
social mobility can lead to stable communities, but when
geographical mobility is not accompanied by social mobility
disorganisation can occur. This line of explanation is not con-
clusive but could be used to explain the high social defect rates
in recent municipal estates in Barry in contrast to older municipal
and recent private housing districts. These results based upon one
small town need replication but the spatial patterns identified once
again contrast with the American model. Other British studies
have revealed a similar decentralisation of delinquency residence
and have identified new clusters in peripheral housing estates.
Some parallelism with these British studies was recorded by Peter
Scott in Hobart, Tasmania, which showed a marked decline of

delinquency rates in the central city between 1954 and 1961, whilst new government housing projects in the suburbs showed high rates.[68]

Adequate studies of delinquency are still rare outside North America and Europe and it is particularly with reference to the non-western world that the need exists for adequate cross-cultural studies. The problems of data which exist in the context of western cities are exaggerated many times in Asia, Africa and Latin America; the difficulty is not so much the reliability of existing data as the availability of relevant information for the study of delinquency and crime. W. Clifford suggested that in Southern Africa comparability with western countries was problematic because of varying definitions of delinquent behaviour.[69] Despite these difficulties and the paucity of rigorous studies, some comment is possible on the spatial patterns of delinquency and crime in non-western cities, although caution must be exercised in relation to any attempt at generalisation. It seems that the ecology of delinquency and crime is in some contrast with both European and American cities and that the differences are related to general ecological structures. A number of older studies for Latin American cities contained some contradictions but tended to identify patterns which were in contrast with American findings. Theodore Caplow's evidence from Guatemala City was that the gradient typical of American cities, by which crime rates declined from centre to periphery, could literally be reversed.[70] The worst slums formed an almost continuous border around the city and these were also areas of high delinquency in which personal and social disorganisation was at a maximum. N. S. Hayner found a somewhat different pattern in Mexico City where, although there was a high concentration of delinquency and social defects in the new shanty-towns of the city edge, rates were also high in some central city areas.[71] The evidence on general ecological structure in Mexico City was that commercialisation of the centre had begun and a zone-in-transition was beginning to emerge. These trends seemed to contain the explanation of differences from Guatemala City: the latter retained a weakly-developed commercial area and a central city still occupied by prestigious families, whilst Mexico City had moved towards similarities within western cities. These two studies suggest that the emergence of low status areas, either as peripheral shanties or central slums, presage high incidence of delinquency; W. Mangin, however, suggested that the shanty-towns or *barriadas* of Lima, although poor and substandard, were not concentrations of social defect: 'There is very little violence, prostitution, homosexuality, or gang behaviour in *barriadas*. Petty thievery is endemic throughout Lima, but *barriadas* seem somewhat safer than most neighbourhoods in this respect, perhaps because there is less to steal.'[72]

A recent study of delinquency in Cordoba, Argentina, by Lois B. De Fleur[73] showed that the general ecological structure reflected a pre-industrial pattern, with the central city housing the prestige groups and a weakly developed transport system. The most squalid slum areas or *villas miserias* were in the intermediate zones of the city although these were by no means the only form of housing development in these zones. The slums were distributed almost randomly and were usually in a specific location which for a number of reasons, such as danger of flooding, the adjacency of industrial land uses or relative isolation, was undesirable to more prosperous sections of the population. The outer zones of the city also contained slum areas. There was a form of gradient in Cordoba's ecological structure, from rich at the centre to poor on the periphery, but patterns were not uniform, land use was mixed, and in almost all districts localised slum areas occurred. Using a sample of 192 offenders, De Fleur analysed spatial patterns of delinquency in relation to this general ecological structure. Her main finding was that the residences of juvenile offenders were often among the deteriorating districts of the *villas miserias* (Figure 63). The exceptions, where offenders apparently lived in the prestige districts, could be explained as servant girls living in the wealthy homes who had been convicted of petty thefts. An investigation of areas of delinquency occurrence showed different patterns, with the highest incidence in areas with the greatest opportunity for crime, and some evidence that many offenders travelled considerable distances to commit crimes. It was in terms of residences of offenders, therefore, that greatest spatial contrasts with American cities emerged: 'The best generalisation would seem to be that most offenders in Cordoba live in the intermediate and far zone of the city.'[74] The general characteristics of the population groups involved are comparable to western experience, in that they form the low status elements of society. These slum dwellers of Cordoba were in fact migrants from rural areas, living in *villas miserias* which were spatially discontinuous and socially disorganised. The links between these groups and the urban society and its institutions were extremely tenuous.

Other parts of the non-western world are even less documented than Latin America. A recent United Nations seminar on crime in Arab states, whilst providing no detailed analysis of the spatial incidence, stressed the potential problems of the ubiquitous shanty-towns: 'Migrants settled in unhealthy huts or

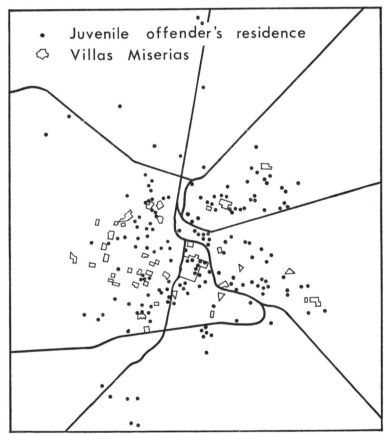

• Juvenile offender's residence
◌ Villas Miserias

Fig 63. *Crime patterns in a non-western city:* Detailed studies of social defect in non-western countries are hampered by lack of data, but this analysis of Cordoba, Argentina, provides some evidence of the geography of delinquency. (After De Fleur, L. 'Ecological Variables in the Cross-Cultural Study of Delinquency' *Social Forces,* 1966–67, with permission from the University of North Carolina.)

barracks and lived in conditions of physical deprivation . . . a comparison of their life with the wealthy causes antagonism . . . one of the major elements of delinquency.'[75] Similar sentiments were expressed by S. K. Weinberg in relation to Ghana where he identified conditions of poverty, overcrowding and destitution as a stimulus to subsistence stealing.[76] Marshall Clinard in an overview of crime and delinquency in less-developed countries described the occurrence of problem neighbourhoods within cities which were impersonal and non-integrated.[77] These were the poor, substandard sections of the city, where high mobility implied a diversity of social norms and values and, inevitably, they were characterised by high rates of deviant behaviour. Much of the emphasis in ecological research on crime and delinquency has been placed on the regional rather than on the intra-urban scale. This is evident in the few relevant analyses of communist countries such as S. Walczak's comment on Poland: 'Maps illustrating the ecology of crime indicate a great concentration of crime in certain regions.'[78] Walczak also observed that crime rates in the large cities were particularly high in comparison to surrounding districts. W. D. Connor's study of crime in the USSR had little spatial context but high rates were seen as the products of a working-class milieu which had characteristics comparable with other industrial societies.[79]

Any attempt to assess the general qualities of delinquency areas and their explanation is inevitably complex in a field in which adequate theories remain elusive. Some facts have come to be accepted: crime is an urban phenomenon and is invariably concentrated in those city neighbourhoods which suffer social and economic impoverishment. The spatial patterning of these problem neighbourhoods varies from one part of the world to another and the classic pattern of the American city is not found elsewhere: a reflection of contrasts in general urban structure. If the simple correlates of social deviancy tend to be repetitive, their interpretation as causal circumstances cannot be universal. There are cultural differences of far-reaching magnitude: within poor areas there are contrasts between organised and disorganised communities; Oscar Lewis in his portrayal of the culture of poverty does not include social deviancy as a normal facet of life.[80] In the quest for an understanding of crime and delinquency, the role of social geography can be articulated. A primary task is to indicate where social deviance occurs and among which groups of people. This objective has been reasonably well achieved in western cities but is hardly started in other parts of the world. Beyond this primary objective, there are contributions towards explanation which can be made, particularly where aggregated data are the scale relevant to understanding. The value of this scale as a source of explanation has been testified by D. Glaser in the context of American cities: 'Most promising research results have come from programmes centred on the urban neighbourhoods where crime and delinquency are most concentrated,'[81] and by M. Clinard in relation to the non-western world: 'There is strong evidence indicating that the neighbourhood rather than the individual or family is often the locus of delinquency and crime.'[82] Although a vast literature exists on social deviance, much remains to be done and several priorities are matched by emerging emphases in geographical approaches. The neighbourhood territory and the social group structure are scales at which most geographical studies have been made. The search for multi-factor solutions parallels the idea of geographical synthesis and new interests in multivariate techniques; the problem of individual behaviour may be illuminated by behavioural procedures developed within human geography. These will not of course provide total answers but they indicate ways in which geographers may proceed beyond the primary task of identifying spatial patterns and the population types which form them. Contemporary reports from most parts of the world portray crime and delinquency as increasing problems. From the United States, which has received most publicity, the evidence is of central city and even suburban streets which are unsafe to walk at night, of elaborate measures to afford protection against criminals and of certain areas of large cities which are out of bounds for large sections of the population. In some non-western cities the acceptance of crime as a way of life for increasing numbers of individuals seems a concomitant of poverty and the lack of legitimate opportunities, and the gulf between the rich who need to protect their interests and the poor who look with envy at their material properties seems wider than ever. At a general level, the appearance of the city in society has always been accompanied by a dramatic increase in known crime and, given this continuing situation, academic approaches to the distribution and explanation of crime have considerable practical application.

URBAN SUB-AREAS, ATTITUDES AND BEHAVIOUR

Studies of social deviance, although concerned with identifying particular delinquency areas, make limited use of the general framework of urban sub-areas. The reasons for this lie in the fact that indices of deviance tend to show a high degree of clustering in small sections of the city and are absent from large parts of the urban area; whilst general ecological structure is therefore relevant it is not operationally significant. Other social patterns, related to differences in attitudes and behaviour, demonstrate more clearly the usefulness of sampling frameworks of urban sub-areas as bases for analyses.

A part of the study of Newcastle-under-Lyme involved using sub-areas as a means of testing attitudes towards neighbourhoods and social visiting.[83] Two sub-areas were chosen which had contrasted characteristics in terms of the classification and within each a random sample of households was chosen to survey by field interviews. The two sub-areas studied were an interwar municipal estate at Knutton and an interwar private estate in the Westlands. The two districts had been distinguished on the basis of rateable value and the contrasted structures of the sample populations showed the sub-areas to be completely different as indicated by the sub-area framework. Both estates had mature populations, a reflection of their interwar period of construction and occupance: the two distinct elements to the Westlands population consisted of stable locals and transient non-locals and these were distinguished in terms of length of residence. The two sub-areas were sharply contrasted in terms of social class and educational attainment, confirming the ranking of the sub-areas by rateable value. In terms of family ties a strong Westlands sub-group, the locals, had strong Staffordshire connections, as did the whole Knutton population. The non-locals in the Westlands, however, had family in many parts of England and Wales and very few in Staffordshire. The pattern of friendship in middle-class Westlands was widespread, often national rather than local in context, and locally confined to districts of similar prestige to the Westlands itself. In Knutton, by contrast, friendship patterns were virtually entirely localised to the estate and the nearby district of Silverdale and a feature was the limited amount of visiting with friends which was recorded. Over half the people interviewed in the Westlands belonged to clubs and associations, typically golf club or conservative club; less than one-fifth of Knutton respondents claimed club membership and workingmen's club and bingo were quoted most frequently. A scaling technique* was used to measure the degree of social integration within each sub-area and both scored poorly on the question of neighbourliness. Westlands people were well disposed towards the area as a place to live, were well aware of its local prestige as a residential district, and deplored municipal house-building in adjacent districts. Knutton people were less satisfied, thought this estate was inferior to more modern municipal housing and identified a local 'rough element'. Over a range of characteristics, therefore, the two ecologically different sub-areas could be shown to have socially different populations.

The social area analysts have completed a number of projects in which similar interviewing procedures have been used to test social area typologies. A study of San Francisco measured differences in participation between inhabitants of contrasted types of social area.[84] Four census tracts were selected which had uniformly low scores on ethnicity, but were strongly contrasted in socio-economic and family status. Mission, a district of low-rent rooming houses, had low scores on both constructs; Pacific Heights, with high-rent apartments, had high socio-economic but low family status; Outer Mission, typically comprising small, single-family dwellings, had low socio-economic but high family status; and St Francis Wood, a prosperous, single-family home district, had high scores on both constructs. The study claimed to demonstrate that participation could be related to residence and that social areas had status as independent variables in the analysis of attitudes and life-styles. Men living in high socio-economic status neighbourhoods belonged to a greater number of associations, attended them more frequently, and held more offices. The type of association was markedly different: labour unions ranked first in low socio-economic status districts, general interest associations, such as Rotary clubs, in high socio-economic status areas. Men in high family status neighbourhoods had more social contacts with neighbours and kin and were more likely to have met their close personal friends in their neighbourhoods. In a similar study in Los Angeles[85] Scott Greer selected four districts with contrasted family status scores and concluded that the high family status areas had more neighbouring and more localised

* See Appendix.

involvement. Wendell Bell has reviewed a whole series of studies in American cities which have made successful use of social areas as sampling procedures.[86]

A further British example was that provided by B. T. Robson in Sunderland[87] where, using principal components analysis to identify sub-area types, he selected seven for more detailed investigation: the questionnaire survey was concerned with the attitudes towards education which were held by the parents of children who were candidates for a school entrance examination (the eleven-plus). The broad contrast which the survey results revealed was between the three working-class districts in which aspirations were low and three districts, two of which were higher status and the third of which was a rooming-house area, where aspirations were high. Robson saw the working-class districts as much more organised on a local community basis; the secondary modern school, to which children who failed the entrance examination would be sent, was physically part of the neighbourhood whereas the grammar school was not. This conflict between community and educational roles was affected by crowded living conditions and large family-size in ways which tended to dampen individual aspirations and promote a collectivist attitude. The middle-class areas were far less locally-oriented with referents which were national rather than local: individualism had greater play but the general priority placed upon education meant high aspirations. The Sunderland study, by its own terms of reference, was based on a series of small samples and replication is needed before generalisations upon educational attitude are possible. Robson's main conclusions, however, were that residential area and social milieu had strong influences upon individual attitudes: 'No matter what the area, the attitudes of individual families were more familiar to those prevailing around them than to those of their objective social class.'[88] This suggestion is in some contrast to recent essays by R. E. Pahl[89] in which geographical location is identified as a less meaningful parameter of difference than social class, although Pahl's context was urban-rural differences in a particular part of London's commuter fringe. Close alignments with Robson's views, however, are found in some of Wendell Bell's summary statements on the utility of social area frameworks: 'It is suggested that the socio-economic characteristics of a neighbourhood population as a unit may be important indicators of the economic reference group of those living in the neighbourhood; and that this reference group provides a set of expectations for the associational behaviour of the residents.'[90] Bell emphasised the works of the Sherifs, who had been interested in adolescent behaviour: 'It is clear . . . that the social areas are real, not only in the sheer perceptual sense of being part of the maps of social reality carried about in individuals' heads, but also in the sense of providing individuals with significant reference groups for gauging their own behaviour as well as the behaviour of others.'[91]

The conclusions reached by Robson and Bell indicate some of the contributions which residential area analysis might make towards the understanding of social patterns within cities. The basic question concerns the relevance of neighbourhood and geographical location in the understanding of life styles. This question has prompted many hypotheses and extreme points of view at either end of the scale of possibilities but current research output has fallen short of definitive statements. The social geographical referent must always be of some significance though the degree of significance will vary considerably over time and place and among different types of subject matter. Other factors —social, psychological or economic—will often be of equal or greater relevance: the problem for the geographer, as for all others concerned with the study of cities, is to recognise the balance and to see the specific contribution of spatial analysis in its proper context of the city as a whole.

THE URBAN NEIGHBOURHOOD

Much of the discussion in this chapter has been concerned with the concept of territoriality and the extent to which social activities can be related in a systematical way to physical space. The neighbourhood unit has been a conscious attempt by planners to introduce territoriality and segmentation as part of their design for urban growth. A clear assumption of the advocates of planned neighbourhoods has been that they are replicating one of the better elements of natural or organic city growth. Lewis Mumford found ample evidence for neighbourhoods in European cities such as Paris, Venice and Florence, characterised by the quarters which possessed focal points such as church or square and some level of local organisation.[92] In these cities natural divisions defined the neighbourhoods more clearly but even in Manhattan, where the

o

monotonous grid-iron morphology seemingly prevented segmentation, distinctive neighbourhoods such as Yorkville and
Greenwich Village had emerged. As Lewis Mumford and others
can demonstrate, neighbourhoods exist: far less clear is their
meaning in terms of the social interaction and association which
the term implies. A classic description of the neighbourhood: 'An
area in which the residents are personally well acquainted with
each other, and are in the habit of visiting one another, or
exchanging articles and services, and, in general, of doing things
together,'[93] places the emphasis upon a particular range of activities and accepts that there are a considerable number, notably
employment, which are not conducted at a neighbourhood level.
Even for this limited range of activities, there are qualifications
which must be made: the differences between different social
classes and between different age-groups, between locals and
non-locals, and the effect of increasing mobility over time;
the scale at which one conceives a neighbourhood in terms of
area, configuration, or population-size. But for the moment, the
concept of the natural neighbourhood, loosely articulated,
provided one stimulus to the formation of the planners' vision of
a neighbourhood unit.

C. H. Cooley, who is usually regarded as an early influence
upon neighbourhood planners, emphasised the role of face-to-face
relationships and a sense of community based upon place which
existed within the various segments of the metropolis.[94] Inherent
in the writing of Cooley and others was an idealism of the village
and the notion that city growth had involved the loss of its
community and qualities. Other origins of the neighbourhood unit
principle are found in social works, often a reaction against the
substandard living conditions of the industrial cities of nineteenth-
century Europe and America. The Garden City movement in
England was in this category whilst the various social settlement
schemes at the turn of the century had an important role. Lewis
Mumford quoted the Toynbee Hall scheme in the East End of
London and the Neighbourhood House scheme in America as
seminal influences on the development of the neighbourhood unit.
The practice of providing community centres to act as focuses
for local population in problem areas of the city had a strong
appeal for Clarence Perry, who emerged as a main driving force
for the adoption of neighbourhoods.[95] A third influence was the
example of garden suburbs in the early part of the twentieth

century, emerging as working expressions of neighbourhoods. Perry acknowledged the influence of Forest Hills Garden in New York which was developed in 1910, and other new suburbs, such as Hampstead in London and Riverside in Chicago, had similar features. Of the results of these influences in terms of planned neighbourhood units, the Radburn, New Jersey, scheme was undoubtedly the best known. Perry's ideas on population-size, boundaries, provision and location of open space, local stores, institutions and internal street system, were incorporated into the plan for Radburn.[96] Traffic/pedestrian segregation was obtained by a peripheral main road and central pedestrian ways, designed to enhance face-to-face relationships. At the centre of each neighbourhood was an elementary school, intended to be a multi-functional building and to act as a community centre. The population of each neighbourhood was calculated in terms of the number of families needed to support an elementary school, which in Radburn was judged to be 7,500 to 10,000 people. Shops and services were gathered in a cluster at the edge of the neighbourhood. The Radburn scheme became the prototype for a planned neighbourhood unit, although there have been many variations upon its basic theme.

The population-size and layout have varied and some planners have been concerned with a hierarchy of neighbourhood units within the overall city. Clarence Stein advocated a more comprehensive hierarchy and at one time intended to build Radburn in three over-lapping neighbourhoods to obtain greater flexibility: both ideas which were to re-emerge much later in neighbourhood planning. In Germany, Walter Gropius developed a hierarchy of urban elements from house to town, one of which was the neighbourhood:[97] a South African scheme suggested a housing unit of 2,600 people, based upon an elementary school.[98] Housing projects along neighbourhood lines were familiar features in British cities in the 1920s and 30s, but it was not until legislative reports of the 1940s that development really started. The Abercrombie Report of 1943[99] suggested neighbourhood units of 6,000 to 10,000 people, based upon the elementary school as the minimum unit for development: the Dudley Report of 1944[100] gave official sanction to the principle and spelt out the form of neighbourhoods which were to find main expression in the new towns. There were differences from the Radburn format; shops and institutions were central rather than peripheral and elementary schools could not be used to determine population-size. Some variations in form of neighbourhoods in new towns resulted from local ideas on design: in Harlow, for example, they were built in clusters to support extra facilities. Outside Britain, neighbourhood units are common in many European countries and in those parts of the world where urban planning is comprehensively practised. Examples are Elizabeth in South Australia, Vandersbijl Park and Sasolburg in South Africa, and the USSR where the micro-districts with 6,000 to 8,000 population, equipped with schools, shops and social facilities and separated from main roads by green open space, are clearly analogous to neighbourhood units.[101]

A number of problems in terms of neighbourhood design have been recurrent and have been differently solved in various schemes. One contentious point is the degree of isolation which a neighbourhood should possess and solutions go to an extreme in some British new towns where green wedges are used to mark boundaries: most recent attempts at neighbourhood planning have moved substantially away from this extreme. The amount of social heterogeneity is another question and views differ from Mumford, who favoured the mixed income group neighbourhood, to Peter Mann,[102] who regarded that kind of social balance as an erroneous interpretation of urban social structure which should be quietly buried. Experience from British new towns has been that social balance has little reality even when it is instilled into design. Other problems include location of facilities, population-size, density and street patterns.

Tests of the viability of planned neighbourhood units are comparatively few, but a study in Stoke-on-Trent, Staffordshire, was designed to measure the extent to which a neighbourhood functioned as a local community and also to test levels of satisfaction.[103] This particular neighbourhood was constructed during the 1950s and by 1965 it contained 3,500 dwellings and a population of 14,000. The neighbourhood (Figure 64) had a centrally-placed shopping precinct containing thirty units, a community hall, a health centre and a church, but the four schools were dispersed through the estate. The general elongated shape of the neighbourhood, partly induced by qualities of the site, adversely affected access to the centre and this was aggravated by the large population-size. A questionnaire survey revealed consistent contrasts in term of local interaction and allegiance to the neighbourhood between the eastern and western edges of the estate and the central housing clusters. People living on the peripheries tended to travel outside the neighbourhood for shopping, made little use of the community hall and were often dissatisfied with the estate as a place to live: all of these characteristics were in contrast with the greater involvement and satisfaction of the residents of centrally-placed sections. The study could offer some guide-lines of the preferred population-sizes and morphology of planned neighbourhood units.

Planning theorists have recently questioned the whole concept of the neighbourhood unit. The main lines of criticism are that the planned neighbourhood imposes an artificial compartmentalisation upon city structure, that it lacks flexibility, and that it is out of phase with the increasing mobility of urban population. C. Alexander expressed his dissatisfaction and, using the language of the theory of sets,[104] suggested that planners building neigh-

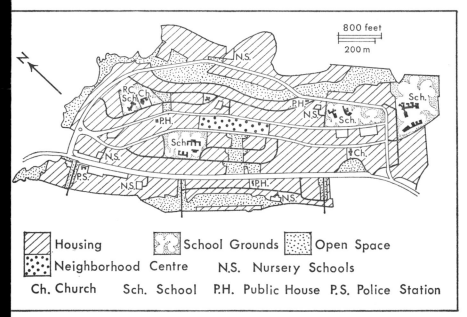

Housing   School Grounds   Open Space

Neighborhood Centre   N.S. Nursery Schools

Ch. Church   Sch. School   P.H. Public House   P.S. Police Station

Fig 64. *A British neighbourhood unit: Ubberley-Bentilee, Stoke-on-Trent:* This neighbourhood had, in 1965, 3,500 dwellings arranged around a centrally placed service area which comprised thirty retail units together with a community hall and some other services.

bourhoods had used the simplistic *tree* concept, with neat independent segments, whereas in fact the more complex *semi-lattice* concept, which allows for overlaps and interdependence, was much more appropriate. Jane Jacobs expressed similar sentiments in her reaction against modern city planning in the United States;[105] she thought that urban renewal was destroying the natural complexity of city life and replacing it by an unnatural simplicity. The neighbourhood unit principle, as articulated by Clarence Perry, does possess some of these inflexible qualities; a fixed population-size, a fixed relationship of neighbourhood residents to supply of schools, shops and other facilities and a limited flexibility for growth. But although this might be demonstrated as an inadequate attempt to relate people's activities and movements to a compartmentalised physical framework, this was not an original objective. Perry's objectives in social terms for neighbourhood units were modest and the 'community' ideas were exaggerated by later adopters of the concept. As Perry identified the priorities, they were those of systematically relating physical amenities to population and of providing a safe environment for pedestrian movement. As they have emerged physically, however, neighbourhood units do appear as inflexible segments of urban form which, if one accepts some measure of architectural determinism,[106] might inhibit movement. Alternative urban forms, however, which retain some qualities of the neighbourhood but possess more apparent flexibility, have proved difficult to achieve.

Elements of neighbourhood planning which identify the need for greater flexibility were evident in the early work of Clarence Stein on over-lapping units and in the cluster design adopted in Harlow new town. Similarly, the unfulfilled plan for a new town at Hook in Hampshire[107] contained proposals for small cul-de-sac housing groups, each serving a primary school, as part of wider neighbourhoods. Choice in terms of movement was increased by varying densities of housing, by minimising barriers and by stressing inter-connections among the various parts of the town. Recent research has tended to vindicate the spirit of the Hook plan and a physical expression of this spirit is emerging in the new town of Columbia, Maryland.[108] Columbia was formed from a hierarchy of 'associational elements' comprising housing clusters, neighbourhoods, villages and town, arranged as a system of over-lapping communities (Figure 65) and related to the school system.

At increasing levels of the hierarchy the number and quality of local services improved, from a few basic services in the housing cluster to the main business centre of the city. Open-endedness and accessibility were, however, key factors in the design so that

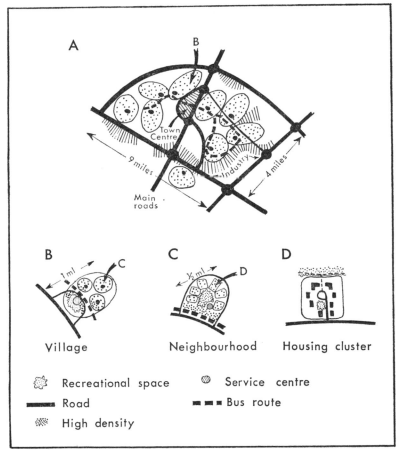

Fig 65. *Neighbourhoods in new town design: Columbia, Maryland:* The plan for Maryland uses neighbourhood in a hierarchical but flexible urban structure of over-lapping units. A. Overall plan with villages arranged around the town centre, main roads and a central bus route; B. Village, comprising a service centre, several neighbourhoods and recreational space. High density housing near centre; C. Neigh-bourhood with a centre, recreational space, several housing clusters, and high density near bus route; D. Housing cluster or the basic residential unit. (From information supplied by the Rouse Company.)

choice could always be made and extensive overlapping was possible. The real community within which each individual lived did not need to conform with the spatial segment within which he was located and could be a function of interest-sharing rather than spatial contiguity. This type of urban planning attempts to maintain the better qualities of the neighbourhood within a more flexible and fluid spatial framework and may well become a prototype for future design. The Columbia plan began by investigating social processes as well as physical facilities.

A wider aspect of this mood for flexibility in neighbourhood units is evident in modern planning theory (see, for example, Figure 66). The main argument is that social interaction as a whole is highly diverse and operates with a bewildering variation for individuals over time and space. An individual at various times in one day may be a parent taking his child to the neighbourhood school, a consultant engineer advising on a project several hundred miles away, and a friend visiting in other parts of the city. Over short spaces of time individuals may physically move virtually anywhere in the world or may, with modern telecommunications, establish contact with dispersed colleagues without leaving a home base: patterns of inter-connection are rapidly increasing in a 'shrinking world'. An awareness of the diminishing constraints of distance has, of course, been current for some time. F. L. Sweetser[109] used the phrase 'relational personal neighbourhoods' to describe patterns which were really indeterminate; McClenahan[110] described a 'communality' as an interest circle characterised by the social nearness of members whose residences could be considerable distances apart. Melvin Webber, however, has become the principal component of this non-spatial or aspatial view and sees, futuristically, a decreasing necessity to locate near anything or anyone as transport and communication technologies continue to improve.[111] Webber distinguished between urban realm and urban place; the former being a non-spatially bounded range of contacts which may vary for an individual according to the particular activity pattern in which he is engaged,* the latter

* Webber's Urban Realms are analogous to de Lauwe's concept of social space (Anne Buttimer, *Geographical Review* 1969, 417–26). De Lauwe described a hierarchy of spaces: familial or the domestic level of inter-action; neighbourhood, containing daily and local movement; economic, containing employment centres; and urban-regional. These are progressively larger and overlapping spatial horizons within which individuals live.

being the segment of space in which he resides and which contains local interaction. There are considerable variations in the scales of urban realm and the amount of involvement in urban place according to the characteristics of individuals. Melvin Webber recognised this with his broad distinction between the *cosmopolite*, the professional with diverse and wide urban realms and limited involvement in local space, and the *localite*, the worker with restricted urban realms and high involvement in local space or neighbourhood. Within this broad distinction there are many further diversities. The housewife is far more a localite than her professional husband, whilst the mature family man is

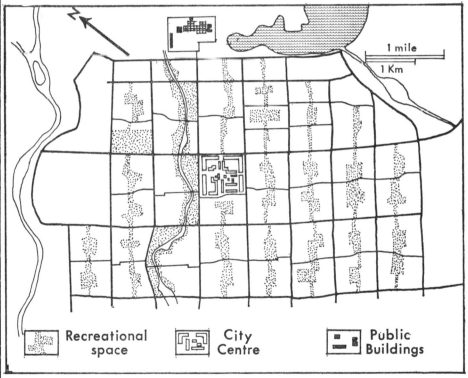

Fig 66. *Design of an Indian new town: Chandigarh:* A grid road system provides flexibility for further growth. (From Jacobs, A. B., 'Observations on Chandigarh', *Journal of the American Institute of Planners,* 1967, reprinted with permission from the author and the American Institute of Planners.)

likely to be more localised than his younger, unmarried colleague.

Melvin Webber sees little place for the neighbourhod in the future city but others, perhaps more realistically, identify a continuing role. The locally-based community remains a major reality for non-mobile sections of society such as children, young mothers, old people and the poor. An example of the continuing significance of neighbourhood territory was provided by Gerald Suttles in his analysis of the Addams area, a Chicago slum.[112] The Addams area (see Figure 67), less than half a square mile in area and occupied by 2,000 people, was a recognised territory within which urban realms were limited and urban place dominant. Various ethnic groups occupied distinctive segments, within each of which social orders and sets of values were established, but retained an identity with the area as a whole. Suttles described provincialism as the most general characteristic of the Addams area; what happened a few blocks away hardly affected the daily routine of commercial transactions, social engagements and family life. This reality of neighbourhood and the dominance of local interaction in the Addams area has been paralleled by findings from several other studies of low income areas. Whereas directly comparable studies in non-western cities are not available, it is likely that urban place is completely dominant for the vast majority of the population. Oscar Lewis observed the minimal organisation which existed in the slums of non-western cities where the culture of poverty prevailed.[113] He suggested that the family, nuclear and extended, formed the major unit of interaction, otherwise there were informal, temporary groupings or voluntary associations and gangs. Even within the worst slums of non-western cities, such as the tenements or endemic shanty towns, a sense of territoriality might arise over time. Generalisation for non-western cities is impossible. Physical movements sometimes appear complex and frequent, but the absence of an adequate transport/communications technology suggests that local place must exert considerable influence. Direct evidence of the non-territoriality of the professional suburb even in western cities is fragmentary but the traits upon which Webber formed his distinction are clearly present. The role of urban place or neighbourhood in the life styles of a suburban Los Angelino, Webber's testing ground, is clearly immeasurably less than was recorded in the Addams area.

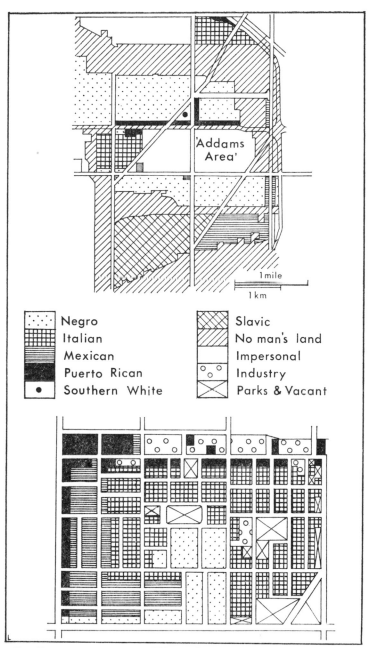

Negro   Slavic

Italian   No man's land

Mexican   Impersonal

Puerto Rican   Industry

• Southern White   Parks & Vacant

'Addams Area'

1 mile

1 km

Fig 67. *Territoriality in modern Chicago:* The inner city maintains its distinctive natural areas, based largely upon ethnic segregation. Diagrams show the position and internal structure of Addams area. (After Suttles, G. D. *The Social Order of the Slum,* Chicago, 1968, copyright 1968 by the University of Chicago.)

Whilst some generalisations on the role of neighbourhood are possible, many more detailed cross-cultural analyses are needed and in western cities increasing emphases in research are placed upon identifying the activity patterns of individuals and upon studying images of the neighbourhood. Research along these lines has only been tentative[114] but some of Terence Lee's[115] published results from Cambridge provide useful guidelines. Housewives in Cambridge were asked to define, on maps, the neighbourhoods within which they lived and information was collected on their activity patterns. The results of the survey showed a high level of individual variation in terms of definitions of neighbourhood, levels of involvement in locality and attitudes but Lee suggested that although there was no close agreement on the meaning of neighbourhood there was what he termed a 'consentaneity of views', implying agreement and interdependence but not necessarily in reciprocal systems. As a finding this lacks precision but does reflect the complex problems which must be faced in an attempt to relate social processes to spatial structure. For some the goal is unattainable[116] but as R. Guttman has suggested: 'It is difficult to accept the conclusion that it makes no difference how these houses are built, where they are located and how they are arranged in space.'[117] One of the more enlightened recent suggestions came from H. Gans and his distinction between potential and effective environments.[118] He suggested that design or physical form only provides the potential environment with the possibilities for social behaviour; the effective environment on the other hand is the product of the physical patterns and the behaviour of the people who occupy them. A distinction should perhaps be made between effective neighbouring, in the sense of exchanging visits and other direct contacts, which is usually limited to small sections of a housing estate and occurs among a few intimates, and an awareness of neighbourhood which would cover a wider area and become operational only for special events.[119] Although there is a diversity of individual attitudes, perceptions and degrees of involvement in neighbourhood, comprehensible broad patterns of variation exist and it is towards the identification of these meaningful generalisations that social geographical research should be aimed. Melvin Webber's arguments of a redundancy of urban place as urban realms become dominant has theoretical credence, but an aspatial society is far in the future for the great majority of the world's population and may be a myth even for the most mobile professional or business executive. There will always be roles for which locality is the arena of collective interaction and the importance of face-to-face relationships is unlikely to disappear. The lessons to be learned for the neighbourhood as a planning unit now seem to have been accepted: more flexibility and integration with the whole are essential and any physical design for neighbourhoods must permit choice and not impose localised patterns of movement.

CHAPTER EIGHT

Movement Within The City

ATHOUGH social geographers have always included mobility in their studies of cities, it has only recently been afforded the kind of emphasis which it deserves. General statements on the broad patterns of movement are useful but more analysis is required of the directions, frequency and purposes of the various types of mobility. Something of the complexity of urban mobility was expressed by T. Hagerstrand: 'Each individual has a moving pattern of his own, with turning points at his home, his place of work and his shopping centre during the week, and his recreation grounds on a holiday or a Sunday.'[1] J. Kofoed attempted to categorise the various elements of mobility in a recent review of person-movement research.[2] He suggested that the three main elements were fields of contact, activities and travel patterns. The individual's field of contact depends upon his spatial location relative to facilities, upon the attractiveness of facilities and his mobility potential. Activities produced varied forms of mobility and whereas work-journeys occur with fixed frequency, social visits are irregular. Similarly, whilst some activities, such as work or school, occur at fixed times of the day and at specific places, others, such as shopping or recreation, may occur at any time within a range of hours and are more flexible in terms of location. Kofoed described travel patterns as the responses to activities:

they are affected by characteristics of the urban system and the quality of physical channels of movement.

Attempts to classify mobility reveal a phenomenon of infinite variability, an awareness of which has prompted many researchers to investigations of the individual or household. Behavioural geography is important at this scale of analysis and has given urban geographers some common ground with concepts, theories and measurement techniques of social psychologists. However, geographers have the particular need even at this scale to produce useful aggregate generalisations. At the macro-scale of the city, intuitively at least, order does exist. Similar activities tend to concentrate in space, as in the central business district, providing common destinations for a range of movements. Work and school attendance hours tend to be closely regulated, thus producing general movements at specific times of the day. For the normal family, journeys to work and to school dominate all others. Beyond this level of order, mobility characteristics can be associated in general terms with different groups of people; higher-income groups are generally the most mobile and the various stages of the family life cycle have different propensities for residential mobility. These correlates of mobility provide the geographer with the bases for generalisations at various levels. At the macro-scale, R. L. Morrill has distinguished between those parts of the world which are spatially-restricted and those which are technically advanced, mobile and inter-dependent;[3] a distinction basically between western and non-western areas. At a micro-scale, F. S. Chapin and others have shown that activity-systems of individuals can range over a short space of time from the short local trip, such as collecting children from school, to much longer business journeys.[4]

Most definitions of mobility are concerned with actual physical mobility and with such distinctions as temporary and permanent migrations. A further distinction can be made, however, between physical mobility and non-physical mobility or communication. The role of communication as a means of interaction has received considerable attention in recent years. The writings of R. L. Meier[5] have particular relevance to geographers, in that he has emphasised the role of communication media, such as newspapers, mail, telephones, radio and television in the process of urban growth. Meier has suggested, for example, that cities and societies could be classified on the basis of their levels of information flows and used the term 'hubit', defined as one piece of meaningful information: the amount of information available over a stated period of time for a city was a function of its size, level of development, and the efficiency of its communications system. Flows of information from cities could also be viewed as an urbanisation process at work; the dissemination of ideas and of social values affects life-styles of individuals who might have little physical contact with the city. These concepts are clearly closely related to M. Webber's views on a non-spatial society[6] and the recurrent difficulty for the urban analyst in this context is one of measurement. Most preliminary work has been through the analysis of telephone calls and this has produced useful results. Comprehensive empirical studies, however, have yet to be completed.

Mobility is clearly a wide-ranging topic and treatment here must be selective. The intra-urban spatial context provides one limitation and within that context some comment will be offered on temporary movements within the city, particularly for work and shopping, but residential mobility is given emphasis. An understanding of the decisions on residence and the ways in which these are put into effect contains vital clues to a comprehension of the social geography of the city. The spatial patterning of residential areas at any one point in time is the end result of a decision-making process on where to live; the fact that those decisions are individual has led to behavioural approaches to this part of social geography.

TEMPORARY MOVEMENTS: THE JOURNEY TO WORK

The daily journey to work, normally involving at least one member of any household, is a predominant movement within the city. The Chicago Area Transportation survey estimated that 40 per cent of all personal travel is work-orientated;[7] J. F. Kain, in another American study, suggested a figure of 44 per cent.[8] Again, the emergence of the longer journey to work has had far-reaching effects within the city. J. E. Vance has described the physical parting of residence and work-place as a fundamental influence upon the shape of the city and as a factor which has allowed the emergence of residential areas which are socially and not occupationally distinguished.[9] This evolutionary process which Vance identifies is at present one difference between western and non-western cities. The recent history of western countries provides evidence of the gradual enlargement of commuting fields as travel facilities have improved and as an acceptance of longer work journeys has become more universal. In North America, commuting fields—or labour-sheds—used to demarcate the metropolis have revealed a functional entity of increasing dimensions;[10] recent studies have referred to a 'shrinking Britain' as the time taken to travel between places has been progressively reduced by transport improvements.[11]

The acceptance of longer work-journeys initially affected the wealthier population groups and has only spread down through the social hierarchy as mass transit and car ownership have increased. Class differences persist and most studies have shown that white-collar workers travel the greatest distances to work. J. F. Kain, in his Detroit study, suggested that the longest work-journeys were made by the higher-income groups who lived in outer suburbs and worked in the inner city: the lower-income groups made shortest work-journeys and lived close to work-place regardless of its location within the city. In this context the journey to work pattern is closely tied to the available housing market and to the residential location process within the city. Most studies of general ecological structure have tended to regard distance as the main part of any explanation of journey-to-work patterns: a simple distance-decay function has been used to summarise the residential location of central city employees, whilst off-centre employment nodes have local concentrations of labour. Increasing physical means of mobility and greater freedom of movement for individuals, however, have diminished the significance of distance. These changes will undoubtedly complicate further the pattern of journey to work within cities, and the greater flexibility of individuals is likely to be matched by greater dispersal of jobs and by diminishing monopoly of large-scale employment locations.

THE JOURNEY TO SHOP

Although less significant in terms of frequency and volume than the journey to work, shopping trips form a significant proportion of total movement within the city. Shopping differs from work in that alternatives can always be considered and much

P

more flexibility is possible in terms of both timing and frequency. The spatial patterning of shopping centres within the city provides the framework within which movements to shop occur. B. J. L. Berry's North American model of intra-urban commercial structure is probably the best known[12] and his typology comprised the central business district, highway oriented ribbons, urban arterial development and specialised functional areas. A hierarchy of business centres, in descending order from the CBD, was described as regional shopping centres, community business centres, neighbourhood centres, and isolated convenience stores. With a modified terminology this classification could serve for western countries: certainly it is broadly recognisable in Europe. For non-western cities, however, different structures exist and the importance of local street markets is considerable. The city's business structure, however, is dynamic and A. L. Mabogunje found that in Nigeria[13] traditional commercial patterns were being replaced by more western forms. Within American cities change is also apparent and many writers have documented the decline of smaller shopping areas as large regional shopping centres are developed in the new suburbs.

An understanding of shopping movements is less well developed at the intra-city level than at the regional scale. Although many of the concepts of central place theory are relevant and have in fact received limited application, there are other conditions which may be peculiar to this scale of analysis. Distance of the consumer from alternative shopping centres has always been the prime consideration of central place theory and, though obviously relevant, the high population densities and limited distances involved at the intra-urban scale reduce its significance. Thus L. Curry argued that the direction and frequency of shopping trips among alternative centres within the city could be best described by probability surfaces rather than in terms of the more traditional trade areas.[14] Others have shown that variations in type of population within trade areas, although always relevant, are likely to be much more important within the city. R. L. Davies isolated the characteristic of income variation and showed that marked contrasts in consumer behaviour did exist between population groups of high and low incomes.[15] Preferences among the higher-income groups were for more specialised and private stores, whilst among lower-income groups chain stores and general stores were preferred. Scales of movements were also obviously different; consumers from lower-income areas were clearly much more dependent on local centres, whilst consumers from high-income areas ranged much more freely throughout the city. In American cities, similar income effects can be observed and, as the wealthy move further away from the city centre, the modern peripheral centres gain in status whilst older centres decline. Besides income, other population characteristics affect shopping trips, such as differences in socio-economic status, ethnicity, age, tastes, preferences and facility to travel. Certainly in North American cities, like Toronto, the various ethnic groups patronise specific centres[16] whilst, more generally, older people are those most likely to be constrained by distance and established allegiance. Within non-western cities the limited evidence suggests much more localised patterns of movement prompted by allegiance to local ethnic centres and an inability—through cost or lack of facilities—to travel more than minimal distances within the city.

RESIDENTIAL MOBILITY

Recent American studies have suggested that one-fifth of the entire population was residentially mobile in any one year and that in California the figure was probably nearer one-quarter.[17] Comparison with W. Albig's study of four American cities in 1930, when he suggested an annual mobility rate of 15 per cent,[18] indicates a gradual increase in levels of residential mobility over time. Even these high figures, derived mainly from census data, may belie the actual levels of mobility, and recent studies of Canadian cities, using city directories, have produced even more dramatic figures.[19] Statistics based on net migration at the end of a five- or ten-year period hopelessly understated mobility because they failed to record the real frequency of residential change. Despite the fact that, over a fifteen-year period, between 60 and 70 per cent of the populations of Saskatoon, Edmonton and Calgary moved away, those cities actually increased in population-size. An estimate of the actual number of moves involved for Edmonton (1948–63) produced a figure close to 1 million.

Several other studies have also suggested that overall mobility rates disguise the fact of exceptionally high rates among some sections of the population. The distinction between 'nomads' and 'residents' was used by Goldstein,[20] and the author's distinction between Staffordians and transients in Newcastle-under-Lyme[21] is paralleled by C. Bell's local/non-local contrasts in Swansea.[22] There are of course other correlates of mobility, such as occupational status and stage in family life cycle, which give high mobility to particular groups.

All the available evidence would suggest that in general North American rates of residential mobility are much higher than in Europe. In Britain, for example, the average annual rate presently runs at between 8 and 10 per cent, but this figure shows signs of gradually increasing. Most European cities, apart from occasional special circumstances, are probably similar to British experience. Data for non-western cities are not easily obtainable but it is likely that residential mobility, although high, has many particular characteristics. The drift into cities from rural areas still accounts for a high number of moves; within cities western-style mobility is the prerogative of a limited section of society and the plethora of temporary dwellings complicates patterns. Recent United Nations surveys have suggested some filtering towards peripheral shanties as individuals improve their status.[23] Conditions peculiar to non-western cities at the present time include the legions of street-sleepers and the continuing tendency, in African society for example, to treat cities as staging points or seasonal work-places in which large sections of the population have few residential ties. Firm data are also lacking for socialist countries though there is a rural to urban drift and far greater central control of residential mobility.

Recent studies on residential mobility in North America show that the great majority of movements are now contained within the city; an overall estimate that two-thirds of all moves are intra-city finds some additional confirmation in the 1966 census for British cities. The study of intra-city mobility is but recently developed and has comparatively few firm concepts. Theories developed in the context of migration at a regional scale are not directly applicable. In terms of motivations, for example, it is apparent that the economic or employment reason for mobility, which has always been recognised as a major element in inter-city moves, has much less importance at the intra-urban scale. Reasons for mobility within the city can be described in terms of a small number of broad categories but there is more complexity. Similarly, it is likely that the simple distance-decay model of regional migration needs much more careful interpretation within the city. A further point of contrast is that whereas at the regional scale one can generally envisage space as unfettered, within the city space is made up of a complex urban environment: the existing urban fabric forms the spatial framework within which residential mobility occurs. Many aspects of this urban fabric, some in constant flux, affect the geographical patterns of residential mobility. The present expanding fringe of the city, urban renewal and rehabilitation projects, provide possibilities for new housing; the available property inventory comprises the housing market; existing qualities of location provide alternatives in cost terms; whilst the broad ecological structure is invested with social values which attract or deter potential movers. Residential mobility is conditioned by the urban fabric but it is also, in the longer term, a process by which that fabric is materially formed and altered. P. H. Rees made this latter point in reference to E. W. Burgess and the concentric zonal model: 'He (Burgess) missed the point of his own model of the city. The movement of people from one residence to another as the city grows is the very mechanism by which zonal and natural areas . . . are created.'[24] It is the aggregative effect of movement by individual households which produces geographical patterns of society within the city and the constraints imposed by the existing urban fabric have considerable influence upon those patterns.

Discussions of residential mobility are necessarily concerned with the movers themselves, the consumers of the housing market. Another vital background to actual mobility, however, is the housing supply involving a complex system of decision-makers such as builders, developers and real estate agents. These 'suppliers' are affected by constraints of the urban fabric and by the contemporary legislative and financial climates. E. J. Kaiser and S. F. Weiss, who proposed an analysis of residential development based on decision-making,[25] have produced a conceptual framework for new development.

Once the phase of initial development is over, new suppliers of housing include finance companies—particularly in their role of mortgage providers—real estate agents and other entrepreneurs. Planning agencies—already important in the development stage—continue to play a role, the significance of which is determined by the powers delegated to them in a particular society. Planners are influential in direct terms through renewal or rehabilitation activities and general zoning policy and less directly through

Table 14   A residential development model

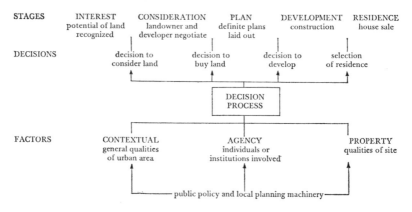

STAGES	INTEREST potential of land recognized	CONSIDERATION landowner and developer negotiate	PLAN definite plans laid out	DEVELOPMENT construction	RESIDENCE house sale
DECISIONS		decision to consider land	decision to buy land	decision to develop	selection of residence

DECISION
PROCESS

FACTORS	CONTEXTUAL general qualities of urban area	AGENCY individuals or institutions involved	PROPERTY qualities of site

public policy and local planning machinery

activities which might affect the quality of residential areas, such as provision of services, major road-building schemes or siting of noxious land-uses. The cumulative contributions of agencies involved in residential development present the housing consumer, at any one point in time, with the overall context within which the decision to move is made.

BEHAVIOURAL APPROACHES TO RESIDENTIAL MOBILITY: THE DECISION PROCESS

Many geographers concerned with intra-urban residential mobility have adopted the individual household as the basic unit of analysis and have used behavioural postulates to form their conceptual frameworks. Julian Wolpert's adaptation of behavioural theory is now regarded as definitive[26] and more recently L. A. Brown and E. G. Moore have attempted to provide an overall perspective of this type of approach.[27] Using concepts such as 'place utility' (the individual's measure of satisfaction for a given location) and 'action spaces' (the locations to which the individual attaches place utilities), Brown and Moore proposed a model of the residential location decision process which is a useful sequence to the developer model devised by Kaiser and Weiss.

The model proposed by Brown and Moore provides a useful

framework in which to discuss residential mobility. It emphasises the need to understand the decision-making process of the individual household and the search procedure through which an actual choice is made.

A seminal work on reasons for residential mobility was P. A. Rossi's *Why Families Move*,[28] which assembled its data from surveys in Philadelphia, and has provided numerous guidelines for subsequent research. Rossi distinguished between voluntary and involuntary moves: the former—accounting for the large majority of moves—occur where a household has a clear choice and the decision is made by assessing alternative courses of action; the latter implies a lack of choice and might arise from dramatic

Table 15   A residential location decision model

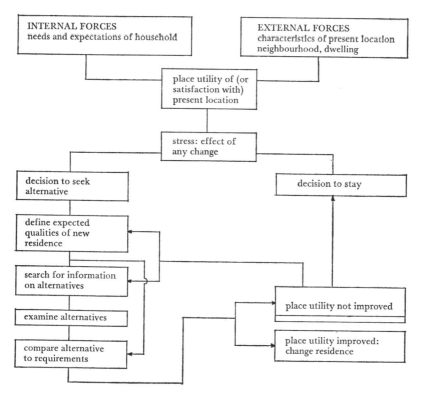

neighbourhood change, such as urban renewal, or major change in family circumstances such as divorce. Geographers have tried to fit the decisions for voluntary moves into a set of behavioural concepts, part of which is implied in the model of Brown and Moore.[29] The individual household is viewed as a simple behaviour system which is subject to continuous stimuli from its immediate environment. Stimuli may constitute 'stressors' which derive from the disparities between the needs and aspirations of an individual household and the actual qualities of its present location: adequate living space, for example, may not be available in the present dwelling. As the model suggests, a household may either stay—adjusting its needs or adapting its environment—or move, where a threshold of stress is reached (level of overcrowding becomes unacceptable) and an alternative exists. Although the terminology may differ, there is general agreement on the kinds of stimuli which lead to moves. All researchers have recognised stage in life-cycle as the dominant motivation for intra-urban mobility; for example, G. Sabagh[30] classified seven life-cycle stages of marriage, pre-child, child-bearing, child-rearing, child-launching, post-child and widowhood. The likelihood of a move for typical families was greatest during the child-bearing and child-launching stages, and least during the child-rearing stage, though household economic circumstances should always be considered as a basic factor in that moves are almost always costly. The association of actual moves with different stages of the life-cycle must also be related to the available range of housing stock at any one point in time. Many lower-income families in Britain, for example, may want to move when increased family size renders their present accommodation unsuitable, but are unable to compete in the private housing market and are dependent upon available vacancies in the public housing sector.

Life-cycle stages are not of course the only reasons for change of residence and Rossi attempted to form an overall measure by means of two indices, 'mobility potential' and 'complaints'. The mobility potential index—strongly related to life-cycle—was computed from three variables, age, household-size and preferences for renting or owning. The combined complaints index was based upon dwelling-unit space, dwelling facilities, accessibility, physical environment, social environment and costs. A survey of voluntary movers showed that almost half moved because of their changing demands for living space, whilst a further 25 per cent had some complaint relating to cost or to neighbourhood. Some differences between renters and owners were apparent, the former being more affected by costs and the latter by neighbourhood. Although Rossi did not rate social mobility highly as a reason for moves, other studies have disagreed and it is likely that if the concept was not limited to major changes of social class but included the desire for increased status as economic circumstances improved, it would be much more significant. Other factors—or stressors—in the decision to move may be connected to qualities of the neighbourhood. Neighbourhoods may change for the worse—in the assessment of an individual household—either physically through deterioration of buildings, landscape, services or adjacent land uses, or socially in terms of the inhabitants. Urban expansion over time has generally been regarded as detrimental to the quality of older neighbourhoods and the general desire to move to suburbs has typified large sections of the American population.

Although general factors are recognised which appear to explain most decisions to move, behaviouralists stress both the individual nature of the decision and the need to account for ways in which people perceive alternatives. A low-density neighbourhood, for example, may be viewed quite differently by two households. Whereas to one its open spaces may appear desirable, to the other these could be a disadvantage: representing a rural prospect to the former and a sense of isolation to the latter. J. Wolpert[31] and others have attempted to allow for this individual variation within what they term the 'mover-stayer' situation. They recognise that even where stimuli to move are apparently high some households may not react. Rossi provided some empirical evidence in this context by conducting a follow-up survey, eight months after his original investigation. He found that his original analyses of reasons for moves produced a prediction which was 87 per cent accurate, but that it did not cover certain unexpected movers and unexpected stayers. The unexpected movers cited reasons such as a windfall or unforeseen event for their change of decision; unexpected stayers had often been influenced by a local change, such as a new landlord, or had been unable to obtain a mortgage, to find a suitable house or to sell their existing dwelling.

Most evidence on reasons for moves, as indeed upon other aspects of residential mobility, is gleaned from North American experience, but a study of Swansea provides some indicators of British conditions. Several neighbourhoods were studied and amongst all but the high-status sample area, reasons for mobility were reminiscent of American experience. Stage-in-life-cycle figured prominently amongst stated reasons, expressed as the need for differently-sized houses; neighbourhood factors, including quality of the built environment and the sociability of people, also scored highly. The high-status area contained two distinctive sub-groups, the locals, whose origins were in the town or nearby and whose moves had all been local, and the non-locals whose moves had all been on an inter-urban rather than an intra-urban scale.[32] Overall reasons for previous change of residence in the high-status sample revealed employment as accounting for 50 per cent of the total; this reflected, however, the non-locals who operated upon a career-orientated national level of mobility. When the locals were analysed as a sub-group, the familiar motivations for intra-urban movement, stage-in-life-cycle in particular, became dominant. A point of significant contrast amongst the low-income populations was that availability of public housing was clearly an important motivation. One survey area was in fact a municipal housing estate and individual house-holds had moved simply because they had been allocated a home; some respondents in low-income districts were waiting for a housing allocation—their only possibility of a change of residence. The study of Swansea was concerned with total mobility within the city, thus containing some inter-urban movement. There were clearly broad comparisons with American experience but also differences: generally mobility rates were much lower, particularly among lower-income groups who were much more constrained by the housing market and financial considerations.

The decision to move does not always lead to a change of residence and both Rossi and behavioural geographers have placed great emphasis upon the research procedures through which alternatives are identified, assessed and acted upon. Rossi used an accounting system, partly based upon the information sources from which potential movers might acquire knowledge of alternative residential locations. Assessment ratings of information sources were based upon newspapers, personal contact, direct observation, real estate agents and windfall; of these, personal contact provided most information. Rossi discovered that a large group, between one-third and one-half of his sample, only viewed one alternative and such evidence of restricted knowledge has been of interest to behaviouralists. Using behavioural terminology, an individual household's 'awareness space' is formed on the basis of contacts and describes that portion of objective reality—the real world—within which decisions can be made. F. E. Horton and D. R. Reynolds used the term 'action space' defined as: 'The collection of all urban locations about which the individual has information and the subjective utility or preference he associates with these locations.'[33] L. A. Brown and E. G. Moore[34] use the idea of awareness space as the mental map or image possessed by the individual; D. F. Marble and J. D. Nystuen's description of a mean information field, as the average spatial extent of an individual's short-term contacts, reveals a similar concept.[35] 'Activity space' or 'All urban locations with which the individual has direct contact as the result of day-to-day activities'[36] is a part of awareness space, but the latter has proved difficult to measure. Activity spaces include work areas, recreational areas, shopping areas and the routes which link them to the household and neighbourhood, but awareness space is also formed from the communications media and indirect contacts and may vary with the perceptiveness of individuals as well as with more tangible attributes such as age, education and occupation. Although theoretically possessing a high degree of individual variability, there are probably considerable overlaps in awareness spaces and common mental maps may exist for sub-sections of the population; there is evidence for example that only places within close proximity of residence are well-known.

Awareness space is a small part of objective reality but is still not in itself the area within which alternatives are considered; 'search space' is that part of awareness space which satisfies the needs and aspirations of the individual households. Search space has geographical expression and can probably be approximated by simple distance-decay functions. It is best defined, however, in terms of what Rossi has called the specifications of the household. One set of specifications relates to the dwelling-unit itself and includes space, appearance and internal design; another set relates to general accessibility and neighbourhood qualities. Although dwelling size is dominant in defining search space, there is also a neighbourhood factor of some significance in American cities. Families often tend to move as short a distance as possible; R. R. Boyce found in Seattle that the average length of an intra-city move was less than three miles and 16 per cent moved less than a half-mile.[37] The area near the present residence is that best known to the household and forms a large part of its awareness space; a move within the same neighbourhood means that a number of requirements, such as accessibility and type of area, are kept constant and search can be limited to dwelling-unit attributes. Other relevant specifications relating to type of people, their ethnic and social composition, can also be maintained.

Search space is also defined in terms of accessibility to institutions within the city. The importance of the city centre as a pivotal point for accessibility has declined in more recent years in America,[38] though it probably retains its significance elsewhere. J. F. Kain suggested that access to workplace remained an important element in residential location,[39] but other institutions which exert an influence are local shopping centres, schools and recreational open space. Rossi found that housing cost was only mentioned by a small percentage of his sample. It seems likely, however, that cost considerations form a very real element which most households would take for granted in defining their search space alternatives. 60 per cent of Rossi's sample named cost as the factor which finally decided their choice. A similar factor is the visual impact of the house and its setting: recently several studies have provided valuable leads in the evaluation of visual appearance of neighbourhoods but effective measurement has proved a difficult task.[40]

This description of residential decision-making makes considerable assumptions about flexibility of households and the housing market and has been developed in the context of North American experience. Elsewhere these precise assumptions do not obtain and there are other constraints upon movement. For large sections of Britain's population, aspirations and preferences must take second place in the application for public housing; in Amsterdam and many other European cities, high-rise apartments are the only available places of accommodation for much of the population. Tokyo holds lotteries for state-owned one-room apartments and choice is negligible for all except an elite. Similarly, throughout the non-western world shelter of any kind is a valued possession and concepts based on decisions and choices have little meaning.

SPATIAL PREFERENCES

Although many of these new concepts in behavioural geography have proved difficult to use in research, rather more success has been apparent in the measurement of spatial preferences. Data are collected by household surveys in which individuals are asked to express their degree of preference for a specific area. Questions usually relate to the residential desirability of neighbourhoods or are tests of familiarity with various parts of the city and responses can be recorded and measured on nominal and ordinal scales.* The attraction of space preference studies is that they attempt to measure the ways in which households perceive alternative residential locations and to analyse individual variation. Measurement techniques and approaches are as yet not fully developed,[41] but promising advances have been made. Expressed preferences are a product of the 'image' possessed by the individual and form a link between reality and behaviour. J. Doherty provided a simple but useful schematic representation:[42]

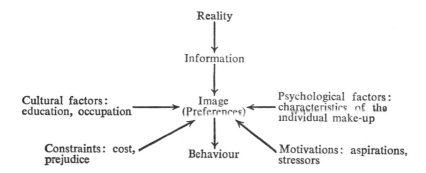

Most studies have either requested individuals to rank alternative locations in order of preference or to place them on a point-scale. Scores are expressed as simple aggregates or averages, though recent analyses favour more sophisticated techniques.

An early study on a regional scale was the analysis of British school-leavers by P. R. Gould and R. R. White.[43] Pupils in

* See Appendix.

twenty-three schools were asked to rank, in order of residential preference, the ninety counties of Britain; a correlation matrix was calculated and principal components analysis was used. Each school showed a marked preference for its own locality and a general preference for the south coastal counties of England. Gould developed the approach with a group of students in Tanzania,[44] who were required to rank the country's sixty districts, to assign a required salary to the district of their first choice and compensating amounts for all other districts and to evaluate each district on five scales which included assessments of friendliness and accessibility. Again using principal components analysis, Gould showed an area of high desirability which extended across the eastern and central parts of the country, generally corresponding with modernised districts. Gould's studies have usually been based on student samples and under laboratory conditions. Field surveys are much more difficult to handle but a preliminary result for South Wales (Figure 68) demonstrates measurement of spatial preference at the regional scale.

A number of studies of space preference within the city have direct relevance to residential mobility. R. J. Johnston used a sample of students in a study of Christchurch, New Zealand;[45] each student was given two lists of fifty residential districts and was required to assess their social standings and residential desirability, each on a five-point scale. Most desired areas were generally located in a sector extending north-west from the city centre, conforming with highest social standing assessments, but there were a number of distinct nodes of preference including proximity to beach, to city centre, and to present residence. In an analysis of Liverpool R. Bordessa attempted to measure perceptions of what space contained and also to account for variability amongst the individuals in his sample.[46] Findings indicated that individual perceptions of areas and their qualities varied with differing characteristics of the individual. The Liverpool study of householders within the city faced problems of interpretation because it departed from controlled samples of students, amongst which high levels of homogeneity can be expected. Within less homogeneous neighbourhood samples, variations in responses are related to attributes such as age, sex, length of residence and education.

In Swansea five contrasted neighbourhoods within the city

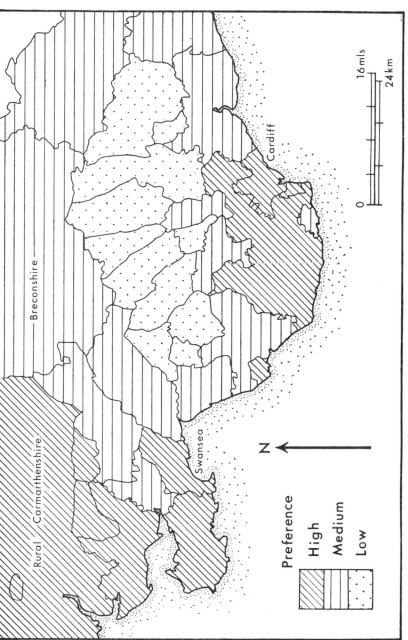

Fig 68. *Spatial preferences in South Wales:* Respondents, from a sample of 250 households in the western part of the region, were asked to score 35 areas within the region on a three-point scale and a factor analytic technique was used to summarise the preferences. More attractive coastal areas and rural peripheries are most preferred and older industrial areas in the central coalfield are least preferred.

were studied and sample populations were required to rank twelve residential districts and ten local authority housing estates in order of preference. A larger number of recognisable districts within the city were aggregated in order to overcome some of the practical problems of household interviews. Each respondent was shown maps locating the areas within the city, but even with this procedure and the limited numbers of areas used, people were unable to rank all alternatives and many equal preferences were recorded.[47] The most-desired area is clearly in the western part of the city (Figure 69), corresponding in fact with the resort districts which possess high local status. Also indicated is some preference for residence close within the city and a high level of desirability attached to the present neighbourhood. Responses on the desirability of municipal estates were of interest in that they could be substantiated from other sources of information in Swansea. By and large, as shown by Figure 70, preference for public housing closely resembled the patterns shown for general residential districts (Figure 69). Two estates in the west—West Cross and Sketty Park—were consistently highly favoured, whilst preferences were also expressed for the estate nearest to present residence and for central city locations. Data from the city housing department on applications for transfers provided further confirmation of this pattern of preference. Although the effect of public sector intervention has been to provide generally equivalent styles of housing in various parts of the city, these neighbourhoods have preference ratings which conform with the general ecological structure.

Hence, studies of spatial preference are being developed within the context of behavioural geography and provide valuable insights in the analysis of residential mobility. Measurement techniques and their interpretation are not problem-free and a preference does not of course mean a decision, but the approach offers considerable scope for further development.

RESIDENTIAL MOBILITY AT THE ECOLOGICAL SCALE: SPATIAL PATTERNS

From the host of individual households making decisions on when and where to move residence and out of the complexity of interacting stimuli, preferences, attractions and constraints, social geographers must attempt to discern some order and to identify

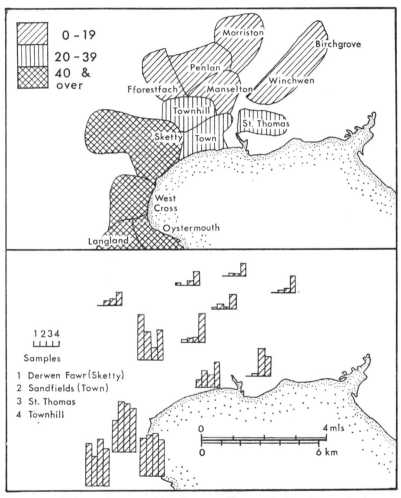

Fig 69. *District preferences within Swansea:* The map is based upon simple percentages (proportion of total sample placing a district in the first three choices) and the contrast between the desirable west and other areas is clear. In the lower map, height of column indicates level of preference.

Ω

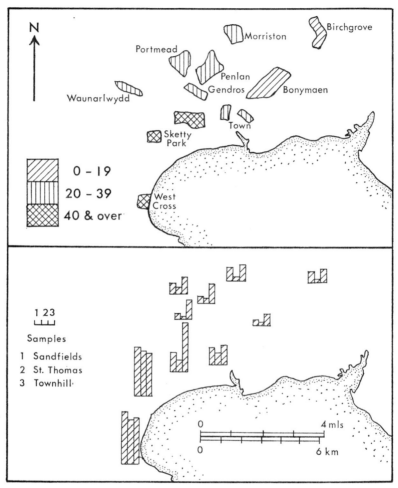

Fig 70. *Local authority preferences within Swansea:* Residential preference for public housing or local authority estates closely mirrors the general rating of residential districts. See also Fig 69.

spatial patterns. Actual moves, the end-results of decision-making, provide data from which geographical patterns of residential mobility can be recognised and analysed. At one level geographers have studied change within districts as the composition of the resident population alters over time. The invasion success process, developed within the context of urban ecology, described a pattern of sequent occupance; Hoyt's original formulation of the sector theory was stated in terms of shifts of high-status residential districts over time.[48] Filtering concepts, whereby housing became available to lower-income groups as former occupants move to new or better accommodation,[49] were derived from Hoyt's original work. A recent study of shifting residential areas was R. J. Johnston's analysis of Melbourne[50] (see Figure 71), whilst similar patterns have been recorded in Winnipeg as high-status areas, formerly close to the city centre, have migrated south and west. The activities of a relatively small group of prestigious families have often proved important influences upon overall urban growth. Hoyt picked out the role of the leaders of the community in providing directions into which future expansion was to occur; Emrys Jones spoke of the social values which became attached to certain peripheral areas in Belfast;[51] whilst in North Staffordshire the movement out of the industrial towns to more amenable districts to the west was led by the owners and managers of the ceramics industry.[52]

Filtering processes of residential change and shifts of status areas have been widely recognised and documented in the literature of social geography, but most earlier studies were descriptive and lacked good analytical techniques. Examples of improvements in this respect are provided by analyses of Negro ghetto expansion in American cities. Large influxes of Negroes have led to a situation in which almost one-third of the American Negro population lived in twenty metropolitan areas in 1950, and the northern Negro population had almost doubled each decade since 1920. The Negro ghetto, non-existent in the nineteenth century, emerged as the in-migrants gradually occupied sub-standard districts in the central city. R. L. Morrill[53] has summarised four factors which have acted to maintain the ghetto: prejudice on the part of white people; the characteristics of the Negroes; discrimination by real estate and financial institutions; and barriers imposed by legal and governmental agencies. These factors are closely replicated in Elizabeth Burney's study of

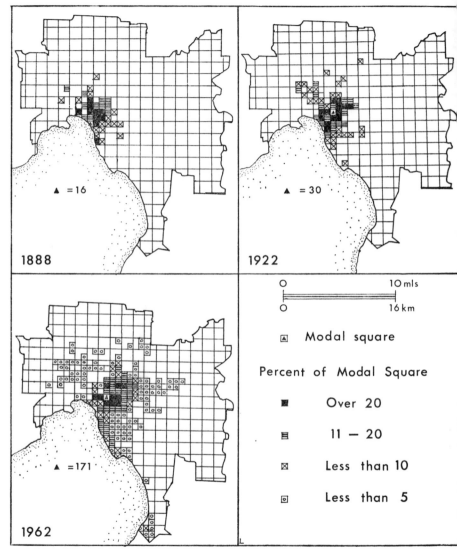

Fig 71. *Shifting status areas in Melbourne:* Territorial shifts of high status areas over time are revealed by this study of Melbourne. (After Johnston, R. J., 'The Location of High Status Residential Areas', *Geografiska Annaler* B, 48, 1966, 23–35, with permission of the author and *Geografiska Annaler*.)

housing segregation in British cities.[54] With continuing pressures from natural population growth and in-migration, the ghetto has had to expand territorially and Morrill has described the form which this expansion has taken. The districts contiguous to the Negro ghetto are typically older white housing areas in which there is instability because of the nearness of the Negroes, the fear of falling land-values and of general socio-economic deterioration. Proximity was crucial in the likely convertibility of residential blocks to Negro occupance; in Philadelphia, white buyers of real estate formed 4 per cent of the total on the edge of the ghetto, compared to 100 per cent between five and seven blocks away. Actual expansion of the ghetto could be described as a block-by-block total transition. Once the initial break had been made, successive vacancies were taken up by Negroes and the process was often promoted by real estate agents who favoured gradual transition along the edge of the ghetto.

Morrill likened the spread of the ghetto to a spatial diffusion process in which block-by-block substitution spread from a point of origin, with the whites as the passive and Negroes as the active agents. A spatial diffusion model of a probabilistic simulated type* was formed and applied to Seattle. Comparing actual with projected patterns of ghetto expansion for 1940–50 and 1950–60, Morrill found good general correspondence which satisfied his terms of reference. The main differences were that the actual pattern extended further to the north. Field checks revealed that insufficient weight had been given to quality and value of homes while topography was also apparently crucial; by 1960 Negroes were rapidly filling in the lower-lying viewless land but were much less successful in ridge properties with good views. H. M. Rose has questioned the suitability of diffusion models,[55] preferring to regard ghetto expansion as an adjustment process, and Morrill himself has referred to his own model as 'quasi-diffusionary',[56] but the contributions of this type of model and of other probabilistic approaches are likely to be considerable in the analysis of residential change (see Figure 72).

Gradual shifts of 'territories', particularly those with special characteristics such as prestige districts and ghettoes, have proved amenable to generalisations, but patterns are more complex when all individual moves are considered. One hypothesis for individual

* See Appendix.

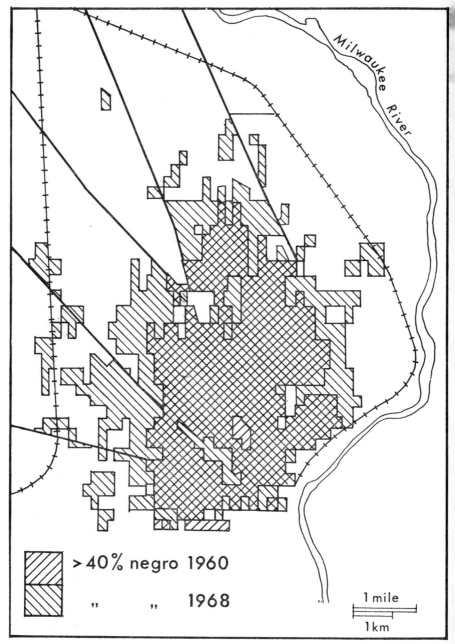

Milwaukee River

///// >40% negro 1960

///// „ „ 1968

1 mile

1 km

Fig 72. *Negro ghetto expansion:* The map identifies the Negro ghetto in Milwaukee in 1960 and simulates its expansion to 1968 (adapted from Rose, H. M., 'The Development of an Urban Sub-System: The Case of the Negro Ghetto', *AAAG* 60, 1970, 1–5, with permission from the Association of American Geographers).

moves which is credible at a general scale but more questionable when analysed in detail, would suggest a progression from the centre outwards. R. J. Johnston in a study of London found that the majority of moves were from the centre towards the periphery, in accordance with a general theory of metropolitan expansion,[57] but his results in Melbourne were less straightforward.[58] In the latter city, there was a relatively complex pattern of movement across the city and some migration towards the centre. Complexity in the directions of moves has been apparent for some time; T. Caplow discovered that only one out of sixteen moves in his Minneapolis sample could be described as 'outward'[59] and others have recognised that only people who choose familism as a life-style will become suburban dwellers.

The fact that spatial patterns of mobility cannot be neatly summarised is in large part a reflection of the complexities of decision-making and the variability of individuals, or at least sub-groups, within the total population. Geographers are, finally, seeking to identify aggregate patterns and their correlates; it is in this context that the link between the micro-scale of behaviouralism and the macro-scale of the spatial generalisation becomes most acute. P. H. Rees proposed a framework which was essentially ecological,[60] but which contained some progression from the decision of the individual household to aggregate spatial patterns. The individual household had achieved a position in social space, defined by its socio-economic status and its life-cycle stage; this position was matched by a dwelling of appropriate dimensions and quality within the constraints of cost. The dwelling possessed a location in a neighbourhood of similar dwellings, and the existence of these differential residential areas gave spatial patterns within the city. For Rees, the urban ecology is a summary of past processes of mobility: 'An orderly social geography results as like individuals make like choices.'[61]

Other approaches have involved identifying spatial patterns of rates of population movement or turnover within the city and investigating their correlates at an ecological scale of analysis. Census data for small areas have provided basic information and several studies have been based upon this source. A British example—an analysis in Swansea—used nineteen variables from the 1966 census. Information was recorded in terms of numbers who had moved residence within the period 1961–6 and it became clear that there were considerable differences between inter-urban and intra-urban moves. The distinction between these two types of mobility is based upon the crossing of a municipal boundary; inter-urban moves may therefore include some whose residential relocation is contained within the same general urban area.

Table 16   Variables used in Swansea mobility study

1. inter-urban mobility
2. intra-urban mobility
3. per cent owner-occupiers
4. per cent social classes I and II
5. per cent in socio-economic groups 5 and 6
6. per cent women at work
7. per cent single-person households
8. per cent single adults
9. per cent working outside municipality
10. per cent with use of all facilities
11. per cent over 65 years
12. per cent in local authority housing
13. per cent in social classes IV and V
14. Sex ratio
15. fertility ratio
16. persons per room
17. per cent of households over five persons
18. per cent in private rented unfurnished tenancies
19. per cent without cars

A correlation matrix produced a clear set of correlates with inter-urban movers; significant at the 0·1 per cent level:

social classes I and II	+0·65	without cars	−0·78
working outside LA	+0·61	social classes IV and V	−0·56
owner-occupiers	+0·56	LA tenants	−0·44
SEGs 5 and 6	+0·36		

For intra-urban movers, there were no significant correlations at the 0·1 per cent level but several at the 5·0 per cent:

LA tenants	+0·27	working outside LA	−0·30
without cars	+0·24	owner-occupiers	−0·25
fertility ratio	+0·21		

A factor analysis of the nineteen variables produced similar results:

Factor One (24·9%)		*Factor Four (8·8%)*	
inter-urban mobility	+0·66	intra-urban mobility	+0·83
social classes I and II	+0·81	working outside LA	−0·60
SEGs 5 and 6	+0·77		
owner occupiers	+0·74		
social classes IV and V	−0·91		
without cars	−0·85		
LA tenants	−0·62		

Mobility at the inter-urban scale is strongly associated with social class and with private house ownership but intra-urban mobility rates are less clearly associated with other variables. There is some association with low social class, with fertility and with local authority tenancy but the correlations are not statistically strong. Spatial patterns of the two forms of mobility allow more detailed interpretation. Figure 73 shows the pattern for inter-urban mobility with the highest rates in the prestigious western districts of the city and in some other new suburbs. These are the residential districts which include a large number of professionals who are mobile for career-connected motives and

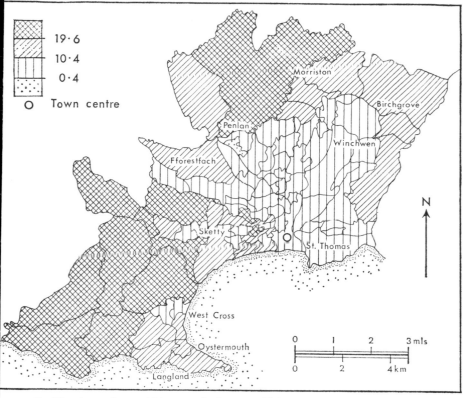

Fig 73. *Inter-urban mobility rates in Swansea:* High rates of inter-urban mobility typify more prestigious western districts of the city.

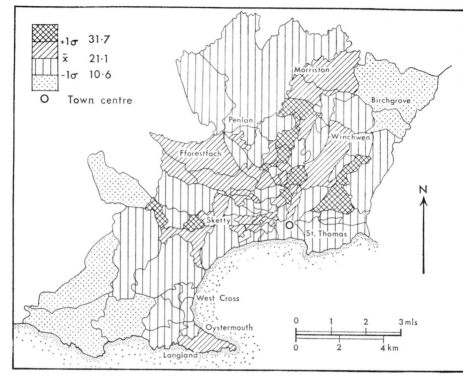

Fig 74. *Intra-urban mobility rates in Swansea:* Rates are generally low with highest rates found both in recent municipal estates and some high status districts.

who are often non-local in origin. Low rates of inter-urban mobility in lower-status areas—the central and eastern parts of the city—reflect constraints upon movement among low-income groups and in particular the constraints upon inter-urban movement among residents of local authority estates whose tenancies are not normally transferable from one city to another. Spatial patterns for intra-urban mobility (Figure 74) are more complex, high rates occur both in recent local authority estates and in several high-status districts. The pattern might be described as bi-modal with life-cycle factors producing high rates in local authority estates—as larger families qualify for housing—and in high-status areas as families move within the private sector. Full interpretation of intra-urban movement is not possible from census data because only turnover is given. Figure 75, however, shows origins and destinations of moves for two sample survey populations. The high-status movers, Derwen Fawr, had longer-distance moves, mainly from lower status areas; the low-status movers, St Thomas, had short-distance moves, many within the same district. It should again be emphasised, from information in the census, that rates of intra-urban movement were low in comparison to North American findings.

Although meaningful patterns can be identified from this type of ecological analysis, E. G. Moore has suggested that aggregate

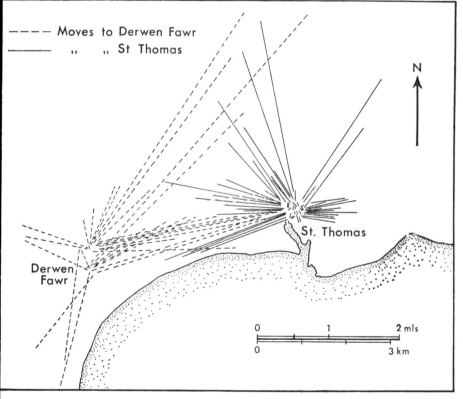

Fig 75. *Intra-urban moves in Swansea:* Individual moves for two contrasted samples (high status Derwen Fawr and low status St Thomas) show more localised movement in the latter and a longer-distance shift to prestige west in the former.

data have deficiencies and should be used with caution in the absence of information upon which to base micro-models.[62] His own work on Brisbane led to the conclusion that if short-term predictions for population turnover were required, then simple models based on distance-decay and accessibility functions were adequate. There were also, however, statistical correlates of mobility which could, within limits, be developed in terms of a causal model. Using population turnover for small areas in Brisbane in 1961 as the main variable, Moore identified indices of age differential, single adults, private housing, owner-occupiers and Australian-born, as potential correlates. This set of indices was justified by reference to past literature. Although the simple correlations between each index and turnover were all highly significant, Moore was not satisfied from his available evidence of the extent to which there were common associations with accessibility to the city centre. Similarly, in an attempt to form a causal model, using methodology developed by H. M. Blalock,[63] a plausible statement could be formed but a number of potential distortions remained. Although caution in the interpretation of statistical correlates is undoubtedly justified, distance from or accessibility to the city centre seems the least likely causal relationship and real associations probably exist between aggregate measures such as tenure and population turnover. The fallibilities of analysis at the ecological scale are well-known but do not render the approach valueless; it remains for further research to test associations in an effective way and to develop a better understanding of movement within the city.

Conclusion

A lengthy conclusion would be inappropriate in a text which has already covered a wide range of topics and has referred to a considerable amount of literature. It is sufficient to re-state some of the main points of emphasis, to reconsider the nature of the geographical perspective, and to attempt some assessment of its relevance to the problems which the city poses.

It has been convenient to take the formal city as a unit and to discuss its internal structure in terms of equally convenient sub-divisions. All these divisions have reality but increasingly they are more profitably viewed for research purposes as inter-related elements of a total urban system, rather than as discrete units. The city itself is the product of the society of which it is part and distinctions between urban and rural have become almost everywhere less significant. In western societies, the distinction has diminished because urban values now permeate society as a whole; there are urbanites living both in compact cities and in open areas, and traditional urban and rural occupations no longer have exclusive meaning. Non-western societies have similarly witnessed a diminution in urban/rural differences and migrants into emerging cities have transferred rural values and life-styles into an urban context. Contemporary cities of the Third World are not the functional equivalent of those in developed countries. It is likely that urban life-styles will become more distinctive in non-western cities as expressions of a modernising process, but it is also likely that other forces for differentiation, such as social class and social status, will often transcend territorial groupings.

Although the effects of increasing mobility and the dissemination of information appear to reduce the friction of distance, it has been argued that, at most scales of human activity, territoriality and spatial contiguity remain significant referents. Spatial location, effective through territoriality and accessibility, is a basic fact which should be incorporated into any explanation of behaviour and attitudes. The spatial referent may often be less important than others but it is always relevant. Even where the means for 'non-physical' communication—mail and telephone—exist and appear sufficient, the face-to-face relationship remains a greatly preferred alternative. This necessity for direct interaction and the continuing relevance of spatial location is an implicit assumption for a social geography of the city. Whilst the theoretical credibility of an aspatial or non-spatial view can be recognised, its applicability to the present-day real world is limited and its attainability is doubtful.

An emphasis on the importance of analysing the spatial context does not ignore other bases for explanation. A sociological context has been elaborated as the natural ally to a social geography of the city, but other contexts need be no less rewarding. Inter-disciplinary approaches, derivative and indigenous theories are all essentials in urban analysis. The geographer constrained in his discipline may achieve little, but with the flexibility to adapt and use the concepts and techniques of other disciplines in addition to his own, he may achieve a great deal. It is hoped that the geographical perspective demonstrated in this text has conveyed these elements of cross-fertilisation and, simultaneously, retained a particular theme of emphasis. Whereas overlaps among various disciplines increase, the priority within each remains distinctive. In each topic discussed in this text, for example, the approach has been to take or to define a territory and subsequently to describe and analyse its characteristics. These characteristics comprise the basic spatial patterns of points, areas or flows; the associations which these elements hold with each other and with the broader urban environment; and the dynamism which they possess when viewed in a temporal dimension. The similarities which this kind of definition of a geographic perspective bears to that of a general system makes it easy to understand why some geographers have adopted the approach of systems analysis. Whilst this practice has considerable value in many cases, the system in itself is not a panacea and such concepts should only be used where they result in positive gains. Similar qualifications could be voiced on the application of quantitative methods to geographical research. Whilst these have undoubtedly improved the quality of much work and have opened up new avenues and insights, they are not always necessary and can, at their worst, be used to dress up inadequacies of hypotheses or data. Both moves towards more general theories, such as systems analysis, and towards increasing quantification, however, have had the important effects of drawing urban geography into a closer alliance with other social sciences and of highlighting the common ground which exists.

Innovations, whether of theories or techniques, have rarely replaced but have rather augmented the existing body of knowledge. It could be argued that the elements which the urban geographer studies have not changed in kind, but that additions have been made and emphases and priorities have altered considerably. Land use and morphology remain important themes but functional relationships and processes are now accorded more priority. The perspective of historical growth and background is still evident but other contemporary non-geographical perspectives, such as the sociological and economic contexts, receive precedence. A macro-scale of study remains with substantial modifications but the value of the micro-scale is increasingly emphasised and—in this context—predictable economic man is complicated by the vagaries of social values. With the subject in a constant state of flux, future emphases in urban geography are difficult to predict. It is likely, however, that emphases on movements and processes are likely to increase, that detailed analyses at the micro-scale will precede attempts at re-stating general theories, and that those techniques which allow predictive analysis may receive closer attention.

Whilst the search for good theory goes on, most geographical studies of the city are concerned with empirical data and are applicable to real problems. In attempting to judge the value of the approaches described in this text to the actual dilemmas facing urban man, a great deal of value judgement is inevitably involved. It could be argued that all extra knowledge adds to our understanding but equally that the problems of cities appear to multiply rather than to diminish with the passage of time and after several decades of intensive academic research. It is true that even the most obvious and relevant findings from academic research rarely find immediate application; the basis of a problem may be thoroughly demonstrated but practical steps to its solution can be prevented for a variety of reasons: there are many political, economic, social and other forces involved in the city, the interests and objectives of which may never coincide. Given these constraints, the impact of academic research may be limited and variable.

The geographical perspective, however, may well have particular advantages which render it more relevant than most to the real problems of the city. Urban planning is multi-faceted in content and expertise but probably has more in common with urban geography than with any other single discipline. Fundamental considerations with space allocation and with spatial interaction characterise both geography and planning. Many approaches, long-established in geography, have passed in modified form into planning procedures; many new planning theories have a spatial context. Cities in advanced countries already pose enormous problems, the cities of developing countries are still emergent and opportunities for constructive control exist. It seems clear that in both 'halves' of the world urban planning will increase and the planning agency, whether it be central or local government, will of necessity become a major force in society. For the practical needs of these agencies and for the understanding of the city, a geographical approach and perspective is likely to remain of considerable importance.

APPENDIX

Some Statistical Terms and Quantitative Procedures

QUANTITATIVE methods have had a considerable impact upon urban geography and inevitably any text must now reflect this trend. At several points descriptions of techniques have been referred to an appendix rather than attempt to include them in the body of the text. The intention here is not to attempt a comprehensive survey of statistical techniques in urban geography but to explain briefly some of the terms which have been used.

DATA

The quality of data used is crucial to any kind of analysis and it is hoped that this point has been sufficiently emphasised. There are substantial qualitative differences between data sets available from various parts of the world and these inevitably influence results. Given a data set, the nature of the statistics affects the type of quantitative technique which can be employed. The main types of data are: nominal, ordinal and interval. *Nominal data*, the crudest form of statistics, lack precise measurement and are only recorded in terms of a number of nominated qualities. Presence or absence of a feature, such as retail stores, is the most basic form of information and may be recorded by 1 or 0 in a binary set. Expressed opinions can be fitted to a three-point nominal scale, such as very good, fair, poor on the adequacy of local shopping facilities. *Ordinal data* again accept the absence of precise measurement but are more sophisticated than nominal data in that they assume an ability to rank alternatives. A number of shopping centres, for example, can not only be evaluated in nominal terms but also ranked in order of quality. *Interval data*

R

possess precise qualities of measurement and numerical expression. If statistics, such as the average sale per head, were known, these could be used as more precise measures of shopping centre quality.

Alternative statistical techniques are available to perform similar measurements, depending upon the kind of data being used. Most techniques have been developed in relation to interval data but these have their equivalent where nominal or ordinal data are involved; these alternatives are usually summarised under the headings of parametric and non-parametric statistics. Most parametric techniques assume a normal distribution—values are evenly distributed on either side of the mean. Where this does not occur, transformations of data are necessary to render them suitable for analysis.

MEASURES OF CORRELATION

Where two sets of statistics are available for the same units, such as the proportions of females and children in the various census districts of a city, it is possible to measure the extent to which the two distributions are associated. Where only two variables are involved, simple correlation may be used to measure their relationship. Measures of correlation are termed co-efficients and score within the range $+1 \cdot 0$ to $-1 \cdot 0$. In the example of women and children, one could logically expect a strong direction association and a co-efficient near to $+1 \cdot 0$. If the data had referred to children and old age pensioners, which one might logically expect to be disassociated, the co-efficient might score near $-1 \cdot 0$. The best known correlation co-efficient for use with interval data is Pearson's product moment, whilst non-parametric equivalents for ordinal data are Spearman's rank order and Kendall's *tau* and contingency co-efficients for nominal data. Correlation co-efficients are normally used to measure linear relationships, though non-linear relationships can be analysed.

Correlation is a measure of statistical relationship and does not imply causality; spurious statistical associations can exist and co-efficients should be carefully interpreted. Problems of scale are very relevant to correlation and most geographical studies adopt an ecological scale, accepting that they are not necessarily concerned with identifying individual patterns of association. Regression analysis is closely related to the problem of correlation and involves the estimation of one variable (the dependent variable) from one or more independent variables. Regression lines are best estimates of the relationships between two variables and can be used for predictive purposes; the least squares method of calculation is that which is most commonly used. When more than two variables are involved, multiple regression and multiple correlation techniques have to be used in order to measure the patterns of association in the matrix of variables.

MEASURES OF SIGNIFICANCE

Correlational and regression techniques provide measures of association but their meaning can only be assessed through the use of tests of significance. These tests determine whether observed samples differ from results which could be expected on the basis of pure chance. Levels of significance most commonly used are 1 per cent and 5 per cent, indicating a probability of no more than one and five cases in a hundred, respectively, that a result could have been obtained by chance. There are many tests of significance but those referred to in the text are the Student's T and Snedecor F procedures.

ANALYSIS OF VARIANCE

A common problem in statistics is that of testing whether two samples differ significantly with respect to some defined property. There are many techniques for comparing two sample mean values and the chi-squared test is the best known procedure for comparing differences between observed and expected frequencies. Analysis of variance allows comparison among three or more sets of data where absolute values are known. A series of samples may be selected and the aim is to judge whether these are meaningful groups or patterns or whether they are no different from the overall population. The technique compares within-sample differences with between-sample differences and significance tests can be used to measure the degree of dissimilarity. If between-sample differences are significantly greater than within-sample differences it can be assumed that the sample is a meaningful group or class.

MULTIVARIATE PROCEDURES

Techniques of multivariate analysis can be used with large numbers of variables and are increasingly widely used in geographical research. Conceptually, such techniques involve the idea of multi-dimensionality and the difficulties of visualising measurement in that space are considerable. The recent surge of interest in these techniques is as much associated with improvements in computer technology as it is with awareness of the need for such procedures: indiscriminate use of these procedures can be misleading and unnecessary. Multiple correlation and multiple regression are basic multivariate procedures but the most widely used techniques can be described under the broad heading of factor analysis.

FACTOR ANALYSIS

There are in fact several types of factor analytic procedures of which principal components analysis and principal axes factor analysis have found widest geographical application. The main difference between these could be summarised by stating that principal components is the more general of the two procedures. All forms of factor analysis are measures of association and the correlation matrix is a basic step; at that step, factor analysis substitutes *communalities* along the diagonal of the matrix in order to reduce the amount of variance, but principal components analysis retains unities along the diagonal and deals with total variance. The objective in factor analysis is, through this adjustment, to eliminate meaningless associations, often referred to as 'random noise'. Rotation procedures, which may be applied to obtained components or factors, improve their specificity and make them less ambiguous. Well-known rotation procedures are varimax, which has a constraint of orthogonality, and promax, which allows obliqueness and is thus more flexible. Orthogonality refers to the respective positions of factors in multi-dimensional space.

Factor analysis accepts a large data input which usually takes the form of variables recorded for observations or territorial units. Quality of input data, the overall balance of variables, and the meaningfulness of the territorial units for which they are recorded, are crucial. All variables should possess normal distributions and some studies have used weightings to compensate for the varying size of territorial units. There are three main outputs to factor analysis: eigen values, loadings and scores. Eigen values are measures of each factor's diagnostic power, which can be expressed as proportions of total variance, and are produced in decreasing order of importance. Leading factors in analyses of types of social areas usually account for around 30 per cent of total variance and thus serve as highly efficient summaries of large data inputs. There are as many factors as there are initial variables and the summation of eigen values equals the number of variables; an eigen value of 1·0 is conventionally taken as a cut-off point in deciding the number of factors to be used in subsequent analysis. Loadings are measures of the association between the original input variables and each factor; they are similar in form to correlation co-efficients and possess values within the range +1·0 to −1·0. It is from the evidence of loadings that individual factors can be characterised (nominated as dimensions such as socio-economic status); cut-off points have tended to be arbitrary but significance tests can be used. For each factor scores are allocated to each observation or territorial unit and allow geographical patterns to be identified. This procedural description refers to R-mode analysis in which the variables form the correlation matrix; Q-mode analysis transposes variables and observations. Factor analysis has had a considerable impact in human geography as a summarising device for large data inputs, as a means of identifying dimensions from the pattern of relationships, and as a basic step in classification procedures. The several forms of factor analytic procedure all have particular merits and choice of procedure should be conditioned by the nature of the problem at hand.

CANONICAL CORRELATION

This analytic procedure is another multivariate measure of asociation which can be used to identify the relationships between dimensions in two matrices, called the criterior and the predictor sets. In the example which was quoted (p. 125), the two data sets comprised morphological variables and socio-economic variables and it could be demonstrated that dimensions from the former, such as inter-war detached housing with particular qualities of form, were associated with dimensions from the latter, namely the higher-status groups.

CLASSIFICATORY PROCEDURES

Classification or taxonomy is a recurrent theme in geographical studies and a very wide range of classificatory techniques have been developed. Techniques of cluster analysis have emerged strongly in more recent years as procedures which can operate for a large number of variables. The type of cluster analysis described in the text involves a step-wise procedure by which initially discrete units are joined according to their similarity or proximity in multi-dimensional space, the dimensions of which are determined by the number of scores recorded for each unit. At each step the two most similar units are combined and become one unit for successive steps; as the analysis proceeds, distinctive clusters emerge until by the ultimate step the formerly separate units have been reduced to one macro-region. Another classificatory scheme referred to in the context of crime studies (p. 213) was predictive attribute analysis in which a classification procedure is used not merely as a descriptive device—allocating individuals to groups on the basis of their similarities—but also as a means of predicting the values of characteristics which have not been directly measured. These inferential qualities have great potential but need careful handling.

SIMULATION

Simulation techniques have found particular application to those aspects of human geography which are concerned with predicting growth patterns over time. Simulation has some advantage over other predictive techniques in that it has flexibility; it has been described as the basis for a stochastic model in which elements of chance can be incorporated. Probability theory is strongly involved in simulation and the most widely used technique in geography is the Monte Carlo method.

MEASUREMENT OF GEOGRAPHIC PERCEPTION

Recent research concerned with perception, such as analyses of spatial preferences, has posed new measurement problems because the data are rarely available in interval form. In some instances, techniques have been devised by which data can be transformed into a form suitable for measurement by normal parametric techniques; in others, such as studies based on ranking of preferences, a non-parametric technique—such as Spearman's rank order co-efficient—can be used. An example of the latter is given by studies which obtain a correlation matrix from a rank order co-efficient and subsequently apply factor analysis to the matrix. Attention has also been focused upon previously little-used procedures designed for nominal data. Scaling techniques, which have been widely used by social psychologists, involve the fitting of quantitative scores to qualitative information. These techniques have application to geographical problems but an adequately tested range of measures has yet to become available in geographic research. An advantage of non-parametric techniques is that they contain fewer basic assumptions about the qualities of data.

SETS AND SYSTEMS

Sets and, more particularly, systems are general scientific methodologies which have strong appeal to geographers as unifying conceptual frameworks and as integrated bodies of techniques. A set is defined as an arbitrary but well-defined collection of objects which are called the elements of the set. The terms 'tree' and 'semi-lattice' which occurred in the context of neighbourhood planning describe two types of set; the former simple with compartmentalised elements, the latter complex with overlapping elements.

A system is less easily defined but generally it could be stated that when the elements of a set belong together because they co-operate or work together, this constitutes a system. A further quality, besides the elements and their inter-relationship, could be the relationship between the elements and their environment. One basic distinction is that between open and closed systems: the former are able to interact with the environment, whilst the latter are not. Although, in reality, geographical work is concerned with open systems, an assumption of the closed system may provide a useful working model.

ACKNOWLEDGEMENTS

My sincere thanks are due to numerous people who have in some way helped in the production of this book. I am grateful to Professor W. G. V. Balchin for his encouragement and for his willingness to make departmental facilities available, and to the rest of my colleagues at Swansea for their interest and contribution towards a convivial working atmosphere. The cartographic illustrations were drawn by Mrs A. Szendro and Mr G. B. Lewis, with some assistance from Mrs Wendy Nelmes. Mr E. Price produced the photographic illustrations and Miss Jenny Davies typed the manuscript. I have been fortunate to have access to such a range of expertise and am extremely grateful to those concerned. Several of the photographic illustrations were provided by my colleagues Mr H. R. J. Davies and Dr J. A. Edwards, and I thank Mr L. G. Moseley for his comments on Chapter 7 and Dr J. P. Dickenson for permission to use his Latin American photographic illustrations. Particular thanks are due to Professor R. Lawton who, besides initiating the process by which I wrote this book, has also edited the manuscript in an extremely detailed and constructive way. Lastly, my thanks to my parents for their consistent interest and support, and to my wife who has affably tolerated my long periods of absence from her company and who has helped in many ways.

DAVID HERBERT

Department of Geography,
University College of Swansea
June 1972

NOTES

No detailed bibliography has been included with the book since the notes to each chapter contain a good deal of bibliographical material and comprise a comprehensive review of the literature. Some general texts on methodology and techniques are listed as notes to the Appendix (p. 312).

CHAPTER ONE

1 The United Nations Organisation has sponsored many inter-disciplinary studies of world urban problems and publications include Hauser, Philip M. (ed), *Urbanisation in Asia and the Far East* (UNESCO 1957) and Hauser, Philip M. (ed), *Urbanisation in Latin America* (UNESCO 1961)

2 The team of consultants assembled by the Rouse Corporation for the planning and development of Columbia, Maryland, USA, covered a wide range of disciplines and expertise
   Also relevant in this context is the work of the Athens Centre for Ekistics in co-ordinating disciplines particularly through its annual Delos Symposium

3 Questions of definition are discussed by Buttimer, Anne, 'Social Geography', *International Encyclopaedia of the Social Sciences*, 6 (1968), 134–45

4 Systems analysis is discussed in a geographical context by Harvey, David, *Explanation in Geography* (Arnold, 1969), 449–80

5 Berry, B. J. L., 'A Synthesis of Formal and Functional Region using a General Field Theory of Spatial Behaviour' in Berry, B. J. L. and Marble, D. F., *Spatial Analysis* (Prentice-Hall, 1968), 419–28

6 Blalock, H. M., *Causal Inferences in Non-experimental Research* (University of North Carolina Press, 1964), 99

7 Berry, B. J. L. and Horton, F. E., *Geographic Perspectives on Urban Systems* (Prentice-Hall, 1970), 250–71

8 The Redcliffe-Maud Report, *Royal Commission on Local Government in England*, 1966-69 (HMSO, 1969)

CHAPTER TWO

1 United Nations Bureau of Social Affairs, Population Division, 'World Urbanisation Trends, 1920–1960' (An Interim Report of Work in Progress) in Breese, Gerald (ed), *The City in Newly Developing Countries* (Prentice-Hall, 1969), 21–53

2 See Davis, Kingsley, 'The Urbanisation of the Human Population', *Scientific American* 213 (1965), 40–53

3 Figures from United Nations, 'World Urbanisation Trends', 28 and 43

4 Figures from Hoyt, Homer and Pickard, Jerome P., 'The World's Million-Population Metropolis', *Urban Land*, 23 (1964), 7–10; and Hoyt, Homer, 'Growth and Structure of Twenty-One Great World Cities', *Land Economics*, 42 (1966), 53–64

5 Blumenfeld, Hans, 'The Modern Metropolis', in Scientific American Book, *Cities* (A. A. Knopf, 1967), 40–57

6 Gottman, Jean, *Megalopolis: the Urbanised North-eastern Seaboard of the United States* (Twentieth Century Fund, 1961)

7 The idea of ecumenopolis appears frequently in the journal *Ekistics*; see 'The Ekistics Grid', *Ekistics*, 19 (1965), 210

8 Sovani, N. V., 'The Analysis of Over-urbanisation', *Economic Development and Cultural Change*, 12 (1964), 113–22

9 Jefferson, Mark, 'The Law of the Primate City', *The Geographical Review*, 29 (1939), 226–32

10 Zipf, G. K., *Human Behaviour and the Principle of Least Effort* (Addison-Wesley, 1949)

11 Stewart, C. T., 'The Size and Spacing of Cities', *The Geographical Review*, 48 (1958), 222–45

12 Berry, B. J. L. and Garrison, W. L., 'Alternate Explanations of Urban Rank-Size Relationships', *Annals of the Association of American Geographers*, 48 (1958), 83–91

13 Wirth, Louis, 'Urbanism as a Way of Life', *American Journal of Sociology*, 44 (1938), 1–24
14 See discussion in Reissman, L., *The Urban Process* (Free Press, 1964), 123
15 Lewis, Oscar, 'The Culture of Poverty', *Scientific American*, 215 (1966), 19–25
16 Abu Lughod, Janet, 'Migrant Adjustment to City Life: The Egyptian Case', *American Journal of Sociology*, 67 (1961), 22–32
17 Hoselitz, B. F., 'Urbanisation: International Comparisons' in Turner, R. (ed), *India's Urban Future* (University of California Press, 1962)
18 Pahl, R. E., *Urbs in Rure : The Metropolitan Fringe in Hertfordshire*, London School of Economics and Political Science, Geographical Papers 2 (1965)
19 Hall, Peter, *The World Cities* (Weidenfeld and Nicolson, 1966), 134–5
20 Best, R. H., 'Competition for land between rural and urban uses' in *Land Use and Resources : Studies in Applied Geography* (Institute of British Geographers, 1968), 89–100
21 Mumford, L., *The City in History* (Pelican Books, 1966)
22 Ibid., 540
23 Fisher, J. C. (ed), *City and Regional Planning in Poland* (Cornell University Press, 1966), 154
24 Cullingworth, J. B., *Town and Country Planning in England and Wales* (Allen and Unwin, 1967)
25 Hall, P., *The World Cities*, 76
26 The Housing, Town Planning etc Act 1919
27 *Town Planning and Ground Exploitation in Amsterdam*, Office of Director of Public Works (Amsterdam, 1967), 23
28 Fisher, J. C., *City and Regional Planning in Poland*, 158
29 Hall, P., *The World Cities*, 169
30 Town and Country Planning (1971), 46–47
31 Eichler, E. P. and Norwitch, B., 'New Towns' in Moynihan, D. (ed), *Urban America* (US Information Service, 1970), 345
32 Williams, D. G., 'The Modal Split', *Town Planning Review*, 42 (1971), 180–94
33 Turner, F. C., 'Highways and Public Transportation', *Metropolitan* (1970), 21–4

34 Town Planning in Amsterdam, 11–12
35 Toynbee, A., 'The Coming World City', *Ekistics*, 182 (1971), 112
36 Lindsay, J. V., *The City* (W. W. Norton, 1969)
37 Davy, J., 'Polluting the Planet', *Ekistics*, 27 (1969), 165–7
38 Ayres, R. U. and Knees, A. V., 'Pollution and Environmental Quality, in Perloff, H. S. (ed), *The Quality of the Urban Environment* (Resources for Future Inc., 1969), 35–71
39 Clawson, M., 'Open (uncovered) Space as an Urban Resource' in Perloff, H. S. (ed), *The Quality of the Urban Environment* (Resources for Future Inc., 1969), 139–175
40 Mabogunje, A. L., *Urbanisation in Nigeria* (University of London Press, 1968), 314
41 Breese, G., *Urbanisation in Newly Developing Countries* (Prentice-Hall, 1966), 5
42 Abrams, C., *Man's Struggle for Shelter in an Urbanising World* (M.I.T. Press, 1964)
43 Turner, J. F. C., 'Uncontrolled Urban Settlement: Problems and Policies' in Breese, G. (ed), *The City in Newly Developing Countries* (Prentice-Hall, 1969), 507–34
44 Rosser, C., 'Housing for the Lowest Income Group: the Calcutta Experience', *Ekistics*, 183 (1971), 126–31
45 McGee, T., *The South-east Asian City* (G. Bell and Sons Ltd., 1967), 145
46 Mabogunje, A. L., *Urbanisation in Nigeria*, 291
47 Report 'Transport and Communication in Asia and the Far East', *Ekistics*, 29 (1970), 14–19
48 McGee, T., *The South-east Asian City*, 20
49 Pye, L. W., 'The Political Implications of Urbanisation and the Development Process' in Breese, G. (ed), *Urbanisation in Newly Developing Countries*, 401–6
50 Doxiadis, C. A., 'Preparing Ourselves for the City of Tomorrow,' *Ekistics*, 27 (1969), 274–9
51 Toynbee, A., 'The Coming World City'

CHAPTER THREE

1   Valuable recent review statements on theories include: Hauser, P. M. and Schnore, L. F., *The Study of Urbanisa-*

tion (Wiley, 1965) and Berry, B. J. L. and Horton, F. E., *Geographic Perspectives on Urban Systems* (Prentice-Hall, 1970)

2   Harvey, D., 'Social Processes and Spatial Form: An Analysis of the Conceptual Problems of Urban Planning', *Papers of the Regional Science Association*, 25 (1970), 47–69

3   Reissman, L., *The Urban Process* (Free Press, 1964)

4   Reissman, L., *The Urban Process*

5   Wirth, L., 'Urbanism as a Way of Life', *American Journal of Sociology*, 44 (1938), 1–24

6   Morris, R. N., *Urban Sociology* (Allen and Unwin, 1968)

7   Sjoberg, G., *The Pre-Industrial City* (Free Press, 1960)

8   Schnore, L. F., 'On the Spatial Structure of Cities in the Two Americas' in Hauser, P. M. and Schnore, L. F., *The Study of Urbanisation* (Wiley, 1965), 347–98

9   McKenzie, R. D., *The Metropolitan Community* (McGraw Hill, 1933)

10 Hall, P., *The World Cities* (Weidenfeld and Nicolson, 1966)

11 McGee, T., *The South-east Asian City* (Bell, 1967)

12 Gottman, J., *Megalopolis, the Urbanised North-eastern Seaboard of the United States* (New York: The Twentieth Century Fund, 1961)

13 Morris, R. N., *Urban Sociology*, xi–xii

14 Hurd, R. M., *Principles of City Land Values* (New York: The Record and Guide, 1903)

15 Reissman, L., *The Urban Process*

16 Park, R. E., 'Suggestions for the Investigation of Human Behaviour in the Urban Environment' in Park, R. E., Burgess, E. W. and McKenzie, R. D., *The City* (University of Chicago Press, 1925)

17 Park, R. E., 'Investigation of Human Behaviour'

18 McKenzie, R. D., 'The Scope of Human Ecology' in Burgess, E. W. (ed), *The Urban Community* (University of Chicago Press, 1925)

19 McKenzie, R. D., 'Scope of Human Ecology'

20 Park, R. E., 'Human Ecology', *American Journal of Sociology*, 42, No 1 (1936)

21 Firey, W. E., *Land Use in Central Boston* (Harvard University Press, 1947)

22 Jones, E., *A Social Geography of Belfast* (Oxford University Press, 1960)

23 Alihan, Milla, *Social Ecology* (Columbia University Press, 1938)

24 Duncan, O. D., 'From Social System to Ecosystem', Sociological Inquiry, 31, No 2 (1961), reprinted in Meadows, Paul and Mizruchi, Ephraim H. (eds), *Urbanism, Urbanisation and Change: Comparative Perspectives* (Addison-Wesley, 1969), 89

25 Wirth, L., 'Human Ecology', *American Journal of Sociology*, 50 (1945), 483–8

26 Quinn, J., *Human Ecology* (Prentice-Hall, 1950)

27 Hawley, A., *Human Ecology* (Ronald Press, 1950)

28 Theodorson, G. A. (ed), *Studies in Human Ecology* (Row, Peterson, 1961), 129

29 Schnore, L. F., 'Spatial Structure of Cities', also Willhelm, Sidney M., 'The Concept of the Ecological Complex: A Critique', *American Journal of Economics and Sociology*, 23 (1964), 241–8

30 Harvey, D., *Explanation in Geography* (Arnold, 1969)

31 Gist, N. P. and Fava, Sylvia Fleis, *Urban Society* (Crowell, 1966), 101

32 Chase, S., *The Proper Study of Mankind* (Harper, 1948), 21

33 Willhelm, S. M., 'Concept of the Ecological Complex'

34 Christaller, W., *Central Places in Southern Germany* (Prentice-Hall, 1966)

35 Burton, I., 'The Quantitative Revolution and Theoretical Geography', *The Canadian Geographer*, 7 (1963), 16

36 Berry, B. J. L. and Horton, F. E., *Geographic Perspectives*, 13–14

37 Houston, J. M., *The Social Geography of Europe*

38 Dickinson, R. E., *The West European City* (Routledge & Kegan Paul, 1951)

39 Smailes, A. E., 'Some Reflections on the Geographical Description and Analysis of Townscapes', *The Institute of British Geographers Transactions and Papers*, 21 (1955), 99–115

40 See, for example, Stedman, M. B., 'The Townscape of Birmingham in 1956', *The Institute of British Geographers, Transactions and Papers*, 25 (1958)

41 Proceedings of the IGU Symposium in Urban Geography, *Lund Series B*, No 24 (1962)
42 Miller, R. and Watson, J. W. (eds), *Geographical Essays in Memory of Alan G. Ogilvie* (Nelson, 1959), 110–43
43 Whitehand, J. W. R., 'Fringe Belts. A Neglected Aspect of Urban Geography', *Transactions of the Institute of British Geographers*, 41 (1967), 223–33
44 Davies, W. K. D., 'The Morphology of Central Places: A Case Study', *Annals of the Association of American Geographers*, 58 (1967), 91–110
45 Horwood, E. M. and Boyce, R. R., *Studies of the Central Business District and Urban Freeway Development* (Seattle: University of Washington, 1959)
46 Chapin, F. S., *Urban Land-use Planning* (University of Illinois Press, 1965)
47 Bourne, L. S., *Private Redevelopment of the Central City* (University of Chicago, Department of Geography, Research Paper No 112, 1967)
48 Openshaw, S., 'Canonical Correlates of Social Structure and Urban Building Fabric: An Exploratory Study', *Department of Geography, University of Newcastle-upon-Tyne Seminar Papers II* (1969)
49 Dyos, H. J., *Victorian Suburb* (Leicester University Press, 1961)
50 Haggett, P., *Locational Analysis in Human Geography* (Arnold, 1965), 9–17
51 Berry, B. J. L. and Horton, F. E., *Geographic Perspectives*, 18
52 Harvey, D., *Explanation in Geography* (Arnold, 1969)
53 Hagerstrand, T., 'Migration and Area' in Hannerberg, D., *et al.* (eds), *Migration in Sweden*, Lund Series B (1957)
54 Bunge, W., *Theoretical Geography*, Lund Series C (1966)
55 Berry, B. J. L., *Essays on Commodity Flows and the Spatial Structure of the Indian Economy* (Department of Geography, University of Chicago Research Paper, III, 1966).
56 Robson, B. T., *Urban Analysis* (Cambridge University Press, 1970)
57 Harvey, D., 'Social Processes and Spatial Form: An Analysis of the Conceptual Problems of Urban Planning', *Papers: The Regional Science Association*, 25 (1970), 47–69

S

58 Clark, Sir Kenneth, remark in BBC series *Civilisation* (1971)
59 Burgess, E. W., 'The Growth of the City', in Park, R. E., Burgess, E. W. and McKenzie, R. D., *The City* (University of Chicago Press, 1925)
    Hoyt, H., *The Structure and Growth of Residential Neighbourhoods in American Cities* (Washington: Federal Housing Administration, 1939)
    Harris, C. D. and Ullman, E. L., 'The Nature of Cities', *The Annals of the American Academy of Political and Social Science*, 242 (1945), 7–17
60 Murdie, R. A., *Factorial Ecology of Metropolitan Toronto 1951–61* (University of Chicago Department of Geography Research Paper No 116, 1969)
61 Hall, P. (ed), *Von Thünnen's Isolated State* (Pergamon, 1966)
62 Berry, B. J. L., 'Internal Structure of the City', *Law and Contemporary Problems*, 30 (1965), 115
63 Sjoberg, G., *The Pre-Industrial City* (Free Press, 1960), Schnore, Leo F., 'On the Spatial Structure of Cities in the Two Americas' in Hauser, P. M. and Schnore, Leo F., *The Study of Urbanisation* (Wiley, 1965), 347–98
64 Hoyt, H., 'Recent Distortions of the Classical Models of Urban Structure', *Land Economics*, 40 (1964), 199–212
65 Alonso, W., 'The Historic and Structural Theories of Urban Form: Their Implications for Urban Renewal', *Land Economics*, 40 (1964), 227–31
66 See, for example, Lowry, I. S., 'A Short Course in Model Design', *Journal of the American Institute of Planners*, 31 (1965), 158–65
67 Chisholm, M., 'Priority Research Areas in Human Geography', *Social Science Research Council, Newsletter*, 11 (1971), 15
68 See, Harvey, D., *Explanation in Geography* (Arnold, 1969), 141–186

CHAPTER FOUR

1 Sjoberg, G., *The Pre-Industrial City* (Free Press, 1960)
2 Vance, J. E., 'Land Assignment in the Pre-Capitalist, Capitalist, and Post-Capitalist City', *Economic Geography*, 47 (1971), 101–20

3   Vance, J. E., 'Focus on Downtown' in Bourne, L. S. (ed), *Internal Structure of the City* (Oxford University Press, 1971), 119–20

4   Proudfoot, M. J., 'City Retail Structure', *Economic Geography*, 13 (1937), 425–8

5   Olsson, W. W., 'Stockholm: Its Structure and Development', *Geographical Review*, 30 (1940), 420–38

6   Murphy, R. E. and Vance, J. E., 'Delimiting the CBD', *Economic Geography*, 30 (1954), 189–222; and 'A Comparative Study of Nine Central Business Districts', *Economic Geography*, 30 (1954), 301–36; and (with Epstein, B. J.) 'Internal Structure of the CBD', *Economic Geography*, 31 (1955), 21–46

7   Davies, D. H., 'Boundary Study as a Tool in CBD Analysis: An Interpretation of Certain Aspects of the Boundary of Cape Town's Central Business District', *Economic Geography*, 35 (1959), 322–45

8   e.g. Weir, T. R., 'Land Use and Population Characteristics of Central Winnipeg', *Geographical Bulletin*, Department of Mines and Technical Surveys (1956), 5–21

9   Davies, D. H., *Economic Geography*, 322–45

10 Herbert, D. T., 'An Approach to the Study of the Town as a Central Place', *Sociological Review* 9 (1961), 273–92

11 Murphy, R. E., *The American City : An Urban Geography* (McGraw Hill, 1966), 290

12 Davies, D. H., 'The Hard Core of Cape Town's CBD', *Economic Geography*, 36 (1960), 53–69

13 Pred, A., 'Impromptu Impressions and Reactions' in Brill, E. J. (ed), *Urban Core and Inner City* (Leiden, 1967), 542–49

14 Vance, J. E., 'Focus on Downtown', 115–16

15 Horwood, E. M. and Boyce, R. R., *Studies of the Central Business District and Urban Freeway Development* (University of Washington Press, 1959)

16 Diamond, D. R., 'The Central Business District of Glasgow', *Proceedings of the IGU Symposium in Urban Geography*, *Lund Series in Geography*, Series B 24 (1962), 525–34

17 Olsson, W. W., op cit

18 Herbert, D. T. and Davies, W. K. D., 'The Central Business District of Swansea: An Introductory Study of Functional Structure', *Swansea Geographer*, 6 (1968), 23–33

19 Scott, P., 'The Australian CBD', *Economic Geography*, 35 (1959), 290–314

20 Smith, L., 'Space for CBD functions' in Bourne, L. S., *Internal Structure of the City* (Oxford University Press, 1971), 356

21 Chapin, F. S. and Logan, H., 'Patterns of Time and Space Use' in Perloff, S. (ed), *The Quality of the Urban Environment* (The John Hopkins Press, 1969), 327

22 Chapin, F. S., *Urban Land Use Planning* (Urbana, University of Illinois Press, 1965)

23 Goddard, J. B., 'Functional Regions within the City Centre: A Study by Factor Analysis of Taxi Flows in Central London', *Transactions of the Institute of British Geographers*, 49 (1970), 161–182

24 Murphy, Raymond E. and Vance, J. E., *Economic Geography*, 31 (1955), 21–46

25 Bowden, M. J., 'Downtown through Time: Delimitation, Expansion and Internal Growth', *Economic Geography*, 47 (1971), 121–35, and Weaver, D. C., 'Changes in the Morphology of Three American Central Business Districts 1952–66', *Professional Geographer*, 21 (1969), 406–10

26 Herbert, D. T., *Some Aspects of Social Geography in the North Staffordshire Conurbation*, unpublished Ph.D. thesis (University of Birmingham, 1964)

27 Davies, W. K. D., Giggs, J. A. and Herbert, D. T., 'Directories, Rate Books and the Commercial Structure of Towns', *Geography*, 53 (1968), 41–54

28 Scholler, P., 'Centre Shifting and Centre Mobility in Japanese Cities', *Proceedings of the IGU Symposium in Urban Geography, Lund Studies in Geography*, Series B 24 (1962)

29 See Prokop, D., 'Image and Functions of the City' in Brill, E. J. (ed), *Urban Core and Inner City* (Leiden, 1967), 22–34

30 Vance, J. E., 'Focus on Downtown' (1971)

31 Pred, A., 'Impromptu Impressions and Reactions' in Brill, E. J. (ed), *Urban Core and Inner City* (Leiden, 1967), 542–9

32 Nelson, R. L., 'Land Values in the US', *Urban Land*, 28 (1969)

33 Hoyt, Homer, 'US Metro Area Retail Shopping Patterns', *Urban Land*, 25 (1966)

34 Vance, J. E., 'Emerging Patterns of Commercial Structure

in American Cities', *Proceedings of the IGU Symposium in Urban Geography, Lund Studies in Geography*, Series B, 24 (1962), 495

35 Allpass, J., 'Changes in the Structure of Urban Centres', *Journal of the American Institute of Planners*, 34 (1968), 170–3

36 Dickinson, R. E., *City and Region* (Routledge and Kegan Paul, 1964)

37 McKeever, J. R., 'What's New in Europe's Urban Development', *Urban Land*, 27 (1968)

38 McKeever, J. R., 'What's New in Europe's Urban Development', *Urban Land*, 27 (1968)

39 Ward, D., 'The Industrial Revolution and the Emergence of Boston's CBD', *Economic Geography*, 42 (1966), 152–71

40 Firey, W. E., *Land Use in Central Boston* (Harvard University Press, 1947)

41 Gans, H., *The Urban Villagers* (The Free Press of Glencoe, 1962)

42 Burgess, E. W., 'The Growth of the City' in Park, R. E., Burgess, E. W. and McKenzie, R. D., *The City* (University of Chicago Press, 1925)

43 Zorbaugh, H., *The Gold Coast and the Slum* (University of Chicago Press, 1929)

44 Wirth, L., *The Ghetto* (University of Chicago Press, 1928)

45 Gist, N. P. and Fava, Sylvia F., *Urban Society* (T. Y. Crowell, 1966), 174

46 Morrill, R. L., 'The Negro Ghetto: Problems and Alternatives', *The Geographical Review*, 40 (1965), 339–61

47 Rose, H. M., 'Metropolitan Miami's Changing Negro Population 1950–1960', *Economic Geography*, 40 (1964), 221–38

48 Friesema, H. P., 'Black Control of Cities: The Hollow Prize', *Journal of the American Institute of Planners*, 35 (1969), 75–9

49 Hunter, D. R., *The Slums: Challenge and Response* (Free Press of Glencoe, 1964)

50 Wilson, J. Q., *Urban Renewal* (MIT Press, 1966)

51 Anderson, M., *The Federal Bulldozer: A Critical Analysis of Urban Renewal, 1949–62* (MIT Press, 1964)

52 Gans, H. J., 'The Failure of Urban Renewal', in Wilson, J. Q., *Urban Renewal* (MIT Press, 1966), 537–57

53 Fried, M., 'Grieving for a Lost Home: Psychological Costs of Relocation' in Wilson, J. Q., *Urban Renewal* (MIT Press, 1966), 359–79

54 Foote, Nelson N. *et al.*, *Housing Choices and Housing Constraints* (McGraw-Hill, 1960)

55 Alonso, W., 'The Historical and Structural Theories of Urban Form: Their Implications for Urban Renewal', *Land Economics*, 40 (1964), 227–31

56 For a discussion of the Toronto case, see Bourne, L. S., 'Market, Location and Site Selection in Apartment Construction', *Canadian Geographer*, 12 (1968), 211–26

57 Davis, J. T., 'Middle Class Housing in the Central City', *Economic Geography*, 41 (1965), 238–51

58 Perloff, H., 'Newtowns Intown', *Journal of the American Institute of Planners*, 32 (1966), 155–61

59 Bourne, L. S., *Private Redevelopment of the Central City* (University of Chicago, Department of Geography Research Paper 112, 1967)

60 Murphy, R. E., *The American City* (McGraw Hill, 1966), 314

61 Griffin, D. W. and Preston, R. E., 'A Restatement of the Transition Zone Concept', *Annals of the Association of American Geographers*, 56 (1966), 339–50; 'The Zone in Transition: A Study of Urban Land Use Patterns', *Economic Geography*, 42 (1966), 236–60; and 'A Reply to Comments on the Transition Zone Concept', *Professional Geographer*, 21 (1969), 232–7

62 Bourne, L. S., 'Comments on the Transition Zone Concept', *Professional Geographer*, 20 (1968), 313–16

63 Bourne, L. S., *Private Redevelopment of the Central City* (1967)

64 Rannels, J., *The Core of the City* (Columbia University Press, 1956)

65 Castle, I. M. and Gittus, E., 'The Distribution of Social Defects in Liverpool', *Sociological Review*, 5 (1957), 43–64

66 See Patterson, S., *Dark Strangers: A Study of West Indians in London* (Penguin Books, 1965); Burney, E., *Housing on Trial* (Oxford University Press, 1967); Jones, P. N., *The Segregation of Immigrant Communities in the City of Birmingham, 1961*, University of Hull: Occasional Papers in Geography No 7 (1967)

67 Hall, P., *The World Cities* (Weidenfeld and Nicolson, 1966), 43–44
68 Rex, J. A., 'The Sociology of a Zone in Transition' in Pahl, R. E. (ed), *Readings in Urban Sociology* (Pergamon, 1968), 211–31
69 Chombart de Lauwe, P. H., *Paris et L'Agglomeration Parisienne*, 1 (Paris, 1952)
70 Mukerjee, R., 'Ways of Dwelling in the Communities of India' in Theodorson, G. A. (ed), *Studies in Human Ecology* (Row Peterson, 1961), 390–401
71 Mukerjee, R., op cit, 305
72 Mukerjee, R., op cit, 398–99
73 Mabogunje, A. L., *Urbanisation in Nigeria* (University of London Press, 1968)
74 Caplow, T., 'The Social Ecology of Guatemala City', *Social Forces*, 28 (1949), 113–135
75 de Blij, H. J., 'The Functional Structure and Central Business District of Lourenço Marques, Mozambique', *Economic Geography*, 38 (1962), 56–77
76 Breese, G. (ed), *The City in Newly Developing Countries* (Prentice-Hall, 1969), 452
77 Abrams, C., *Man's Struggle for Shelter in an Urbanising World* (MIT Press, 1968)
78 Mabogunje, A. L., *Urbanisation in Nigeria*, 235
79 Lewis, O., *The Children of Sanchez* (Random House, 1961), and *Five Families* (Basic Books Inc., 1959)
80 Turner, J. F. C., 'Uncontrolled Urban Settlement: Problems and Policies' in Breese, G. (ed), *The City in Newly Developing Countries* (Prentice-Hall, 1969), 507–31
81 Mabogunje, A. L., *Urbanisation in Nigeria*, 226
82 Meier, R. L. and Hoshino, I., 'Cultural Growth and Urban Development in Inner Tokyo', *Journal of the American Institute of Planners*, 35 (1969), 210–22
83 Meier, R. L., 'Exploring Development in Great Asian Cities: Seoul', *Journal of the American Institute of Planners*, 36 (1970), 379

CHAPTER FIVE

1 Ginsburg, N., 'Tasks of Geography', *Geography*, 54 (1969), 401–9

2   Buttimer, Anne, 'Social Space in Interdisciplinary Perspective', *Geographical Review*, 54 (1969), 417–26 and Hall, E. T., *The Silent Language* (Premier Books, New York, 1965)

3   Harvey, D., 'Social Processes and Spatial Form: An Analysis of the Conceptual Problems of Urban Planning', *Papers of the Regional Science Association*, 25 (1970), 47–69

4   See Buttimer, Anne, op cit

5   Rees, P. H., 'Concepts of Social Space: Toward an Urban Social Geography', in Berry, B. J. L. and Horton, F. E. (eds), *Geographic Perspectives on Urban Systems* (Prentice-Hall, 1970), 306–94

6   See Buttimer, Anne, op cit, and Chombart de Lauwe, *Paris et l'Agglomeration Parisienne* (Paris, 1952)

7   Rees, P. H., op cit

8   See Robinson, W. S., 'Ecological Correlations and the Behaviour of Individuals', *American Sociological Review*, 15 (1950), 351–7; Goodman, L. A., 'Some Alternatives to Ecological Correlation', *American Journal of Sociology*, 44 (1959), 610–25; Duncan, O. D., Cuzzort, R. P. and Duncan, B., *Statistical Geography; Problems in Analysing Areal Data* (Free Press of Glencoe, 1961)

9   Spence, N. A. and Taylor, P. J., 'Quantitative Methods in Regional Taxonomy', in Board, C. *et al.* (eds), *Progress in Geography*, 2 (Arnold, 1970)

10   Smailes, A. E., 'Towns', in Watson, J. W. and Sissons, J. B. (eds), *The British Isles: A Systematic Geography* (Nelson, 1964), 380–402

11   Thurston, H. S., 'The Urban Regions of St Albans', *Transactions of the Institute of British Geographers*, 19 (1953), 107–21

12   Conzen, M. R. G., 'Alnwick, Northumberland, a Study in Town Plan Analysis', *Transactions of the Institute of British Geographers*, 27 (1960)

13   Openshaw, S., 'Canonical Correlates of Social Structure and Urban Building Fabric: An Exploratory Study', *Department of Geography, University of Newcastle-upon-Tyne, Seminar Papers*, 11 (1969)

14   Johnston, R. J., 'Towards an Analytical Study of the Townscape: The Residential Building Fabric', *Geografiska Annaler*, 51 B (1969), 20–32

15 Amato, P. W., 'Residential Amenities and Neighbourhood Qualities', *Ekistics*, 28 (1969), 180–4

16 Jones, P. N., 'Colliery Settlement in the South Wales Coalfield, 1850 to 1926,' *University of Hull, Occasional Papers in Geography*, 14 (University of Hull Publications, 1969)

17 Musil, J., 'The Development of Prague's Ecological Structure', in Pahl, R. E. (ed), *Readings in Urban Sociology* (Pergamon, 1968), 232–59

18 Park, R. E., 'Human Ecology', *American Journal of Sociology*, 42 (1936), 1–15

19 Alihan, Milla, *Social Ecology* (Columbia University Press, 1938)

20 Zorbaugh, H. W., *The Gold Coast and the Slum* (The University of Chicago Press, 1929)

21 Wirth, Louis, *The Ghetto* (University of Chicago Press, 1928)

22 Wirth, Louis, *The Ghetto*

23 Hatt, P., 'The Concept of the Natural Area', *American Sociological Review*, 11 (1946), 423–7

24 Hurd, R. M., 'Principles of City Land Values' (*New York Record and Guide*, 1903)

25 Hoyt, H., *The Structure and Growth of Residential Neighbourhoods in American Cities* (United States Government Printing Office, 1939)

26 Herbert, D. T. and Williams, W. M., 'Some New Techniques for Studying Urban Sub-Divisions', *Applied Geography II*, Geographia Polonica, 3 (Warsaw, 1964), 93–117

27 Jones, R., 'Segregation in Urban Residential Districts: Examples and Research Problems', in *Proceedings of the I.G.U. Symposium in Urban Geography* (Lund, 1962), 433–46

28 Robson, B. T., 'An Ecological Analysis of the Evolution of Residential Areas in Sunderland', *Urban Studies*, 3 (1966), 120–42

29 Jones, E., *A Social Geography of Belfast* (Oxford University Press, 1960)

30 Form, W. H., Smith, J., Stone, G. P. and Cowhig, J., 'The Compatibility of Alternative Approaches to the Delimitation of Urban Sub-Areas', *American Sociological Review*, 19 (1954), 434–40

31 McElrath, D. C., 'The Social Areas of Rome: A Comparative Analysis', *American Sociological Review*, 27 (1962), 376–91

32 Berry, B. J. L. and Rees, P. H., 'The Factorial Ecology of Calcutta', *American Journal of Sociology*, 74 (1968–69), 445–91

33 Robson, B. T., *Urban Analysis: A Study of City Structure* (Cambridge University Press, 1969)

34 Census of Canada, 1961. Dominion Bureau of Statistics, Ottawa, Canada. A description of census tract delineation prefaces each city volume in the census tract series

35 Jones, E., *A Social Geography of Belfast*, 204

36 Shevky, E. and Williams, Marilyn, *The Social Areas of Los Angeles* (University of California Press, 1949) and Shevky, E. and Bell, W., *Social Area Analysis: Theory, Illustrative Application and Computational Procedures* (Stanford University Press, 1955)

37 Bell, W., 'Economic, Family and Ethnic Status: An Empirical Test', *American Sociological Review*, 20 (1955), 45–52

38 Shevky, E. and Williams, Marilyn, *The Social Areas of Los Angeles* and Bell, Wendell, 'The Social Areas of the San Francisco Bay Region', *American Sociological Review*, 18 (1953), 39–47

39 Van Arsdol, M. D., Camilleri, S. F. and Schmid, C. F., 'The Generality of Urban Social Area Indices', *American Sociological Review*, 23 (1958), 277–84

40 Herbert, D. T., 'Social Area Analysis: A British Study', *Urban Studies*, 4 (1967), 41–60

41 A correlation of 0·03 between fertility and women at work ratios was obtained by Warnes, A. J. in an unpublished study of Chorley, Lancs: and of 0·11 for Cardiff by Inder, R. A., 'Social Area Analysis', *The Swansea Geographer*, 9 (1971), 73–82

42 McElrath, D. C., op cit

43 Anderson, T. R. and Egeland, J. A., 'Spatial Aspects of Social Area Analysis', *American Sociological Review*, 26 (1961), 392–9

44 Hawley, A. H. and Duncan, O. D., 'Social Area Analysis: A Critical Appraisal', *Land Economics*, 33 (1957), 337–45

45 Jones, F. L., 'Social Area Analysis: Some Theoretical and Methodological Comments illustrated with Australian Data', *British Journal of Sociology*, 19 (1968), 424–44

46 Udry, J. R., 'Increasing Scale and Spatial Differentiation: New Tests of Two Theories from Shevky and Bell', *Social Forces*, 42 (1964), 403–13

47 Anderson, T. R. and Bean, L. L., 'The Shevky-Bell Social Areas: Confirmation of Results and a Re-Interpretation', *Social Forces*, 40 (1961), 119–124

48 Beshers, J. M., *Urban Social Structure* (Free Press of Glencoe, 1962)

49 Reissman, L., *The Urban Process* (Free Press of Glencoe, 1964)

50 Morris, R. N., *Urban Sociology* (Allen and Unwin Ltd., 1968)

51 Udry, J. R., op cit

52 Bell, W. and Moskos, C., 'A Comment on Udry's Increasing Scale and Spatial Differentiation', *Social Forces* 42 (1964), 414–17

53 A similar case is argued by Timms, D. W. G., *The Urban Mosaic* (Cambridge University Press, 1971), 141; see for a more general assessment of social area analysis, 123–210

54 Lewis, Oscar, 'The Culture of Poverty', *Scientific American*, 215 (1966), 19–25

55 Anderson, T. R. and Bean, L. L., op cit

56 See Timms, D. W. G., *The Urban Mosaic* (1971)

CHAPTER SIX

1 See Berry, B. J. L. and Horton, F. E. (eds), *Geographic Perspectives on Urban Systems* (Prentice-Hall, 1970)

2 Derived from 1961 *Census of Canada*. Population and Housing characteristics by Census Tracts: Winnipeg

3 Murdie, R. A., 'The Factorial Ecology of Metropolitan Toronto: 1951 and 1961' (*Department of Geography, University of Chicago Research Paper*, 116, 1969)

4 Rees, P. H., 'Concepts of Social Space: Toward an Urban Social Geography', in Berry, B. J. L. and Horton, F. E. (eds), *Geographic Perspectives on Urban Systems* (Prentice-Hall, 1970), 306–94

5 Janson, C. G., 'The Spatial Structure of Newark, New Jersey', *Acta Sociologica*, 11 (1968), 144–69

6 Murdie, R. A., op cit

7 Brown, L. E. and Horton, F. E., 'Social Area Change: An Empirical Analysis', *Urban Studies*, 7 (1970), 271–88

8 Pederson, P. O., *Modeller for Befolkningsstruktur og Befolkningsudvikling i Storbymorader Specielt med Henblik pa Storkobenhavn* (Copenhagen State Urban Planning Institute, 1967)

9 Sweetser, F. L., 'Factor Structure as Ecological Structure in Helsinki and Boston', *Acta Sociologica*, 9 (1965), 205–25

10 Herbert, D. T., 'Principal Components Analysis and British Studies of Urban-Social Structure', *The Professional Geographer*, 20 (1968), 280–3

11 See Herbert, D. T., 'Principal Components Analysis and Urban-Social Structure: A Study of Cardiff and Swansea', in Carter, H. and Davies, W. K. D. (eds), *Urban Essays: Studies in the Geography of Wales* (Longmans, 1970), 79–100

12 Musil, J., 'The Development of Prague's Ecological Structure', in Pahl, R. E. (ed), *Readings in Urban Sociology* (Pergamon, 1968), 232–59

13 Jones, F. L., 'Social Area Analysis: Some Theoretical and Methodological Comments illustrated with Australian data', *British Journal of Sociology*, 19 (1968), 424–44

14 Berry, B. J. L. and Rees, P. H., 'The Factorial Ecology of Calcutta', *American Journal of Sociology*, 74 (1968–69), 445–91

15 Abu Lughod, J. L., 'Testing the Theory of Social Area Analysis: The Ecology of Cairo, Egypt', *American Sociological Review*, 34 (1969), 198–212

16 Berry, B. J. L. and Rees, P. H., op cit

17 Abu Lughod, J. L., op cit

18 Abu Lughod, J. L., op cit

19 Rees, P. H., op cit

20 Van Arsdol, M. D., Camilleri, S. F. and Schmid, C. F., 'The Generality of Urban Social Area Indices', *American Sociological Review*, 23 (1958), 277–84

21 McElrath, D. C., 'The Social Areas of Rome: A Comparative Analysis', *American Sociological Review*, 27 (1962), 376–91

22 Van Arsdol, M. D., Camilleri, S. F. and Schmid, C. F., 'The Generality of Urban Social Area Indices', 282

23 Berry, B. J. L. and Rees, P. H., 'The Factorial Ecology of Calcutta', 491

24 Berry, B. J. L. and Rees, P. H., 'The Factorial Ecology of Calcutta', 491

25 Timms, D. W. G., *The Urban Mosaic* (Cambridge University Press, 1971), 146

26 See Mabogunje, A. L., *Urbanisation in Nigeria* (University of London Press, 1968); McGee, T., *The South-east Asian City* (Bell, 1967) and Schnore, L. F., 'On the Spatial Structure of Cities in the Two Americas', in Hauser, P. M. and Schnore, L. F. (eds), *The Study of Urbanisation* (Wiley, 1965)

27 Jones, P. N., *The Segregation of Immigrant Communities in the City of Birmingham, 1961* (University of Hull, Occasional Papers in Geography, 7, 1967) and Pickett, K. G., 'Migration in the Merseyside Area', in Lawton, R. and Cunningham, C. M. (eds), *Merseyside : Social and Economic Studies* (Longmans, 1970), 108–48

28 Musil, J., op cit

29 Dawson, A. H., 'Warsaw: an Example of City Structure in Free Market and Planned Socialist Environments', *Tijdschrift voor Economische en Social Geographie*, 62 (1971), 104–113

30 Sweetser, F. L., op cit

31 Beshers, J. M., *Urban Social Structure* (Free Press of Glencoe, 1962)

32 Rees, P. H., op cit

CHAPTER SEVEN

1 Beshers, J. M., *Urban Social Structure* (Free Press of Glencoe, 1962), 113–26

2 Hirschi, T. and Selvin, H. C., *Delinquency Research : An Appraisal of Analytic Methods* (Macmillan, 1967)

3 Lambert, R., *Nutrition in Britain 1950–1960* (Codicote Press, 1964)

4 Beshers, J. M., *Urban Social Structure*, 110

5 See Stamp, L. D., *The Geography of Life and Death* (Collins, 1964)
6 Rowntree, B. S., *Poverty, A Study of Town Life* (Macmillan, 1901)
7 Coates, K. and Silburn, R., *St Ann's* (Nottingham University, 1967)
8 De, S. N., 'Cholera in Calcutta', Chapter 3 of *Cholera, Its Pathology and Pathogenesis* (Oliver and Boyd, 1961)
9 Pyle, G. F., *Some Examples of Urban Medical Geography*. Unpublished M.A. dissertation (University of Chicago, 1968)
10 Dunham, H. W., 'The Ecology of Functional Psychoses in Chicago', *American Sociological Review*, 2 (1937), 467–79
11 Mintz, N. L. and Schwarz, D. T., 'Urban Ecology and Psychosis', *International Journal of Social Psychiatry* (1964)
12 Castle, I. M. and Gittus, E., 'The Distribution of Social Defects in Liverpool', *Sociological Review*, 5 (1957), 43–64
13 Gittus, E., '*Sociological Aspects of Urban Decay*', mimeographed, University of Newcastle-upon-Tyne
14 Timms, D. W. G., 'The Spatial Distribution of Social Deviants in Luton, England', *The Australian and New Zealand Journal of Sociology*, 1 (1965), 38–52
15 Giggs, J. A., '*Schizophrenia in Nottingham C.B.: 1963–1969*', mimeograph (1971), University of Nottingham
16 Levin, Y. and Lindesmith, A., 'English Ecology and Criminology of the Past Century', *Journal of Criminal Law and Criminology*, 27 (1937), 801–16
17 Mayhew, H., *London Labour and the London Poor* (1864), described by Levin, Y. and Lindesmith, A. in Theodorson, G. A. (ed), *Studies in Human Ecology* (Row, Peterson, 1961), 16–19
18 See Theodorson, G. A. (ed), *Studies in Human Ecology*, 19
19 Burt, C., *The Sub-Normal School Child Vol. 1, The Young Delinquent* (University of London Press, 1925)
20 Booth, C., *Life and Labour of the People*, Appendix to Vol. 2 (Williams and Norgate, 1891)
21 Shaw, C. R. and McKay, H. D., *Juvenile Delinquency and Urban Areas* (University of Chicago Press, 1942)
22 Burgess, E. W. and Bogue, D. J., *Contributions to Urban Sociology* (University of Chicago Press, 1964), 609
23 See Dunham, H. W., op cit; Reckless, W. C., 'The Distribu-

tion of Commercialized Vice in the City: A Sociological Analysis', *Publications of the American Sociological Society*, 20 (1926), 164–76

24 Schmid, C. F., 'Urban Crime Areas', *American Sociological Review*, 25 (1960), 527–42 and 655–78

25 Schmid, C. F., op cit

26 Castle, I. M. and Gittus, E., op cit

27 Beynon, E. D., 'Budapest: An Ecological Study', *Geographical Review*, 33 (1943), 256–75

28 Beynon, E. D., 'Budapest: An Ecological Study', in Theodorson, G. A. (ed), *Studies in Human Ecology* (Row Peterson, 1961), 366

29 Scott, P., 'Delinquency, Mobility and Broken Homes in Hobart', *Australian Journal of Social Issues*, 2 (1965), 10–22

30 Lind, A. W., 'Some Ecological Patterns of Community Disorganization in Honolulu', *American Journal of Sociology*, 36 (1930), 206–20

31 Shaw, C. R. and McKay, H. D., op cit

32 Trasler, G., 'Theoretical Problems in the Explanation of Delinquent Behaviour', *Education Research*, 6 (1963–64), 42–9

33 Burgess, E. W. and Bogue, D. J., op cit, 487–91

34 Mays, J. B., 'Crime and the Urban Pattern', *Sociological Review*, 16 (1968), 241–55

35 Lander, B., *Towards an Understanding of Juvenile Delinquency* (Columbia University Press, 1944)

36 Burgess, E. W. and Bogue, D. J. (eds), op cit, 489

37 Chilton, R. J., 'Continuity in Delinquency Area Research: A Comparison of Studies for Baltimore, Detroit, and Indianapolis', *American Sociological Review* (1964), 71–83

38 Srole, L., 'Social Integration and Certain Corollaries: An Explanatory Study', *American Sociological Review*, 21 (1956), 709–16

39 Mays, J. B., *Growing Up in the City* (Liverpool University Press, 1954), 147–8

40 Cohen, A., *Delinquent Boys: The Culture of the Gang* (Routledge and Kegan Paul, 1956)

41 Mayhew, H, *London Labour and the London Poor*

42 Burgess, E. W. and Bogue, D. J. (eds), *Contributions to Urban Sociology*, 593

43 Thrasher, F., *The Gang* (University of Chicago Press, 1927)
44 Mays, J. B., 'Crime and the Urban Pattern', *Sociological Review*, 16 (1968), 243
45 Cloward, R. A. and Ohlin, L. E., *Delinquency and Opportunity : A Theory of Delinquent Gangs* (Free Press of Glencoe, 1960)
46 Palmore, E. B. and Hammond, P. E., 'Interacting Factors in Juvenile Delinquency', *American Sociological Review*, 29 (1964), 548–54
47 Palmore, E. B. and Hammond, P. E., op cit
48 Wootton, B., *Social Science and Social Pathology* (Allen & Unwin, 1959), 68
49 Sullenger, T. E., 'The Social Significance of Mobility', *American Journal of Sociology* (1950), 559–64
50 Freedman, R., 'Cityward Migration, Urban Ecology, and Social Theory' in Burgess, E. W. and Bogue, D. (eds), *Contributions to Urban Sociology* (University of Chicago, 1964), 178–200
51 Willie, C. V. and Gerschenovitz, A., 'Juvenile Delinquency in Racially Mixed Areas', *American Sociological Review*, 29 (1964), 740–4
52 Mays, J. B., op cit
53 Willie, C. V., 'Relative Contributions of Family Status and Economic Status in Juvenile Delinquency', *Social Problems*, 4 (1967), 326–34
54 Quinney, R., 'Crime, Delinquency and Social Areas', *Journal of Research in Crime and Delinquency*, 1 (1964), 149–54
55 Schmid, C. F., op cit
56 Hirschi, T. and Selvin, H. C., *Delinquency Research: An Appraisal of Analytic Methods*
57 Wilkins, L. T., 'Crime, Cause and Treatment: Recent Research and Theory', *Education Research*, 4 (1961–62), 18
58 McNaughton-Smith, P., *Some Statistical and Other Numerical Techniques for Classifying Individuals* (London, HMSO, 1965)
59 Boggs, Sarah L., 'Urban Crime Patterns', *American Sociological Review*, 30 (1965), 899–908
60 Mays, J. B., op cit
61 Mays, J. B., op cit, 253
62 Clinard, M., 'The Organization of UCD services in the

Prevention of Crime and Juvenile Delinquency, with Particular Reference to Less Developed Countries', *International Review of Criminal Policy*, 19 (1962)

63   Jacobs, Jane, *Death and Life of Great American Cities* (Random House Inc., 1961)

64   Morris, T., *The Criminal Area* (Routledge and Kegan Paul, 1957)

65   Ibid

66   Timms, D. W. G., 'The Spatial Distribution of Social Deviants in Luton, England', *Australia and New Zealand Journal of Sociology*, 1 (1965), 38–52

67   Giggs, J. A., 'Socially Disorganized Areas in Barry: A Multi-variate Analysis', in Carter, H. and Davies, W. K. D., *Urban Essays: Studies in the Geography of Wales* (Longmans, 1970), 101–43

68   Scott, P., 'Delinquency, Mobility and Broken Homes in Hobart', *Australian Journal of Social Issues*, 2 (1965), 10–22

69   Clifford, W., 'Problems in Criminological Research in Africa South of the Sahara', *International Review of Criminal Policy*, 28 (1965).

70   Caplow, T., 'The Social Ecology of Guatemala City', *Social Forces*, 28 (1949), 113–35

71   Hayner, N. S., 'Criminogenic Zones in Mexico City', *American Sociological Review*, 11 (1946), 428–38

72   Mangin, W., 'Mental Health and Migration to Cities: A Peruvian Case', in Meadows, P. and Mizruchi, E. H. (eds), *Urbanism, Urbanization, and Change: Comparative Perspectives* (Addison Wesley, 1969), 316

73   De Fleur, Lois B., 'Ecological Variables in the Cross-Cultural Study of Delinquency', *Social Forces*, 45 (1966–67), 556–70

74   Ibid, 568

75   Third United Nations Seminar for the Arab States on the Prevention of Crime and the Treatment of Offenders.

76   Weinberg, S. K., 'Urbanisation and Male Delinquency in Ghana', *Journal of Research in Crime and Delinquency* (1965), 85–94

77   Clinard, M., op cit

78   Walczak, S., 'Planning Crime Prevention and Control in Poland' *International Review of Criminal Policy*, 26 (1968), 47

79   Connor, W. D., 'Juvenile Delinquency in the USSR: Some

T

Quantitative and Qualitative Indicators', *American Sociological Review*, 35 (1970), 283–97

80 Lewis, Oscar, 'The Culture of Poverty', *Scientific American*, 215 (1966), 19–25

81 Glaser, D., 'New Trends in Research on the Treatment of Offenders and the Prevention of Crime in the USA', *International Review of Criminal Policy*, 23 (1965), 9

82 Clinard, M., op cit

83 Herbert, D. T., *Some Aspects of Social-Urban Geography in the North Staffordshire Conurbation*. Unpublished Ph.D. thesis (University of Birmingham, 1964)

84 Bell, W. and Force, M. T., 'Urban Neighbourhood Types and Participation in Formal Associations', *American Sociological Review*, 21 (1956), 25–34, and 'Social Structure and Participation in Different Types of Formal Associations', *Social Forces*, 34 (1956), 345–50; Bell, W. and Boat, M. D., 'Urban Neighbourhoods and Informal Social Relations', *American Journal of Sociology*, 62 (1957), 391–8

85 Greer, S., 'Urbanism Reconsidered: A Comparative Study of Local Areas in a Metropolis', *American Sociological Review*, 21 (1956), 19–25

86 Bell, W., 'Urban Neighbourhoods and Individual Behaviour', in Meadows, P. and Mizruchi, E. H. (eds), *Urbanism, Urbanization, and Change: Comparative Perspectives* (Addison Wesley, 1969), 120–46

87 Robson, B. T., *Urban Analysis: A Study of City Structure with Special Reference to Sunderland* (Cambridge University Press, 1969)

88 Ibid

89 Pahl, R. E., *Spatial Structure and Social Structure*, Centre for Environmental Studies Working Paper, 10 (1968)

90 Bell, W., op cit, 136

91 Sherif, M. and C. W., *Reference Groups* (Harper and Row, 1964); see Bell, W., op cit, 137

92 Mumford, L., 'The Neighbourhood and the Neighbourhood Unit', *Town Planning Review* (1954), 256–70

93 Definitions of Neighbourhood are discussed in Dickinson, R. E., *City and Region* (Routledge, 1964), 203–9

94 Cooley, C. H., *Social Organization* (New York, 1909)

95 Perry, C., 'The Neighbourhood Unit: A Scheme of Arrangement for the Family Life Community', in *A*

Regional Plan for New York and Its Environs, Vol. 7 (1929)

96 See Gallion, A. B. and Eisner, S., *The Urban Pattern* (D. Van Nostrand, 1963), 125–7

97 See, Brown, M., 'Urban Form', *Journal of the Town Planning Institute*, 52 (1966), 3–10

98 For a general statement on earlier neighbourhood development, see Dahir, J., *The Neighbourhood Unit Plan, its Spread and Acceptance* (Russel Sage Foundation, New York, 1947)

99 Abercrombie, L. P., *Greater London Plan, 1944* (HMSO, 1945)

100 Dudley Report: *Design of Dwellings* (HMSO, 1944)

101 See Hall, P., *The World Cities* (Weidenfeld and Nicolson, 1966), 170–2, for discussion of Moscow's micro-districts

102 Mann, Peter, 'The Socially Balanced Neighbourhood Unit', *Town Planning Review*, 29 (1958), 91–8

103 Herbert, D. T. and Rodgers, H. B., 'Space Relationships in Neighbourhood Planning', *Town and Country Planning* (1967), 196–8

104 Alexander, C., 'A City is not a Tree', *Design* (1966)

105 Jacobs, Jane, *Death and Life of Great American Cities*

106 Broady, M., *Planning for People* (National Council for Social Services, 1968)

107 London County Council, *The Planning of a New Town* (1961)

108 Hoppenfeld, M., 'A Sketch of the Planning-Building Process for Columbia, Maryland', *Journal of the American Institute of Planners*, 33 (1966), 398–409

109 Sweetser, F. L., 'A New Emphasis for Neighbourhood Research', *American Sociological Review*, 7 (1942), 525–33

110 McClenahan, B. A., 'The Communality: The Urban Substitute for the Traditional Community', *Sociol. Soc. Research*, 30 (1945), 264–74, and *The Changing Urban Neighbourhood* (University of California Press, 1929)

111 Webber, M., 'Order in Diversity: Community Without Propinquity' in Wingo, L. (ed.), *Cities and Space* (The John Hopkins Press, 1963)

112 Suttles, G. F., *The Social Order of the Slum* (University of Chicago Press, 1968)

113 Lewis, O., op cit
114 Relevant studies include Chapin, S., and Hightower, H. C., *Household Activity Systems : A Pilot Investigation* (University of North Carolina, 1966); Buttimer, Anne, '*Exploring Attitudes Toward Residential Environment in Selected Districts of Glasgow*'. Unpublished mimeo (1971), Clark University, USA
115 Lee, T. R., 'Urban Neighbourhood as a Socio-Spatial Scheme', *Human Relations*, 21 (1968), 241–67
116 See Pahl, R. E. (ed), *Readings in Urban Sociology* (Pergamon, 1968), 74–208
117 Gutman, R., 'Site Planning and Social Behaviour', *Journal of Social Issues*, 4 (1966), 103–115
118 Gans, H., *The Levittowners* (Allen Lane, 1967)
119 See Bell, C., *Middle Class Families* (Routledge & Kegan Paul, 1968)

CHAPTER EIGHT

1 Hagerstrand, T., 'Migration and Area', quoted in Wolforth, J., 'The Journey to Work', in Bourne, L. S. (ed), *Internal Structure of the City* (Oxford University Press, 1971), 244
2 Kofoed, J., 'Personal Movement Research: A Discussion of Concepts', *Papers of the Regional Science Association*, 24 (1970), 141–55
3 Morrill, R. L., *The Spatial Organisation of Society* (Wadsworth, 1970)
4 Chapin, F. S., 'Activity Systems and Urban Structure: A Working Scheme', *Journal of the American Institute of Planners*, 34 (1968), 11–18
5 Meier, R. L., *A Communication Theory of Urban Growth* (Cambridge, Mass., 1962)
6 Webber, M., 'Culture, Territoriality and the Elastic Mile', *Papers of the Regional Science Association*, 13 (1964), 59–69
7 Chicago Area Transportation Study, see Berry, B. J. L. and Horton, F. E., *Geographic Perspectives on Urban Systems* (Prentice-Hall, 1970), 512–56
8 Kain, J. F., 'The Journey to Work as a Determinant of Residential Location', *Papers of the Regional Science Association*, 9 (1962), 137–60

9 Vance, J. E., 'Housing the Worker: the Employment Linkage as a Force in Urban Structure', *Economic Geography*, 42 (1966), 294–325

10 Berry, B. J. L., Goheen, P. G. and Goldstein, H., *Metropolitan Area Classification: A review of Current Practice, Criticisms and Proposed Alternatives*, Working Paper No. 28, US Bureau of the Census, 1968

11 Hall, P., 'Britain's Uneven Shrinkage', *New Society* (1966), 18–19

12 Berry, B. J. L., Commercial Structure and Commercial Blight, Research Paper No. 85, *Department of Geography Research Series*, University of Chicago (1963)

13 Mabogunje, A. L., *Urbanisation in Nigeria* (University of London Press, 1968)

14 Curry, L., 'The Geography of Service Centres within Towns', *IGU Symposium in Urban Geography, Lund* (1960), 31–53 and Huff, D. L., 'A Probability Analysis of Shopping Centre Trading Areas', *Land Economics*, 53 (1963), 81–90

15 Davies, R. L., 'Effects of Consumer Income Differences on Shopping Movement Behaviour', *Tijdschrift voor Economische en Social Geographie*, 60 (1969), 111–21

16 The point is made by several studies at a regional scale in Canada, such as Murdie, R. A., 'Cultural Differences in Consumer Travel', *Economic Geography*, 41 (1967), 211–33

17 See, for example, Rossi, P. H., *Why Families Move* (Free Press of Glencoe, 1955)

18 Albig, W., 'The Mobility of Urban Population', *Social Forces*, 11 (1933), 351–67

19 Du Wors, R. E., Beaman, J. and Olmsted, A., *Dynamics of Residential Populations in Six Prairie Cities*, paper presented to American Sociological Association in 1965 and other mimeographs at University of Saskatchewan.

20 Goldstein, S., 'Repeated Migration as a Factor in High Mobility Rates', *American Sociological Review*, 19 (1954), 536–41

21 Herbert, D. T., *Some Aspects of Social Geography in the North Staffordshire conurbation*. Unpublished Ph.D. thesis (University of Birmingham, 1964)

22 Bell, C., *Middle Class Families* (Routledge, 1968)

23 Turner, J. F. C., 'Uncontrolled Urban Settlement: Problems and Policies', in Breese, G. (ed), *The City in Newly Developing Countries* (Prentice-Hall, 1969), 507–34

24 Rees, P. H., 'Concepts of Social Space', in Berry, B. J. L. and Horton, F. E. (ed), *Geographic Perspectives on Urban Systems* (Prentice-Hall, 1970), 307

25 Kaiser, E. J. and Weiss, J. F., 'Public Policy and the Residential Land Development Process', *Journal of the American Institute of Planners*, 36 (1970), 30–7

26 Wolpert, J., 'Behavioural Aspects of the Decision to Migrate', *Papers of the Regional Science Association*, 15 (1965), 159–69

27 Brown, L. A. and Moore, E. G., 'The Intra-Urban Migration Process: A Perspective', *Geografiska Annaler B*, 52 (1970)

28 Rossi, P. A., *Why Families Move* (Free Press of Glencoe, 1955)

29 See also Horton, F. E. and Reynolds, D. R., 'Effects of Urban Spatial Structure on Individual Behaviour', *Economic Geography*, 47 (1971), 36–48 and Rushton, G., 'Behavioural Correlates of Urban Spatial Structure', *Economic Geography*, 47 (1971), 49–58

30 Sabagh, G., Van Arsdol, M. D. and Butler, E. W., 'Some Determinants of Intra-Metropolitan Residential Mobility: Conceptual Considerations', *Social Forces*, 48 (1969), 88–98

31 Wolpert, J., op cit

32 Bell, C., *Middle Class Families*

33 Horton, F. E. and Reynolds, D. R., op cit, 37

34 Brown, L. A. and Moore, E. G., op cit

35 Marble, D. F. and Nystuen, J. D., 'An Approach to the Direct Measurement of Community Mean Information Fields', *Papers of the Regional Science Association*, 11 (1963), 99–110

36 Horton, F. E. and Reynolds, D. R., op cit

37 Boyce, R. R., 'Residential Mobility and its Implications for Urban-Spatial Change', *Proceedings of the Association of American Geographers*, 1 (1969), 22–6

38 See, for example, Yeates, M., 'Some factors affecting the Spatial Distribution of Chicago Land Values', *Economic Geography*, 41 (1965), 57–70

39 Kain, J. F., 'The Journey to Work as a Determinant of

Residential Location', *Papers of the Regional Science Association*, 9 (1962), 137–60

40 Peterson, G. L., 'A Model of Preference: Quantitative Analysis of the Perception of the Visual Appearance of Residential Neighbourhoods', *Journal of Regional Science*, 7 (1967), 19–31

41 See Rushton, G., op cit

42 Doherty, J. M., 'Developments in Behavioural Geography', *L.S.E. Department of Geography Graduate Discussion Paper*, 35 (1969)

43 Gould, P. R. and White, R. R., 'The Mental Maps of British School Leavers', *Regional Studies*, 2 (1968), 161–82

44 Gould, P. R., 'The Structure of Space Preferences in Tanzania', *Area* (1969), 29–35

45 Johnston, R. J., *Social Status and Residential Desirability: A Pilot Study of Residential Location Decisions in Christchurch, New Zealand*. Mimeo (1968), University of Christchurch, New Zealand

46 Bordessa, R., 'Perception Research in Geography: An Appraisal and Contribution to Urban Perception', *University of Newcastle, Department of Geography Seminar Paper*, 8 (1969)

47 See Gould, P. R., 'Structuring Information on Spacio-Temporal Preferences', *Journal of Regional Science*, 7 (1967), 260

48 Hoyt, H., *The Structure and Growth of Residential Neighbourhoods in American Cities* (Washington, 1939)

49 See, Smith, W. F., 'Filtering and Neighbourhood Change', in Bourne, L. S. (ed), *Internal Structure of the City* (Oxford University Press, 1971), 170–9

50 Johnston, R. J., 'The Location of High Status Residential Areas', *Geografiska Annaler B*, 48 (1966), 23–35

51 Jones, E., *The Social Geography of Belfast* (Oxford Univ. Press, 1960)

52 Herbert, D. T., *Some Aspects of Urban-Social Geography in the North Staffordshire conurbation*. Unpublished Ph.D. thesis (University of Birmingham, 1964)

53 Morrill, R. L., 'The Negro Ghetto: Problems and Alternatives', *The Geographical Review*, 55 (1965), 339–61

54 Burney, E., *Housing on Trial* (Oxford University Press, 1967)

55 Rose, H. M., 'The Development of an Urban Sub-system: the Case of the Negro Ghetto', *Annals of the Association of American Geographers* 60 (1970), 1–5

56 Morrill, R. L., 'Waves of Spatial Diffusion', *Journal of Regional Science*, 8 (1968), 2

57 Johnston, R. J., 'Population Movements and Metropolitan Expansion', *Transactions of the Institute of British Geographers*, 46 (1969), 69–91

58 Johnston, R. J., 'Some Tests of a Model of Intra-Urban Population Mobility: Melbourne, Australia', *Urban Studies*, 6 (1969), 34–57

59 Caplow, T., 'Incidence and Direction of Residential Mobility in a Minneapolis Sample', *Social Forces*, 27 (1949), 413–17

60 Rees, P. H., 'Concepts of Social Space', in Berry, B. J. L. and Horton, F. E., *Geographic Perspectives on Urban Systems* (Prentice-Hall, 1970), 311–13

61 Rees, P. H., op cit, 313

62 Moore, E. G., 'The Structure of Intra-Urban Movement Rates: An Ecological Model', *Urban Studies*, 6 (1969), 17–33 and 'Comments on the Use of Ecological Models in the Study of Residential Mobility in the City', *Economic Geography*, 47 (1971), 73–85

63 Blalock, H. M., *Causal Inferences in Non-Experimental Research* (University of Carolina Press, 1964)

APPENDIX

Statistical texts by geographers:

Grogory, S., *Statistical Methods and the Geographer* (Longmans, 1964)

Cole, J. P. and King, C. A. M., *Quantitative Geography* (Wiley, 1968)

King, L. J., *Statistical Analysis in Geography* (Prentice Hall, 1969)

Toyne, P. and Newby, P. T., *Techniques in Human Geography* (Macmillan, 1971)

Hoel, P. G., *Elementary Statistics* (Wiley, 1960)

More general statistical texts:

Spiegel, M. S., *Statistics* (Schaum, 1961)

Siegel, S., *Nonparametric Statistics* (McGraw Hill, 1956)

Methodological texts by geographers:
Haggett, P., *Locational Analysis in Human Geography* (Arnold, 1965)
Harvey, D., *Explanation in Geography* (Arnold, 1969)

For a fuller statement on factor analysis see Rummel, R. J., 'Understanding Factor Analysis', *Journal of Conflict Resolution*, II (1967) 444–80, whilst a standard text is Harman, H., *Modern Factor Analysis* (University of Chicago Press, 1961)

For a review of the literature on classification techniques, see Spence, N. A. and Taylor, P. J., 'Quantitative Models in Regional Taxonomy', in Board, C. *et al.* (eds) *Progress in Geography*, 2 (Arnold, 1970), 1–64

INDEX

Page numbers in *italic type* indicate illustrations.